The Philosophy of George Berkeley

A FIFTEEN-VOLUME
FACSIMILE SERIES REPRODUCING
CLASSIC STUDIES AND INCLUDING
FOUR NEVER-BEFORE-PUBLISHED TITLES

EDITED BY
George Pitcher
Princeton University

A GARLAND SERIES

Money, Obedience, and Affection

ESSAYS ON BERKELEY'S MORAL AND POLITICAL THOUGHT

Edited by
Stephen R. L. Clark

GARLAND PUBLISHING, INC.
NEW YORK & LONDON 1989

For a complete list of the titles in this series,
see the final pages of this volume.

These facsimiles were made from copies in
Yale University Library.

Library of Congress Cataloging-in-Publication Data

Money, obedience, and affection.
    (The Philosophy of George Berkeley ; v. 3)
    1. Berkeley, George, 1685-1753. 2. Ethics, Modern—
18th century. 3. Economics—History—18th century.
I. Clark, Stephen R. L. II. Series.
B1348.M66 1988   170'.92'4   88-11304
ISBN 0-8240-2445-1

Printed on acid-free, 250-year-life paper.
Printed in the United States of America

ACKNOWLEDGMENTS

The publisher and editor gratefully acknowledge the permission of the authors and the following journals and organizations to reprint the copyright material in this volume; any further reproduction is prohibited without permission:

Editions Universa for material in *Revue Internationale de Philosophy; Journal of the History of Ideas*; Aberdeen University Press for material in the *British Journal of the Philosophy of Science; The Philosophical Review; Hermathena*; the Southern Economic Association for material in the *Southern Economic Journal*; Peter Owen, Ltd. for material from *Studies in the Theories of Money 1690-1776*; The University of Chicago Press for "Berkeley—Precursor of Keynes or Moral Economist on Underdevelopment," by I.D.S. Ward, from the *Journal of Political Economy* 67, copyright © 1959 by The University of Chicago Press.

INTRODUCTION

George Berkeley's contribution to philosophy, as it is studied in most universities, consists of *The Principles of Human Understanding I* (1710), *Three Dialogues between Hylas and Philonous* (1713), and perhaps *A New Theory of Vision* (1709) and its *Vindication* (1733). Students are expected to answer questions on Berkeley in papers entitled "The British Empiricists" or perhaps "Early Modern Epistemology," and the usual assumption is that he occupies an uneasy interval between John Locke and David Hume—the original "Englishman, Irishman and Scotsman"! That he is usually also entitled "Bishop Berkeley" (although all the aforementioned works—except the *Vindication*—were written in his twenties, while he was, in effect, a struggling research fellow) is only intended to convey that his churchmanship left him without the courage to carry his sceptical principles far enough.

    Modern philosophers have also been inclined to review Berkeley's immaterialist arguments entirely in the abstract, as contributions to an epistemological or metaphysical debate having no strong connection with everyday life and morals. A collection of essays on Berkeley's moral and political philosophy is therefore likely to be regarded as a marginal or eccentric exercise. But Berkeley's whole immaterialist enterprise was part of a consciously adopted strategy to subvert fashionable, Enlightenment thought, which he saw as a real and pressing danger to civil society. He was not engaged in abstract theorizing, but in moral and political action. "Socrates' whole employment," he wrote to Percival, "was the turning men aside from vice, impertinence, and trifling speculations to the study of solid wisdom, temperance, justice and piety, which is the true business of a philosopher" (27.12.1709: Rand 1914, p. 68). Berkeley's lifelong aim was to educate men to "zeal for religion and love of their country" (*Proposal* 1725: 7, p.348: see Leary)*.

On the more usual view Berkeley was a minor member of the Enlightenment, where that is understood to mean the project conceived in the seventeenth century of rebuilding the edifice of human knowledge from the ground up, dispensing with the archaic and ill-founded theses of older philosophy. "To our infinite regret," so Berkeley makes Lysicles declare in *Alciphron* (1732: one the great philosophical dialogues, written on Rhode Island during his American venture), "nothing can be done so long as there remains any prejudice in favour of old customs and laws and national constitutions which, at bottom, we very well know and can demonstrate to be only words and notions" (3, p.212). But Lysicles is the enemy of Berkeleian philosophy and practice: Berkeley was well aware that to introduce a "general scepticism into human knowledge [was to] break down the hinges on which civil government, and all the affairs of the world, turn and depend" (3, p.225: Euphranor speaks). "We who believe a God are entrenched within tradition, custom, authority and law," and should not voluntarily abandon these entrenchments until we are forced out of them by reasoned argument (3, p. 143: Euphranor speaks). The self-image of modern philosophers, heirs of the Enlightenment, requires them to "think for themselves," in such terms as any rational inquirer could think of for herself, and without relying on received opinion. But Berkeley did not suppose himself to be a "free-thinker" or a sceptic:

> Our present impending danger is from the setting up of private judgement, or an inward light, in opposition to human and divine laws. Such an inward conceited prin-

---

*All quotations from Berkely, unless otherwise stated, are from the Luce-Jessop edition of *The Collected Works: Berkeley*, 1948.

ciple always at work and proceeding gradually and steadily, may be sufficient to dissolve any human fabric of polity or civil government (*Discourse* 1738: 6, p. 217; see Petrella).

His strategy was to begin from sceptical principles in order to subvert them, as Philonous declares to Hylas. "The same principles which at first view lead to scepticism, pursued to a certain point, bring men back to common sense" (*Dialogues*: 2, p. 263). William Blake had the same optimistic thought: "if the fool would persist in his folly he would become wise" (Blake 1966 p. 151). The minute philosophers, in the phrase Berkeley borrowed from Cicero (3, p. 46), had denied us any right to believe doctrines that could not be directly demonstrated (to them) from self-evident principle or from immediate sensory experience. Berkeley pointed out that since they also believed that our immediate experience was not of things in themselves, they were therefore committed to a denial of all extra-experiential reality.

He was similarly inclined to point out the oddities of contemporary mathematical and physical theory, as embodying contradictions and indemonstrable principles of a kind that were regularly criticized in theological or moral discourses. "That philosopher is not free from bias and prejudice who shall maintain the doctrine of force and reject that of grace, who shall admit the abstract idea of a triangle, and at the same time ridicule the Holy Trinity!" (*Alciphron*: 3, p. 296: Euphranor speaks). And again: "With what appearance of reason shall any man presume to say that mysteries may not be objects of faith, at the same time that he himself admits such obscure mysteries to be the objects of science?" (*The Analyst* (1734): 4, p. 69).

> To me it seems evident that if none but those who had nicely examined, and coul themselves explain, the principle of individuation in man, or untie the knots and answer the objections which may be raised even about human personal identity, would require of us to explain the divine mysteries, we should not often be called upon for a clear and distinct idea of a person in relation to the Trinity, nor would the

difficulties on that head be often objected to our faith (3, p. 298: Euphranor speaks).

To exist, so Berkeley said in a phrase too often truncated, was either "percipi or percipere (or velle, i.e. agere)" (*Commentaries* 429: 1, p. 53). All that experience or right reason can show us are objects and subjects, items of information and the wills or spirits that contemplate and originate that information. Berkeley's own analysis of what it was to be a subject was lost, if it was ever wholly formulated, when volume II of the *Principles* was lost during his tour of Italy (2, p. 282). The crucial point in that volume must have been that the identity of such a subject did not rest in the ideas it had, but in its practical determination, the will (see *Commentaries* 194a ["Qu. whether Identity of Person consists not in the will"], 478a, 643). There are undoubtedly difficulties with the doctrine (which goes back at least to Aristotle: see Clark 1975 ch. 3.2), but they are not those which critics usually suppose. Berkeley was in no danger of ending his days as a solipsistic phenomenalist, unable to conceive of any phenomena than those immediately present to his own senses, though it may be true of him—as it was of the youthful Newman—that there were for him "two and two only absolute and luminously self-evident beings, [him]self and [his] Creator" (Newman 1967 p.4). On the contrary, he emphasises the obvious truth that none of us can construct the edifice of human knowledge on the basis merely of our own sensations (3, p. 143; 6, p. 206). "So Swift is our passage from the womb to the grave" that no one could learn much by his own experience (*Sermon on Immortality* 1708: 7, p. 14). Where the "minute philosophers" pretend to an ahistorical grasp of truth, enabling them to reject traditional belief and practice on the grounds that they and their friends managed not to see the world in traditional categories, Berkeley reckoned that we should begin not from our own experience, at the most banal, but from the testimony and enthusiasm of the ages. We must begin from testimony (6. p. 218), and distrust it only when obvious contradictions emerge. It is, so he insists, the common sense of humankind that provides us with a beginning, even if our eventual conclusions seem distant from such common sense. "There is a vast Majority on the side of Imagination or Spiritual Sensation" (Blake 1966 p. 794). Just so a later Anglo-Irishman "began telling people that one should believe whatever had been believed in all countries and periods, and only reject any part of it after much evidence, instead of starting all over afresh and only believing what one could prove" (Yeats 1955 p. 78; see Newman 1979 p. 286). Doctrines that require us to deny our common experience, and say, for example, "the Wall is not white, the fire is not hot & c" are at a disadvantage—"we Irishmen cannot attain to these truths" (*Commentaries* 392: 1, p. 47)—but our present and past experience does not embrace the universe. "If the doors of perception were cleansed every thing would appear to man as it is, infinite" (Blake 1966 p. 154). The unseen worlds of glory that surround us only wait for our eyes to open.

> The believer may expect a happyness large as our desires, & those desires not stinted to ye few objects we at present receive from some dull inlets of perception, but proportionate to wt our faculties shall be wn God has given the finishing touches to our natures & made us fit inhabitants for heaven (*Sermon on Immortality* 1708: 7, p. 12).

Enlightenment thought, then and now, also makes assumptions about the proper emotional style of empirical enquiry, as if those experiences that are borne in on us when we remain distant and uninvolved are more "reliable" than those made manifest to a loving delight in God's universe. But Berkeley reckoned, as his remarks on moral truth (*Commentaries* 676: 1, p. 82) suggest, that it was what we were inclined to say enthusiastically, and what preserved in us the proper spirit of obedient faith, that was most reliable. In an early piece of philosophical science fiction, Berkeley imagines the effect of philosophical snuff: Ulysses Cosmopolita thereby investigates the subjective experience of a deracinated freethinker, and finds it populated by terrors entirely of his own devising, "men in black, of gigantick size, and most terrifick forms" (*Guardian Essays on the Pineal Gland* 1713: 7, pp. 188f).

Can no method be found to relieve [freethinkers] from the

> terror of that fierce and bloody animal an English parson? (3, p.209: Crito speaks).

Truth, in matters moral and metaphysical, does not consist in a "correspondence" of our ideas with things outside the mind, but in such propositions as "make proper impressions on [our] mind, producing therein love, hope, gratitude, and obedience, and thereby become a lively operative principle, influencing [our] life and actions, agreeably to that notion of saving faith which is required in a Christian" (3, p. 297: Euphranor speaks). Or as Euphranor is made to say on an earlier page (a little misleadingly), "is not the general good of mankind to be regarded as the rule or measure of moral truths, of all such truths as direct or influence the moral actions of men?" (3, p. 60; see 6, p. 211). Objective reality was not the narrow sphere of the value-neutral scientist (supposing any such creature ever existed), but the realm manifested to that life which is God's presence in us. This is certainly not to say, as some have supposed, that Berkeley cares less about "the truth" than Mandeville does (as Monro 1975 p. 256): on the contrary, Berkeley cares about truth, and can say why; what he disputes is the idea that men such as Lysicles (3, p. 62) can have any reason to seek out or publicize "the truth" when they (and even we) would be much better off if we did not believe them.

It is those who enjoy a landscape that truly possess it (*Guardian Essay on Pleasures* 1713: 7, p. 195), and to describe it aright we must describe it with the sort of affection that does not seek to keep its object only for itself. "The same atheistical narrow spirit centering all our cares upon private interest and contracting all our hopes within the enjoyment of this present life equally produceth a neglect of what we owe to God and our country" (*Essay toward Preventing the Ruin of Great Britain* 1721: 6, p. 79). "A fool sees not the same tree that a wise man sees" (Blake 1966 p. 151). "The tree which moves some to tears of joy in the Eyes of others only a Green thing that stands in the way. ... To the Eyes of the Man of Imagination, Nature is Imagination itself" (Blake 1966 p. 793).

So far from being solipsistic, Berkeley insisted that "man

ought not to consider himself as an independent individual, whose happiness is not connected with that of other men, but rather as the part of a whole, to the common good of which he ought to conspire, and order his ways and actions suitably, if he would live according to nature" (3, p. 63: Euphranor speaks). There is a principle of mutual attraction in our souls that draws us together in communities, clubs, families, friendships, and all the various species of society (*Guardian Essay on the Bond of Society* 1713: 7, p. 226). Those lesser forms of society themselves take shape within that "great City, whose author and founder is God, in which the civil laws are no other than the rules of virtue and the duties of religion, and where every one's true interest is combined with his duty" (3, 129: Crito speaks). When a younger Berkeley said "I'd never blame a Man for acting upon Interest. He's a fool that acts on any other principle" (*Commentaries* 542: 1, p. 68), it was with no intention of giving his support to egotism.

Berkeley's notions of cause, of spirit, of identity are "empirical" in a sense. They are not "innate ideas," for we have no "ideas" of them at all, any more than we have ideas of virtues and vices (*Commentaries* 660: 1, p. 79), but they are those notions that we find we require to speak about what we immediately know ourselves to be. "Certain dispositions and tendencies will not fail to shew themselves, at proper periods, and in certain circumstances; which affections are properly said to be natural or innate" (*Sermon on the Will of God* 1751: 7, p. 130). He comes very close to a Kantian insistence that being a subject, a spirit, involves a capacity to learn the language of nature and to lay claim to memories and projects. "There are properly no ideas, or passive objects, in the mind but which were derived from sense: but there are also besides these her own acts and operations; such are notions" (*Siris* 1744, 308: 5, p. 142). Unlike later empiricists he did not endorse the view that words only have meaning insofar as they symbolize or evoke ideas—a view he considered and rejected (*Commentaries*, 637: 1, p. 78; *Alciphron*: 3, p. 292). If "the meaning is the use" there are many uses of language, and many ways of making sense. Berkeleian notions of cause, spirit, virtue, or identity are not "empirical" in the sense that they are to be identified with anything that can be an object of experience.

> Although terms are signs, yet having granted that those signs may be significant, though they should not suggest ideas represented by them, provided they serve to regulate and influence our wills, passions or conduct, you have consequently granted that the mind of man may assent to propositions containing such terms, when it is so directed or affected by them, notwithstanding it should not perceive distinct ideas marked by those terms (3, p. 296f: Euphranor speaks).

Our understanding of such terms is grounded in what we immediately experience ourselves to be, not as objects but as subjects. "The only original true notions that we have of freedom, agent or action are obtained by reflecting ourselves, and the operation of our own minds" (3, p. 318).

Newman and Berkeley reached very similar conclusions (though Newman disclaimed any knowledge of Berkeley: Vargish 1970 p. 21), but expressed them, temperamentally, in opposite ways. For Newman—and for W.B. Yeats—the phenomenal world was a dream, and truth lay in what was borne in upon the soul when she allowed the spirit of prayerful obedience to arise in her. Berkeley accepted much the same criteria of tradition and saving faith, but the conclusion was not, in Berkeleian terms, that this phenomenal world was exactly a dream. When Yeats spoke of "Goldsmith and the Dean [i.e., Swift], Berkeley and Burke" as "four great minds that hated Whiggery" (Yeats 1950 p. 272), he identified Berkeley as "God-appointed Berkeley that proved all things a dream" (Yeats 1950 p. 268). It is easy to conclude that Yeats must have misunderstood. The eminent Berkeleian scholar, A.A. Luce, was justly incensed by the suggestion that Berkeley was a limp-wristed visionary mooning after the infinite (see Berman 1985). On the contrary, Berkeley was adamant that all the common things of life were real and present only on his view of them, that it was the Lockean materialists who had turned the world of common day into a drifting illusion, that it was they who imagined that "reality" must be forever hypothetical. Berkeley also scorned those who neglected common duties and loyalties and preferred their private whims and fantasies to the good of the commonwealth. He was not caught away from common sense and common goods to live in fairyland (on which destination see Clark 1987b). "Whatever the world thinks," he wrote in *Siris* (350: 5, pp. 157f), "he who hath not much meditated upon God, the human mind and the summum bonum, may possibly make a thriving earthworm, but will most indubitably make a sorry patriot and a sorry statesman."

Yeats misjudged the Bishop and the practical reformer, but if we remember that for Yeats a dream was not absolute or constant unreality, we can understand and endorse his point. Berkeley could, like Ulysses Cosmopolita, "look out of the eye of a saint or out of a drunkard's eye" (Yeats 1950 p. 272), and not imagine that things "really were" just as the "levelling, rancorous, rational sort of mind" supposed. We can even agree with Yeats's judgement that Berkeley was, at least in his youth, a mischievous and rebellious spirit, though rejecting Yeats's misapprehension that he grew up to be an episcopal humbug. "I am young, I am an upstart, I am a pretender, I am vain, very well" (*Commentaries* 465: 1, p. 58). But he did also seriously intend to be a good believing Christian. "He that acts not to the obtaining of eternal Happyness must be an infidel at least he is not certain of a future Judgement" (*Commentaries* 776: 1, p. 93). His proofs of immaterialism were weapons in a war against what he perceived as a narrow, egotistical spirit that had forgotten the wider realms of God's creation, and our duties in it. Both Yeats and Berkeley saw themselves as Irishmen, but not as Catholics. Both sought to arouse their nation to a proper independence of mind and manners as, they thought, Great Britain sank lower into being, not merely wicked, but wicked on principle (6, p. 53, 84). Yeats, of course lent his—qualified—support to rebellion, whereas Berkeley, knowing how such rebellion must usually increase the very evils against which it acts (see *Passive Obedience* 1712: 6, p. 41ff), urged the duty of passive obedience. "The ills of rebellion are certain, but the event doubtful:" (*Advice to the Tories* 1715: 6, p. 55). The spirit of rebellion, of "laughing ecstatic destruction," grows as "a religious fear and awe of God, the centre that unites and the cement that connects all human society" (*Discourse to Magistrates* 1738: 6, p. 219) declines or is rooted out. Yeats hoped for a new revelation as that rebellious spirit, the "rough beast slouching toward Bethlehem to be born" (Yeats 1950 p. 211), took concrete shape in the next age of the world. Berkeley, perhaps with greater realism, thought that "the prevailing notions of order, virtue, duty and Providence" were what made the world habitable (*Discourse to Magistrates* 1738: 6, p. 202), and that in the general decay of manners, "the Age of Monsters was not far off" (6, p. 221). "A general corruption of manners never faileth to draw after it some heavy judgement of war, famine or pestilence" (*Essay toward Preventing the Ruin of Great Britain* 1721: 6, p. 79). If Berkeley expected a "fifth [act to] close the Drama of the Day" (*Verses on America* 1726: 7, p. 373) it was not in the spirit of the Fifth Monarchy men who hoped to disturb the public peace (see 6, p. 161).

These are genuine and vital differences, but Yeats did not worship destruction for its own sake, nor Berkeley worship order. Both saw currently fashionable society as the product of an unimaginative, grasping mentality, and put their hope in what was currently despised, old-fashioned faith and virtue. "The finger of God will unravel all our vain projects" (*Ruin*: 6, p. 71), unless through architecture, sculpture, painting (and literature) we fill men's minds with great ideas, "spiriting them up to an emulation of worthy actions" (6, p. 82). Berkeley, like Yeats, hoped for a new age, optimistically located in the Americas,

In happy climes, the seat of innocence,
where nature guides and virtue rules,
where men shall not impose for truth and sense,
the pedantry of courts and schools
(7, p. 373; see further on his American connections and influence, Conroy 1960, Gaustad 1979).

Yeats, like Berkeley, believed that it was by recalling their fellow citizens to traditional wisdom, "right reason and the maxims of antiquity," that they would best serve the commonwealth. Both believed that the world of humane endeavour and imaginative excellence was not simply a human fiction, a drama played out against an intrinsically unmeaning universe, but rather reality itself, accommodated to our finite view.

Goldsmith and Burke, Swift and Berkeley, so Yeats said, all "understood that wisdom comes of beggary" (Yeats 1950 p. 272). At first sight it is not a judgement that Berkeley—who spent his episcopate in schemes to raise the expectations and desires of the Irish peasantry that they might escape from beggary—would have quite accepted. "To feed the hungry and clothe the naked, by promoting an honest industry, will, perhaps, be deemed no improper employment for a clergyman who still thinks himself a member of the commonwealth" (*Querist*: 6, p. 103; see *Open Letter to Roman Priests* 1749: 6, p. 235ff). But Yeats perhaps had in mind the poverty of Plato's philosopher, longing for the wisdom that he does not now possess (Plato, *Symposium* 201d ff). If so, he caught Berkeley's drift: the failure of the minute philosophers was not that they were ruled by base desires but that their desires and expectations were too feeble. "Faith is not indolent perception, but an operative persuasion" (3, p. 301: Crito speaks), and one way to lay hold upon that saving faith is to awaken one's imaginative and loving involvement in "that purple sky, those wild but sweet notes of birds, the fragrant bloom upon the trees and flowers, the gentle influence of the rising sun ... and a thousand nameless beauties of nature [that] inspire the soul with secret transports" (*Dialogues*: 2, p. 171). "Sensual pleasure is the summum Bonum" (*Commentaries* 769: 1, p. 93), and it is "by an improvement of sensual enjoyment" that "the whole creation will be consumed and appear infinite and holy ... whereas it now appears finite and corrupt" (Blake 1966 p. 164).

Mandeville's belief that it was inconsistent with Christian virtue to enjoy the world, and that those pursuits that were indispensable to the maintenance of a civil society were therefore of the nature of vice (Mandeville 1954 p. 18f), seemed to

Berkeley to subvert a necessary distinction between real and fantastical pleasures: "men who are indisposed to a due exertion of their higher parts are driven to such [fantastical] pursuits from the restlessness of the mind, and the sensitive appetites being easily satisfied" (*Guardian Essay on Pleasures* 1713: 7, p. 194; see J.D. Johnston). Berkeley agrees with Mandeville in enquiring "Whether the bulk of our Irish natives are not kept from thriving, by that cynical content in dirt and beggary which they possess to a degree beyond any other people in Christendom? Whether the creating of wants be not the likeliest way to produce industry in a people? And whether if our peasants were accustomed to eat beef and wear shoes, they would not be more industrious? (*Querist* 19-20: 6, p. 106; Hutchison, Ward). But such wants were not, of themselves, vicious, nor would the wealth and prosperity of a nation be preserved save by "frugal fashions in the upper rank and comfortable living in the lower." "Show your charity," he begged the Roman clergy of Ireland, "in clothing the naked and feeding the hungry, which you may do by the mere breath of your mouths [by making them sensible of the sin and folly of sloth]" (6, p. 236; see Leyburn 1937 on Berkeley's changing attitude to the Roman church).

We shall know the truth when we have embraced our duty to God and the city. "I do not pretend," he wrote to Samuel Johnson, the American divine, "that my books can teach truth. All I hope for is that they may be an occasion to inquisitive men of discovering truth, by consulting their own minds, and looking into their own thoughts" (2, p. 282). It was not an Enlightenment aphorism, but an echo of Plato's insistence that truth was not to be found in any books, but only in the response of the philosophical soul to the intimations of immortal beauty by which we are surrounded. "Whether one, whose end is to make his countrymen think, may not gain his end, even though they should not think as he doth?" (*Querist* 1.315: 6, p. 161).

II

It is my contention, in brief, that Berkeley is only well understood when we see him as a traditional, Anglican, moral philosopher, opposed both to the minute philosophers and to those rigorists (by whom Mandeville seems to have been influenced) who played into the enemy's hands by proposing that "real Christians" must abandon the world to the evil one. Like other educated men of his day he knew the ancient texts as well as contemporary ones, and did not suffer from the modern delusion that philosophy began with Descartes. As both his moral purpose and his acquaintance with ancient texts are obvious it is odd that so little has been written on his moral and political philosophy. It is commonly claimed, if excuse is needed, that he did not write on these matters systematically, but there is ample material in the corpus for commentary. There are, at the very least, as many neat and sometimes sophistical arguments on moral and political affairs as on epistemological. Witness his argument for the claim that God cannot wish us only to love those who are good, on the ground that it is obedience to God's command which itself defines that class. We cannot be required to love and assist only those who love and assist those whom God requires us to assist, since there would be no such people until the command was being obeyed (6, pp. 20ff):

> Antecedent to the end proposed by God, no distinction can be conceived between men; that end therefore itself, or general design of Providence, is not determined or limited by any respect of persons. It is not therefore the private good of this or that man, nation, or age, but the general well-being of all men, of all nations, of all ages of the world which God designs should be procured by the concurring actions of each individual.

Pitcher's response (1977 p. 236), that there might be other God-given laws obedience to which defines the class of beings whom God commands us to love and assist, perhaps neglects Berkeley's central claim, that God, as a being of infinite goodness, must require the good of His creatures. The commandments on which hang all the Law and the Prophets are to love: the only question must be, whom? The argument, whether finally sound or not, has the same mind-stretching delicacy as those to be found in the *Principles* or the *Dialogues*. Like them it is not an abstract argument, but one directed against real and pressing dangers of his day (and ours), especially the notion that only the Wise, or the Elect, or the Revolutionary Front merit any respect, such as "flatter themselves that they alone are the elect and predestinate of God, though in their lives and actions they shew a very small degree either of piety toward God or charity toward man" (*Sermon on the Mystery of Godliness* 1731: 7, p. 91; see Clark 1987c).

It was in the course of preparing an essay on "God-appointed Berkeley and the General Good" (Clark 1985c) for Foster and Robinson's tercentennial collection of *Essays on Berkeley*, that I sought out such commentary on Berkeley's moral and political philosophy as exists. It is one of the few areas of philosophical enquiry where one can come fairly quickly to the conclusion that one has something like a complete bibliography, and be correspondingly aware of the curious gaps in scholarly commentary. Those who have written at length on his general (which is to say, his early) philosophy do sometimes mention and discuss the *Sermon on Passive Obedience* (1713: 6, pp. 15ff), which Urmson (1982 p. 72) reckoned the "only important document" for a study of Berkeleian moral philosophy. It is no surprise that nearly half the papers collected in this present volume are on that work. No surprise: but it ought to be a matter of regret that so little has been written on other issues. It should not have escaped scholars' notice that Berkeley (quite apart from incidental remarks in the traditionally studied works, and in the *Commentaries*) also wrote *An Essay toward Preventing the Ruin of Great Britain* (1721), several essays and sermons (mostly to be found in volume 7 of the *Collected Works*), *Alciphron* (1732), *The Querist* (1735-37), *A Discourse to Magistrates* (1738), and *Siris* (1744). But of general commentators only Ritchie 1967 and Wild 1936 go much beyond the beaten path.

Like Olscamp, I find it difficult to understand the neglect especially of *Alciphron*, in which at least the following problems are discussed:

> Probability as a sufficient ground for faith; determinism against free will; the qualitative distinction between pleasures; the general good as a criterion for moral behavior; the nature of the general good; the way we learn what our individual good is, and the relation between private and public good; the claim that there is a "moral sense," and its relation, if there is such a sense, to our moral knowledge and behavior; the role of reason in ethics, and the emotive functions of ethical terms (Olscamp 1970 p. 5).

To this list one could add: the nature of moral truth; individuals considered as parts of wholes; the importance of tradition and prejudice; limits on public tolerance of dissent; the economic value of virtuous behavior. It is also in *Alciphron* that we can see most clearly what Olscamp has identified as the "key" to Berkeley's philosophy, his conception of Nature as the Speech of God.

Some of the neglect can perhaps be attributed to odium anti-theologicum, and to the disapproving belief that Berkeley did not play fair with Shaftesbury or Mandeville. It could indeed be argued that Berkeley's own experience of ill-informed and malevolent attack (see Bracken 1965) should have warned him to be more cautious in his criticisms. But I suspect that more detailed and careful study of the texts under review would show Berkeley to have allowed his opponents some excellently contrived speeches, and to have been very much to the point in his mockery. Commentary so far has been too partisan; if Berkeley did not play fair, neither have a host of critics. Viner's remark that although Berkeley had more opponents than Mandeville, and Mandeville more critics than Berkeley, "Berkeley more than any other critic seems to have gotten under Mandeville's skin, perhaps because Berkeley alone made effective use against him of his own weapons of satire and ridicule" (1958, pp. 322ff), should serve as a reminder that Mandeville at least did not think Berkeley an unworthy opponent (see also Ritchie 1967).

III

The *Sermons on Passive Obedience* (published as single revised text in 1712), although they are most discussed (here by Orange, G.A. Johnston, Broad, Conroy, and Kupfer), are somewhat untypical productions both because they at least purport to be set out in the demonstrative mode that Berkeley expressly denounces as making "a dictionary of words" (*Commentaries* 690: 1, p. 82: see Olscamp 1970 pp. 61ff vs Conroy), and because he elsewhere identifies the source of sovereignty precisely in the consent of the subjects (21.10.1709: Rand 1914 p. 62), and suggests that a demand for total passive obedience to the de facto sovereign is inconsistent with the principles of the Glorious Revolution of 1688. Yeats's assertion that the published text was "a long, unreadable essay on utilitarianism, written to save his face" (Yeats 1961 p. 399) tells us more about Yeats than about Berkeley, but we should at least consider the possibility that the published text is not quite what he first said. It may be that he was once again arguing from an opponent's principles, on this occasion those of Tory opposition to that Revolution and to the Hanoverian succession, in order to establish what those Tories rejected. The rising water of Philonous's fountain, exemplifying the fate of sceptical or subversive principles, "is forced upward, in a round column, to a certain height; at which it breaks and falls back into the basin from whence it rose" (*Dialogues*: 2, p. 262). In the abstract, the overthrow of James II was illegitimate, since sovereigns should not be resisted, but in the concrete situation of the early 1700s, the beneficiaries of that overthrow must now be acknowledged sovereign: Berkeley, after all, always objected to merely abstract argument. But it is also worth recalling that our present perception of that Revolution, as a triumph for Lockean social contract theory, was not necessarily that of loyal Anglicans in the early eighteenth century. The choice was not between the Divine Right of Monarchs and Social contract, between a Sovereign Monarch and a Sovereign People, for the Sovereign was to be identified with the King in Parliament.

It was not that the king had been too absolute, but that the wrong king had been too absolute; it was not that the monarchy was to be thoroughly limited, but that a Catholic monarchy was to be excluded. The Revolution, as the expression of the via media, was a rejection of revolutionary innovation in favor of a church and state polity approved by the long usage of history, the ancient precedent of the law, and the spirit of reformed Christianity (Straka 1962 p. 37).

That was Berkeley's view as well: some of his contemporaries, absurdly, supposed that he was advocating Jacobite principles; modern readers, as absurdly, suppose that he would have condemned rebellion against the likes of Hitler—"which is a notion so absurd, so repugnant to common sense, that the foundation on which it is built may justly be called in question" (6, p. 44). Loyal Anglicans did not suppose that James had been overthrown, but that the throne had been left vacant by his withdrawal, and the accession of William and Mary providentially vindicated. Civil authority did not derive from the people (see Tussman 1957). To upset that order now would be to foment rebellion to the manifest disadvantage of the commonwealth, to betray their oaths of allegiance and prefer private fantasy to the will of God revealed in history.

Even Olscamp's useful full-length study (1970) is so far out of sympathy with Berkeley's God-centredness, as to do him less than justice. It sometimes also fails to take account of Berkeley's concern with pressing problems of his day. As the only such full-length study, containing many insights, for example, into the relationship between Berkeley's morality and later utilitarianism, it remains an essential tool for those who would study Berkeley in greater depth. "The 2 Great Principles of Morality: the Being of a God & the Freedom of Man" (*Commentaries* 508: 1, p. 63). The latter topic has been discussed in the context of contemporary Berkeleian studies (as by Hershbell, Pitcher 1981, Taylor 1985, and Olscamp 1970 pp. 91ff). Those out of sympathy with theocentrism are bound to find some difficulty in Berkeley's contention both that human beings must be supposed to be free, and morally accountable, and that God is the only cause of all that occurs in the phenomenal world, without benefit of secondary causes. Berkeley could retort against those theists of his day who believed in such material causes, operating within a law-governed universe merely ordained by God, that the problem was just as great for them (*Dialogues*: 2, p. 236). Atheistical criticism requires a different response, which seems to be that our freedom lies only in our capacity either to accept things as God would have us accept them or to prefer our private dreams, as investigated by Ulysses Cosmopolita (7, pp. 188ff: see above). We cannot actually get anything done in the public world without God's assistance, and what is actually done (by God's will and judgement) cannot be thought evil (cf. Pitcher 1977 pp. 99ff). Guilt, as Hershbell points out, lies only in the will. Our only duty is to conform ourselves to His will, "to propose to our selves nobler views such as to recreate and exalt the mind with a prospect of the beauty, order, extent and variety of natural things" (*Principles* 109: 2, p. 89). What really is is what God would have us know: "Evil, defect, negation is not the object of God's power" (*Siris* 320: 5, p. 147). All that is evil is our delusion, all that is accomplished by our mere will is nothing but the objects of individual—and perhaps social—imagination (see Clark 1988).

> For aught we know, this spot, with the few sinners on it, bears no greater proportion to the universe of intelligences than a dungeon doth to a kingdom. It seems we are led not only by revelation, but by common sense, observing and inferring from the analogy of visible things, to conclude there are innumerable orders of intelligent beings more happy and more perfect than man, whose life is but a span, and whose place, this earthly globe, is but a point, in respect of the whole system of God's creation. We are dazzled indeed with the glory and grandeur of things here below because we know no better. But I am apt to think if we know what it was to be an angel for an hour, we should return to this world, though it were to sit on the brightest throne in it, with vastly more loathing and reluctance than we would now descend into a loathsome dungeon or sepulchre (3, p. 172: Euphranor speaks; see Plato, *Republic* 7.514aff, whose Cave Berkeley explicitly evokes at *Siris* 263: 5, p. 124).

The world Berkeley describes, remember, and our imagined travels around it, are not to be conceived spatially (*Siris* 270: 5, p. 127): what is "here below" is what is manifest to our corrupted affections, and our "being an angel for an hour" is being acquainted with a larger segment of a heavenly reality. Those things "which eye hath not seen nor ear heard neither hath it entered into the heart of man to conceive" will be made evident to us on our entry into eternal life (7, p. 184), which is to say into a closer union with that "watchful, active, intelligent, free spirit in whom we live and move and have our being (*Theory of Vision Vindicated*: 1, p. 251). What percepts we encounter, what regions of the infinite realm of experience we visit, depends on the direction or character of our will. "Actions leading to heaven are in my power if I will them, therefore I will will them" (*Commentaries* 160: 1, p. 22). That he later rejected this dictum (to judge from the marginal note) is perhaps a mark of his growing realization of the real weakness (and moral ambiguity) of our desires. "Strange impotence of men. Man without God. Wretcheder that a stone or tree, he having only the power to be miserable by his unperformed wills, these having no power at all" (*Commentaries* 107: 1, p. 18: also obelized: see Taylor 1985). Actions commonly so-called are not in my power just if I will them, for palsy, lightning, neighbours or world's end may intervene. What alone is in my power is the will to submit (or not) to God, to make what Jonathan Edwards was to call "the cordial consent of beings to Being in general" (see Holbrook 1973 pp. 102ff: there is, I believe, a fascinating study to be made of the relationship of Edwards and Berkeley). "A peaceful submission and compliance in things lawful is the indispensable duty of every Christian" (*Sermon on Religious Zeal* 1709: 7, p. 26).

So long as our wills are coincident with his, we enjoy calm and peace, and cheerfulness, neither disturbed within by any remorse for our own actions nor mortify'd by any outward accidents: not engaged in vain pursuits, nor worried by fantastical appetites, but content to satisfy the demands of nature and reason (*Sermon on the Will of God* 1751: 7, p. 137).

That resolute theocentrism marks, as Broad points out, a major difference between Berkeley and the utilitarians he is sometimes, rather patronisingly, said to have anticipated (as by G.A. Johnston). The welfare, or reasonably supposed welfare, of humankind may be the criterion of moral truth, but it is not the ground of moral duty. We should act in accordance with those rules (see Kupfer) that seem to be required for the general good, for that is what we must suppose God wants us to do, and it is in obedience to Him alone that we have any hope of heaven. Such heavenly happiness, it ought to be obvious, is not—in Berkeley's conception any more than in Aristotle's (see *Nicomachean Ethics* 1.1097b8ff.)—granted to solitary individuals, but to members of family, nation, and the Great City which ancient philosophers had addressed (see Clark 1985, 1987).

Some elements of Berkeleian ethics almost amount to "making a dictionary of words": "God ought to be worship'd. This easily demonstrated when once we ascertain the signification of the word God, worship, ought" (*Commentaries* 705: 1, p. 86). But what exactly the reasonable man will suppose to be God (i.e., that which demands worship as of right) and what he will understand of God's speech to us are not such trifling matters, but must be learnt from personal and ecclesiastical experience. There are accordingly both a priori and a posteriori elements in Berkeleian ethics (Broad, G.A. Johnston, Conroy: see Olscamp 1970 pp. 6ff.).

A much less original Anglican writer, J.B. Morris, managed to say clearly what secular moralists have missed: a moral rule, say against incest, is not to be adopted because incest always leads to disaster, nor because we don't know when it would and therefore choose to play safe. The fact that it does so often lead to disaster is God's way of proclaiming His opposition to it: "supposing that there is no presage of conscience whatsoever against such matches, yet the fact that progeny produced from such unions soon dwindle away and degenerate is as much a declaration of God's will against them as a presage of conscience beforehand would be" (Morris 1843, p. 185). God does not forbid such matches because they lead willy nilly to disaster: they could not lead to disaster at all unless He chose to mark His disapproval like that. We may be warned off them by the thought of what may come: they are to be regarded as morally forbidden because it is God who thus warns us off. Such moralists will not regard those occasions when we can be confident that disaster will not ensue from some breach of generally accepted rule as exceptions to a rule of thumb, wherein the "reasonable man" will act by his own best grasp of the consequences. They will simply be occasions when God lets us off our due punishment: the ground of obedience to the rule would be just the same as ever. Even if the wicked were always to flourish, the believing moralist would remain assured that God had given him sufficient reason to understand that wickedness was not approved.

IV

Leary's study of Berkeley's social theory, beginning from the *Guardian Essay on the Bond of Society* (1713: 7, pp. 225ff), makes a useful transition to his economic philosophy. This latter was not, as Wisdom absurdly contended, a response to Berkeley's personal digestive problems (Wisdom 1953 p. 165), any more than his advocacy of tar-water was the fantasy of an "hypochondriacal recluse." There is, of course, an analogy between his economic and his metaphysical theory. Just as he saw that "matter," as conceived by the materialists, was an unnecessary postulate, so also he saw that bullion was not the essence of wealth. Material being, in common sense reality, was what we could touch, eat, and fondle: material wealth was likewise the measure of what we could enjoy. The richest gold mine in the world would be a liability if it rendered people lazy, proud, and dastardly (see J.D. Johnston). But Berkeley was not the source of these insights: John Law had taken the decisive step, in 1705, of identifying credit as the soul of commerce (Hekscher 1955, p. 234), and Berkeley's main difference from other "paper money mercantilists" was that he had, as Hutchison points out, the experience of living in a "depressed economy, distressed area, under-developed country and an exploited colony all at once" (see also Vickers). Ireland was not allowed to compete with English manufactories, but there were other industries (cheese, fisheries, pottery, carpets, cider, paper, linen) that could be cultivated if the obsession with bullion was forgotten.

The economic side of Berkeley's thought has been of some patriotic significance in twentieth-century Irish politics (see Hone 1934; Yeats 1961, p.396ff.), though it may well be doubted that his efforts to show how Ireland might prosper, even in the shadow cast by the British mainland, have had much to do with the problems of modern Eire and Ulster (just as Yeats failed to persuade his fellow countrymen that Berkeley's larger philosophy could help them against English "materialism"). J.D. Johnston did a great deal to bring his economic theory to light, especially in a succession of articles in *Hermathena* (represented in the present collection by his "Synopsis of Berkeley's Monetary Philosophy"), and in Johnston 1970. Economic historians (e.g. Hutchison, Petrella, Vickers, and Ward) have often given Berkeley more credit than philosophers for a lively contribution to the debate (notably, but not exclusively, in The *Querist* 1735-37: 6, pp. 87ff.).

Lovers of Berkeley have hardly been able to refrain, in recent years, from citing some of his questions: "Whether she would not be a very vile matron, and justly thought either mad or foolish, that should give away the necessaries of life from her naked and famished children, in exchange for pearls to stick in her hair, and sweetmeats to please her own palate?" (*Querist* 175: 6, p. 119). "Whether there can be a greater reproach on the leading men and the patriots of a country, than that the people should want employment? And whether methods may not be found to employ even the lame and the blind, the dumb, the deaf and the maimed in some or other branch of our manufactures?" (367: 6, p. 135). "Whether the North and the South have not, in truth, one and the same interest in this matter?" (3.141: 6, p. 177).

These, and other, quotations may seem alarmingly apposite. It must be our first care to remedy "the dirt, and famine, and nakedness of the bulk of our people" (*Querist* 106: 6, p. 114: see Vickers), and the duty of government is to achieve "some harmony of interests from the cacophony of individual interests" (Petrella). "To feed the hungry and clothe the naked by promoting an honest industry" (6, p. 103: see above) is also, and preeminently, the proper function of government, and not something to be left to the magical operations of any invisible hand. But despite J.D. Johnston's efforts to show that Berkeley had anticipated Keynes, it is important to recognize that Berkeley was not a Keynesian, and still less disposed to agree with modern "left-wing" philosophies. *Pace* Hutchison, Berkeley was not in the least likely to agree with Mandeville, or with Keynes. The latter disingenuously or confusedly declared that "for another hundred years we must pretend to ourselves and to every one else that fair is foul and foul is fair, for foul is useful and fair is not: avarice and usury and precaution must be our gods for a little longer still" (Keynes 1931 p. 372). To which Berkeley would have replied that such "wickedness on principle" (6, pp. 53, 84; 3, p. 76) was certain to bring on us the hatred of God and man, and that the idleness which Keynes imagines to be "real virtue" is as bad.

A "zeal for the public" (6, p. 81), aroused by great art and historical reminiscence, was Berkeley's proposed remedy for the factiousness, self-interest, and folly of his day. "It is impossible for either party [Whig or Tory] to ruin the other without involving themselves and their posterity in the same ruin" (*Ruin*: 6, p. 82). But the nation was not the only nor the most important social form. "The English have contributed more to destroy the Indians' bodies by the use of strong liquors than by any means to improve their minds or save their souls. ... Our first Planters imagined they had a right to treat Indians on the foot of Canaanites or Amalekites, [and had] an irrational contempt of the Blacks, as Creatures of another Species, who had no right to be instructed or admitted to the sacraments" (*S.P.G. Anniversary Sermon* 1932: 7, pp. 122f). A truer spirit requires us to act by those laws that a "reasonable agent would choose to obey if he were perfectly fair and not biased" (as

Kupfer rephrases Crito's message: 3, p. 139), and to see that we can and must enter into friendly relations even with those who, by existing social convention, are slaves. Berkeley did not advocate the wholesale release of slaves, of course: partly for practical reasons, that the slaves would at least be better off if planters did not suppose that baptism brought instant emancipation (in that they would allow them to be educated and baptised), and partly because he did not rule out temporary slavery as a solution to the social problem of the willingly indolent or feckless in regions much closer home than the Americas (6, p. 136: see Clark 1985b). *The Querist* is dedicated to the welfare of Ireland, and other essays and sermons to the welfare of Great Britain: but it was the whole of humankind whose welfare, in the end, was his criterion of moral truth. As Pitcher (1977 p. 235) has observed, his actual arguments seem to require him to go further still: it must be the welfare of the whole created universe, so far as we can affect it for good or ill, that must be our criterion, and we can affect far more than he allowed (see Clark 1987a). To that the one qualification must be added that in the last resort the only real harm that can be done to a free spirit is to be corrupted, and that harm can only be self-inflicted. We may fear or deeply regret those ideas that we encounter in God's video game, but they are never really evil. It is not even clear how exactly Berkeley thinks we can help to corrupt another soul, and he may have held that the non-human, not being corruptible by us, cannot be what God would have us trouble ourselves about.

For the most part, however, he remains true to that original insight, that what we call Nature is God's speech to us, that discoverable "laws of nature" are "a grammar for the understanding of nature" (*Siris* 252: 5, p. 120), which reveals to us an idea, an effect of "a divine Love and Intellect, [which are] not themselves obvious to our view, or otherwise discerned than in their effects." Since God has set in us such dispositions as lead us to seek pleasures for ourselves and those whom, by His providence, we care for, that must be what He requires of us on our journey into a fuller union with Him. "In valuing

Good we reckon too much the present and our own" (*Commentaries* 851: 1, p. 100), but reason can lead us to see that we are only parts of a larger whole, on which our happiness depends. That whole, the created universe animated by the divine will and intellect, is to be kept in motion and in devotion, as the object not merely of our sensual affections, but of the intellectual passion for truth, which is to say, of our desire to be set right, to be in tune, to see what God sees and would have us see.

> The eye by long use comes to see even in the darkest cavern: and there is no subject so obscure but we may discern some glimpse of truth by long poring over it. Truth is the cry of all, but the game of a few (*Siris* 368: 5, p. 164).

I hope that this collection of articles, and these pointers toward such Berkeleian topics as have not yet received their due, may encourage others to start poring.

Stephen R. L. Clark

BIBLIOGRAPHY

Berkeley, G.   1948 *Collected Works*, eds. A.A. Luce and T.E. Jessop (Thomas Nelson: Edinburgh).

Berman, D.   1985 "George Berkeley: Pictures by Goldsmith, Yeats and Luce": *Hermathena* 139. 1985 pp. 9–23

Blake, W.   1966 *Collected Works*, ed. G. Keynes (Clarendon Press: Oxford).

Boswell, J.   1963 *Life of Johnson* (Clarendon Press: Oxford).

Bracken, H.M.   1965 *The Early Reception of Berkeley's Immaterialism* (Nijhoff: The Hague).

Clark, S.R.L.   1975 *Aristotle's Man* (Clarendon Press: Oxford)

———.   1985a "Hume, Animals and the Objectivity of Morals": *Philosophical Quarterly* 35, pp.117–33

———.   1985b "Slaves and Citizens": *Philosophy* 60, pp.27–46

———. 1985c "God-appointed Berkeley and the General Good": Foster and Robinson 1985, pp. 233–53

———. 1987a "Animals, Ecosystems and the Liberal Ethic": *Monist* 70, pp.114–33

———. 1987b "How To Believe in Fairies": *Inquiry* 30, pp. 337–55.

———. 1987c "The City of the Wise": *Apeiron* 1 (N.S.), pp.63–80

———. 1988 "Soft as the Rustle of a Reed from Cloyne": P. Gilmour, ed., *Essays on the Enlightenment* (forthcoming).

Conroy, G.P. 1960 "Berkeley and Education in America": *Journal of the History of Ideas* 21, pp.211ff.

Foster, J. and Robinson, H.M. 1985 eds., *Essays on Berkeley: A Tercentennial Celebration* (Clarendon Press: Oxford).

Gaustad, E.S. 1979 *George Berkeley in America* (Yale University Press: New Haven).

Hekscher, E.F. 1955 *Mercantilism*, tr. M. Shapiro, ed. E.F. Soderlund (Allen & Unwin: London).

Holbrook, C.A. 1973 *The Ethics of Jonathan Edwards* (University of Michigan Press: Ann Arbor).

Hone, J.M. 1934 "Berkeley and Swift as National Economists": *Studies* 23, p pp.421ff.

Johnston, J.D. 1970 *Berkeley's Querist in Historical Perspec-*

	tive (Dundalgan Press: Dundalk).
Keynes, J.M.	1931 *Essays on Persuasion* (Macmillan: London).
Leyburn, E.D.	1937 "Bishop Berkeley: The Querist": *Proceedings of the Royal Irish Academy* 44, Section C, 75ff.
Mandeville, B.	1954 *A Letter to Dion*, ed. B. Dobree (University Press of Liverpool: Liverpool).
Morris, J.B.	1843 *Towards the Conversion of the Hindus* (London).
Monro, H.	1975 *The Ambivalence of Mandeville* (Clarendon Press: Oxford).
Newman, J.H.	1967 *Apologia pro Vita Sua*, ed. M.J. Svaglic (Clarendon Press: Oxford).
———.	1979 *An Essay in Aid of a Grammar of Assent* (University of Notre Dame Press: Notre Dame, Indiana; 1st ed. 1870).
Olscamp, P.J.	1968 "Some Suggestions about the Moral Philosophy of George Berkeley": *Journal of the History of Philosophy* 6, pp.147ff.
———.	1970 *The Moral Philosophy of George Berkeley* (Nijhoff: The Hague).
Pitcher, G.	1977 *Berkeley* (Routledge & Kegan Paul: London).
———.	1981 "Berkeley on the Mind's Activity": *American Philosophical Quarterly* 18,

pp.221–27

Rand, B. 1914 *Berkeley and Percival* (Cambridge University Press: Cambridge).

Ritchie, A.D. 1967 *George Berkeley: A Reappraisal* (Manchester University Press: Manchester).

Straka, G.M. 1962 *Anglican Reaction to the Revolution of 1688* (State Historical Society of Wisconsin: Wisconsin).

Taylor, C.C.W. 1985 "Action and Inaction in Berkeley": Foster and Robinson 1985, pp.221–25

Tussman, J. 1957 "Berkeley as a Political Philosopher": S.C. Pepper, K. Aschenbrenner, and B. Mates, eds., *George Berkeley* (University of California Press: Berkeley), pp.122ff.

Urmson, J.O. 1982 *Berkeley* (Oxford University Press: Oxford).

Vargish, T. 1970 *Newman: The Contemplation of Mind* (Clarendon Press: Oxford).

Viner, J. 1958 *The Long View and the Short* (Free Press: Glencoe).

Wisdom, J.O. 1953 *The Unconscious Origin of Berkeley's Philosophy* (Hogarth Press: London).

Yeats, W.B. 1950 *Collected Poems* (Macmillan: London, 2nd ed.).

———. 1955 *Autobiographies* (Macmillan: London).

———. 1961 *Essays and Introductions* (Macmillan: London).

CONTENTS

1. C. D. Broad, "Berkeley's Theory of Morals," *Revue Internationale de Philosophie*, 7 (1953), 72–86 . . . 2

2. Graham P. Conroy, "George Berkeley on Moral Demonstration," *Journal of the History of Ideas*, 22 (1961), 205–214 . . . 17

3. Jackson P. Hershbell, "Berkeley and the Problem of Evil," *Journal of the History of Ideas*, 31 (1970), 543–554 . . . 27

4. T. W. Hutchison, "Berkeley's *Querist* and Its Place in the Economic Thought of the Eighteenth Century," *British Journal of the Philosophy of Science*, 4 (1953-4), 52–77 . . . 40

5. G. A. Johnston, "The Development of Berkeley's Ethical Theory," *Philosophical Review*, 24 (1915), 419–430 . . . 67

6. Joseph Johnston, "A Synopsis of Berkeley's Monetary Philosophy," *Hermathena*, 55 (1940), 73–86 . . . 79

7. Joseph Kupfer, "Universalization in
   Berkeley's Rule-Utilitarianism,"
   Revue Internationale de Philosophie,
   28 (1974), 511–531 93

8. David E. Leary, "Berkeley's Social Theory:
   Context and Development," *Journal of the
   History of Ideas,* 38 (1977), 635–649 115

9. Hugh W. Orange, "Berkeley as a
   Moral Philosopher," *Mind,* 15 (1890),
   514–523 130

10. Frank Petrella, "George Berkeley's Theory of
    Economic Policy and Classical Economic
    Liberalism," *Southern Economic Journal,*
    32 (1965–6), 275–284 141

11. Douglas Vickers, "George Berkeley,"
    Chapter 8 from *Studies in the Theories
    of Money, 1690–1776,* by Douglas Vickers
    (London: Peter Owen Ltd.; 1960), 141–169 . . 151

12. Ian D. S. Ward, "George Berkeley:
    Precursor of Keynes or Moral Economist on
    Underdevelopment," *Journal of Political
    Economy,* 67 (1959), 31–40 181

Berkeley's Theory of Morals

by C. D. Broad

Berkeley had intended to treat ethics systematically in Part II of the *Principles*, but the manuscript of this was lost and he never re-wrote it. The main source now available for his views on this topic is the *Discourse on Passive Obedience*. This can be supplemented in certain minor respects by statements in some parts of the *Alciphron* and in some of Berkeley's essays in the *Guardian*. Here I shall confine myself entirely to the *Discourse*.

The contents of this were originally delivered as sermons in the chapel of Trinity College, Dublin, Berkeley published them first in 1712. The subject was a delicate and exciting one at the time and for long afterwards. Queen Anne's reign was nearing its end; she was to die in the late summer of 1714. In accordance with the Act of Settlement of 1701 she was to be succeeded by George, Elector of Hanover. In the end this change took place fairly smoothly, because the leaders of the Whigs were better prepared and more united than those of the Tories. But it was touch-and-go when it happened, and for years beforehand the question of who would succeed Queen Anne had been a matter of controversy and political intrigue. Now the doctrine of passive obedience was regarded as a typically Tory and Jacobite principle; though it would, on certain interpretations of it, favour *any* government that was once firmly in the saddle. Berkeley was suspected at the time of Jacobitism in consequence of his support of this doctrine.

Berkeley's political conclusion is that rebellion of a subject against the supreme authority of the country of which he is a citizen is, in all circumstances, wrong. He carefully defines his terms; but I am not here concerned *directly* with the political question, and shall therefore not consider the precise meaning of the principle. Here I am concerned with the doctrine only as an introduction to Berkeley's general view of ethics.

In order to prove that rebellion is unconditionally wrong Berkeley thinks it necessary and sufficient to show that it is a breach of what he calls a *negative* ' moral rule or law of nature '. and that all such rules are rigidly binding on everyone at all times and places and under all conditions. Now, in order to show this, he has to discuss such general questions as the essential features and the sanctions of ' laws of nature ' in this technical sense, the criterion by which to determine whether a proposed moral precept is or is not a ' law of nature ', and so on. It is his answers to these general questions which constitute his theory of ethics. But some important points in his general theory emerge only in the replies which he makes to plausible objections to his doctrine that rebellion is a breach of the law of nature. I propose now to try to state the general theory in isolation from its particular political applications.

(1) Fundamental Moral Precepts

Berkeley conducts his discussion in terms of what he calls ' laws of nature '. He is aware that this phrase is ambiguous, and says that he uses it to mean : ' A rule or precept for the direction of the voluntary actions of reasonable agents '. In the other sense, which is much the more usual nowadays, it means: ' Any general rule which we observe to obtain in the works of nature independent of the wills of men '. I shall substitute for the phrase ' law of nature ', when used in the ethical sense in which Berkeley uses it, the phrase ' fundamental moral precept '.

(1,1) *The criterion for such precepts*

Berkeley says that it is generally agreed that there are certain fundamental moral precepts which are unconditionally binding upon all men. But there are great differences of opinion about the criterion by which we are to judge whether a proposed moral precept is of this kind or not. He mentions various criteria which have been suggested, e.g., *innateness* and *universal consent*. Before considering his own criterion it will be worth while to note what he says about *innateness* in this connexion.

He does indeed assert that the fundamental moral precepts are 'stamped on the mind'. But he is careful to qualify this. All that he will admit is that there are innate antipathies to *some* kinds of action which are in fact wrong. But antipathies to certain kinds of action are often due simply to early training, and it is difficult or impossible to distinguish these from genuinely innate antipathies. Berkeley's conclusion is as follows. It is a mistake to assume that, when a strong antipathy is felt towards an act, the act must therefore be a breach of a fundamental moral precept. It is equally a mistake to assume that, where no such antipathy is felt, the act is *not* a breach of such a precept. In all cases, he says, we must decide what is and what is not a fundamental moral precept 'not by any emotion in our blood and spirits, but by ... sober and impartial reason'. This brings us to Berkeley's own criterion.

In the first place, we must remember that he held that the following *factual* propositions can be established by reason without appeal to revelation. (1) That human beings survive the death of their present bodies and thereafter exist for ever. (2) That God exists, that he is perfectly good, that he enjoys eternally all possible perfections, and that he alone can make a man eternally happy or miserable. (3) That the only rational creatures whom a man can affect for good or ill by his actions are himself and other human beings. These three factual propositions are essential premisses in Berkeley's argument.

The argument from them may be put as follows. Suppose that a man had reason to believe that God commands him to act in a certain way in all situations of a certain kind. Then there would be two quite independent reasons for acting in that way in such situations. (1) It is self-evident that the relationship of God as creator to men as his creatures imposes on them a *moral duty* to obey God's orders to them. (2) It must also in the long run be to his *interest* to obey. Our welfare and illfare throughout eternity are in the hands of God, and it is reasonable to suppose that he will reward obedience and punish disobedience to his commands.

So far the argument is purely hypothetical. The next question is this. Have we any ground, independent of revelation, to believe that God has commanded or forbidden men to act in certain ways in all situations of a certain kind? And, if so, how can we tell in detail what he has commanded or forbidden?

The next stage of the argument is as follows. Berkeley says that we must proceed by investigating two questions, viz. (1) What is the general purpose of God with regard to mankind? And (2) what methods would be best fitted to accomplish that end? An intelligent and good being would not issue orders to others arbitrarily. He would do so only in so far as he had an end in view, which he desired to be achieved by their voluntary actions, and because he knew that that end would be most effectively attained by their always acting in accordance with certain rules in all situations of certain kinds.

As regards the *end* which God desires that human voluntary actions shall bring about, Berkeley's conclusion is as follows. That end is the *general* well-being of the whole human race throughout the *whole* of its life on earth. His argument for this may be put as follows:—

(1) Since God is perfectly good, the end which he desires to be achieved by human action must be some kind of good state of affairs somewhere. Since God's own state is automatically one of eternal bliss, this good state of affairs must be a state of some finite created being or beings. Since human action can affect only human beings, any good result attainable by human action must be a state of some one man, or some class of men, or the whole human race.

(2) Berkeley now argues that we must accept the third of these alternatives. He states clearly the premisses of his argument, but the argument itself is very condensed and I do not find it easy to follow. The explicit premisses are these. (i) God, being perfectly *just*, would not favour one individual

or one class of men over the rest of mankind on any other ground than the *superior moral desert* of that individual or of the members of that class. (ii) Moral desert arises *entirely* from conformity to the commands of God. It is therefore logically impossible that any human being should have any moral desert *prior to* the issue of commands by God to men. Therefore, unless and until God had issued commands to men, and they had had opportunities to obey or to flout them, it is logically impossible that any individual or class of men should have deserved better or worse treatment from God than any other.

(3) So far the position is quite clear. I suggest that the argument would continue somewhat as follows, if the steps were made explicit. (i) God could not have desired that one individual or class should become better off than another until *after* he had issued commands and some men had obeyed and others had disobeyed them. (ii) But *before* God issued any commands to men he must have had some end in view to be attained by human action. For, otherwise, he would have had no motive for issuing commands. Therefore the end, in view of which God issued commands to men, cannot have had any reference to the welfare of any individual or class of men rather than any other. It must have been the welfare of the whole human race without regard to person or race or period.

Granted that this must be the end which God desires to be attained by human action, we now come to the second question. What *means* would God adopt? Berkeley says that there are *prima facie* two alternative ways in which the well-being of mankind as a whole might be promoted by issuing general injunctions to all individuals. These might be called the *direct* and the *indirect* method. The direct method would be to command everyone to act on each occasion in such a way as he then judges to be most likely to maximise human welfare. The indirect method is described as follows by Berkeley. It would consist in enjoining upon everyone ' the observation of certain determinate established laws, which, if universally practised, have, from the nature of things, an essential fitness to promote the well-being of mankind'.

The objection to the *indirect* method is that obedience to such determinate rules may, in particular cases, lead to great suffering on the part of many innocent persons. To the *direct* method there are at least two serious objections. One is its extreme vagueness. Even the wisest and the best of men would often be completely at a loss to know what to do and what to avoid doing, if he had nothing but the principle of universal beneficence to guide him. The second objection is that no-one could make a reasonably certain judgment about the rightness or wrongness of another person's action on any occasion. However ill the action may look, the agent could always say that he judged it to be the most benefic act open to him in the situation. Berkeley considers that the objections to the direct method are overwhelmingly greater than the objections to the indirect method. He therefore holds that we can safely conclude that God would adopt the *indirect* method.

If this argument be accepted, we can conclude that there must be various specific fundamental moral precepts, and we can give a criterion for deciding whether a proposed moral rule is or is not one of them. A fundamental moral precept is any rule of conduct which is enjoined by God upon all men in all situations of a certain assigned kind. It is a law binding upon men *because* enjoined upon them by God, who has a *moral right* to command his creatures. Now we can take as enjoined upon us by the will of God any rule of conduct with regard to which we can see that the general well-being of mankind would be promoted by *all* men acting in accordance with it *on all relevant occasions*.

Later on Berkeley restates this criterion more guardedly. Since all the fundamental moral precepts are enjoined by God with a single end in view, they will form a coherent *system*. Berkeley describes this as 'a system of rules or precepts, such that, if they be *all* of them at all times and places by all men observed, they will necessarily promote the well-being of mankind, so far as that is attainable by human action'. Presumably what he means is this. Any single rule of conduct, e.g., 'Never give a false answer to a question', might *still* be a fundamental moral precept, even if acting upon it in all relevant circumstances would *not* necessarily promote the well-being of mankind in a society in which certain other fundamental moral precepts, e.g., ' Thou shalt do no murder ', were habitually flouted. Berkeley thinks it plain that such maxims as ' Thou shalt not forswear thyself ' and ' Thou shalt not steal ', answer to this revised criterion, and are therefore commands issued by God, which men are therefore under an obligation to obey.

(1,2) *Relation of Berkeley's doctrine to Utilitarianism*

Before going further it will be well to emphasise the following distinctions which Berkeley brings out very clearly. (1) We must distinguish between the *criterion* for deciding whether a suggested rule is or is not a fundamental moral precept, and the *ground* of our obligation to act in accordance with it if it is a fundamental moral precept. The *criterion* is whether universal action in accordance with it would or would not promote the welfare of mankind. This is a criterion, because it is safe to assume that God would command men to act on any precept which answers to it, and on no others. But it is *not* the ground of our obligation to act in accordance with such a precept. What makes any moral precept binding on us is simply that God has ordered us to act in accordance with it, and that we, as his creatures, have a manifest duty to obey the commands of our creator. Thus Berkeley's doctrine is fundamentally different from ordinary Utilitarianism. For that makes utility the one and only *ground* of obligation. (2) We must distinguish between the criterion for deciding whether a suggested rule is a fundamental moral precept, and the criterion for deciding whether a particular action in a particular situation is morally permissible. The latter criterion is simply whether the action in question does or does not conflict with any of the fundamental moral precepts which are relevant to the situation.

In view of all this, Berkeley quite consistently holds that it is never permissible to break a moral precept which answers to the criterion for being fundamental, even when it seems perfectly obvious that to obey it will be less conducive to human welfare than to disobey it. We must distinguish, he says, between the *general tendency* of obeying a moral rule and the *accidental consequences* of obeying it in a certain particular case. If and only if the general tendency is beneficent, we can conclude that the rule is enjoined on us by God; and in that case it is our duty to obey it, even in particular cases where the accidental consequences will be bad. It would be inconsistent with God's *wisdom* to allow a breach of one of his commands (e.g., his prohibition of adultery) to be retaliated by a breach of another of them (e.g., his prohibition of murder). But, on the other hand, it would be inconsistent with God's *justice*, if he did not eventually reward those who have obeyed his commands and punish those who have flouted them. There is another world for the recompense of virtue which has been unfortunate and of sin which has been successful here below, and we must await it patiently.

(1,3) *Positive and negative moral precepts*

We can now deal with a distinction which Berkeley regards as very important, viz., the division of moral precepts into positive and negative, or commands and prohibitions.

According to him, it may be logically impossible under certain circumstances for a person to obey all the positive precepts which are relevant to the situation in which he has to perform a voluntary action. Suppose, e.g., that he has been given certain information under promise of secrecy, and that he is now asked a question which he cannot answer truly without revealing the facts thus imparted to him. Then it is literally impossible for him to obey *both* the precepts 'Keep your promises' and 'Answer questions truly'. In regard to positive precepts Berkeley says: 'The exercise of them admits of suspension, limitation, and diversity of degree'. In case of a conflict, such as I have illustrated, the agent must consider the realtive urgency of the various positive precepts involved. But, according to Berkeley, there are no exceptions to fundamental *negative* precepts or prohibitions. For, he says, it is always 'plainly consistent and possible that any man should, at one and the same time, abstain from all manner of positive action whatsoever'. To go back to our example. You can obey both the negative precepts, 'Never break your promises' and 'Never answer questions falsely', by simply refusing to answer when asked a question such that a true answer to it would break a promise.

It will be of interest to consider the logical position for ourselves. A moral *prohibition* in such cases is precisely equivalent to a moral *obligation* to adopt one or other of two mutually exclusive types of response to the situation. One of these is positive and the other negative. Thus, e.g., to say that it is morally forbidden to give a lying answer to a question, is equivalent to saying that it is morally obligatiory *either* to give a truthful answer *or* to decline to answer at all. Similarly, to say that it is morally forbidden to give an answer which will break a promise, is equivalent to saying that it is morally obligatory *either* to give an answer which respects the promise *or* to decline to answer at all. Now, if X is morally obligatory and Y is morally obligatory, then the conjunction $X \& Y$ is morally obligatory. In the present case both X and Y are disjunctions, and so $X \& Y$ is the conjunction of two disjunctions. It is in fact the complex disjunction: 'Either to give an answer which is *both* truthful and respects the promise *or* to decline to answer at all'. But by hypothesis the case under discussion is one where *no* answer can both be truthful and respect the promise. Therefore the first alternative is *impossible*. But, if it is morally obligatory *either* to do A *or* to do B, and it is impossible to do A, then it is morally obligatory to do B. Therefore, in the case supposed, it is morally obligatory to decline to answer.

It should be noted that the 'negativity' of the obligatory alternative in such cases must not be exaggerated. To give no answer to a question is 'negative', as compared with answering truly or answering it falsely, in the sense that it involves no *overt* bodily action relevant to the situation. But to maintain silence under threats and torture is a mode of response which involves immense positive effort of will.

Berkeley has now to deal with the objection that even some *negative* precepts, which seem to answer to his criterion for being enjoined on us by God, appear to admit of exceptions. An alleged instance would be the precept 'Do not kill', when considered in refence to a soldier in battle or an executioner performing the duties of his office. Berkeley was neither a pacifist nor an objector to capital punishment.

His answer is as follows. A negative moral rule may be expressed in terms which are too vague or too general. In that case we must begin by substituting a more specific term, e.g., 'murder' for 'kill'. It seems to me that there is a risk that this expedient may reduce a prohibition to a platitude. What, after all, is 'murder' but *unjustifiable* homicide? And is it not a mere platitude to issue the command: 'Never commit unjustifiable homicide'?

However that may be, Berkeley's answer continues as follows. After making the appropriate substitution we must apply the old criterion. If you find that the intrinsic tendency of following the amended rule in all relevant situations is benefic, you can conclude that it is a fundamental negative precept and that no breach of it is permissible. Otherwise, the rule is not fundamental, and it may sometimes be permissible or even obligatory to break it. Berkeley holds, of course, that there are certain negative moral precepts which survive the test.

(1,4) *Fundamental moral precepts and physical laws*

As we have seen, Berkeley clearly recognises the distinction between 'laws of nature', in the technical sense of fundamental moral precepts, and 'laws of nature' in the modern sense of established regularities of sequence and co-existence among natural phenomena. But he holds that there are certain analogies between the two.

On *any* form of theism which makes God a creator, the laws of physics and of psychology would presumably be expressions of God's will. But on Berkeley's form of theism they are much more direct expressions of it than they would be on most other forms of that doctrine. What we call 'the external world' is for Berkeley a series of sensations generated telepathically in our minds by God. In doing this God freely chooses to follow certain rules of co-existence and sequence, and these are the laws of physics.

The analogy between them and the fundamental moral precepts is this. The rules which God follows in generating sensations in us are well adapted to promote our welfare in general. In the first place, it is of immense advantage to us that there should be a system of rules of *some* kind, so that we may know what sensations to expect under assignable conditions. Secondly, Berkeley thinks that the *particular* rules which God has chosen to follow are such as are on the whole greatly to our benefit. Now, in spite of this, these rules lead in particular cases, e.g., earthquakes, explosions of atomic bombs, etc., to most unpleasant consequences. Yet even in such cases God does not forbear to generate sensations in accordance with his customary routine, though he could do so if he would. We know, then, that God does not depart from the rules which he has freely imposed on his own volitions in generating sensations in us, even in cases where to all appearance an exception would be more conducive to human welfare than strict observance. It therefore seems reasonable to suppose that he would not wish us to depart from the generally and intrinsically beneficent rules which he has enjoined upon our volitions, even when a breach of them would to all appearance be beneficial to mankind.

(1,5) *Fundamental moral precepts and tender emotion*

There is one other point worth mentioning before leaving Berkeley's doctrine of fundamental moral precepts. He insists that we must not allow either personal affection or a desire for the general happiness to induce us to break any of the fundamental negative rules. The following quotation expresses this very forcibly. ' Tenderness and benevolence of temper are often motives to the best and greatest of actions, but we must not make them the sole rule of our actions. They are passions rooted in our nature, and, like all other passions, must be restrained... Otherwise they may... betray us into as great enormities as any other unbridled lust '. He thinks that they are in a way more dangerous than the less respectable passions, because breaches of the fundamental moral rules motived by them have a specious appearance of goodness and generosity.

(2) GOOD AND EVIL

Berkeley says that self-love is ' the most universal ' and the most deeply engraven in our hearts ' of all principles.

It is therefore natural to each of us to consider all things and events and actions from the standpoint of whether they are likely to increase or diminish his own happiness. If and only if he thinks them likely to do the former, he calls them 'good'. If and only if he thinks them likely to do the latter, he calls them 'bad'. Berkeley goes even further in this direction. He says that it is the whole business of a person's life to apply his faculties to preserve his own happiness and to avoid his own unhappiness.

He asserts, however, that a person's judgments as to what constitutes or contributes to his own happiness alter with the degree of his enlightenment and the extent of his experience. At first one considers only sensible pleasure and unpleasure. But, even if we confine our attention to sensible pleasures, we soon learn that what produces immediate pleasure may lead to unpleasant sensations later, and that what produces immediate displeasure may be a necessary condition of highly pleasant sensations in the future. Such considerations may make us, even when we confine our attention to the pleasures and unpleasures of sensation, revise our earlier judgments as to what is good and what is bad.

Beside this Berkeley draws a distinction between what he calls the 'nobler' and the 'less noble' faculties of the soul. By the former he seems to mean those which involve *specifically human* powers and dispositions. By the latter he seems to mean those which we share with non-human animals. He describes the pleasures connected with the exercise of the nobler faculties as 'far more excellent' than those of mere sensation. This would be true even if there were only this present life. But a rational being can know that he is immortal and that there is a Supreme Being who alone can make him eternally happy or miserable. He can know that this Being has issued certain commands, which it is obligatory upon him to obey. And he may reasonably assume that obedience to those commands will be rewarded, and disobedience to them punished. So each of us has to take account, in his estimates of good and evil, of the infinitely longer life which he will lead after death.

So far Berkeley seems to be committed to a form of psychological hedonism. If so, he could not consistently admit that anyone's *motive* for obeying God's commands is the fact that he sees them to be obligatory upon him and desires to do his duty as such. A person might, indeed, see clearly that obedience to the commands of his Creator is obligatory upon him as a creature. But this could not move him to obey them, since he would have no desire to do what is right as such or to avoid what is wrong as such. His only possible motive would be hope of happiness or fear of unhappiness either in this world or the next.

Berkeley seems also be to committed to a form of ethical hedonism rather like J. S. Mill's. Nothing is intrinsically good except pleasant experiences or intrinsically bad except unpleasant ones; but the degree of goodness or badness of such an experience depends, not only on its hedonic intensity and its duration, but also on certain of its non-hedonic qualities.

Both these positions are, I think, internally consistent; but whether Berkeley himself consistently maintains them, or clearly envisages their implications, is more doubtful. In this connexion we should notice the following points, which he makes in his answers to certain objections that he thinks might be brought against his views.

(1) In answer to the allegation that self-preservation is the first and fundamental law of nature, Berkeley says that he can admit this only if it be interpreted as follows. It is a *psychological* fact about men and other animals that there is implanted in each individual an instinct of self-preservation, which is the earliest, the deepest, and the most lasting of all appetites. But, he says, it does not follow (and it is manifestly untrue) that a person is under a *moral obligation* to preserve his own life, which over-rides all his other obligations. Each of us is, no doubt, under a *prima facie* obligation to avoid doing things that may endanger the life of *any* man. But there is no moral rule which obliges a man to prefer the preservation of his own *life* or his own *temporal good* to the preservation of that of any other man. Still less is there any moral rule which obliges each man to prefer his own life or his own temporal good to the performance of *every other moral duty*. Berkeley remarks that the very fact that the instinct of self-preservation is so strong and so universal

would make any such rule superfluous, and therefore we can have no reason to believe that God would have enjoined such a rule upon us.

(2) Berkeley says explicitly that 'there is implanted in mankind a natural tendency or disposition to social life '. We can safely draw this conclusion, he says, from the following two facts. (i) We find men of all races and at all periods living in societies of some kind. (ii) This tendency to form civil societies is bound up with certain *specifically human* characteristics. Berkeley is thinking, no doubt, of the power of speech, the power of remembering and of conceptually reconstructing the past in thought, the power of anticipating and providing against future contingencies, and so on.

(3) Berkeley seems to hold that *specifically moral* goodness consists in, or is derived exclusively from, obeying God's laws, and that *specifically* moral badness consists in, or is exclusively derived from, disobeying them. For he holds that it is in this respect and in no other that men acquire *merit* or *demerit*, and that God allots to each in the long run the amount of non-moral good or evil (i.e., happiness or unhappiness) which his *moral* goodness or badness deserves. So far as this result is not achieved in this life God brings it about by rewards and punishments in the life to come.

In conclusion we may perhaps sum up Berkeleys's position as follows. God's ultimate end for mankind is an *eternal* state of affairs in which non-moral good and evil (i.e., happiness and unhappiness) are distributed among men in accordance with their moral desert. This moral desert arises solely from obedience or disobedience to rules of conduct which are enjoined by God as a means to men's *temporal* happiness without regard to desert. Presumably, then, Berkeley recognises a purely non-moral value and disvalue in happiness and unhappiness respectively, and a purely moral value and disvalue in obedience and disobedience respectively to God's commands. Like Kant (and, I should be inclined to add, like all sensible persons), he holds that the *complete* good involves both moral and non-moral goodness. It is in fact a state of affairs in which moral goodness is unmixed with moral evil and is accompanied by the amount of non-moral good which it deserves. But, in so far as the former condition fails to be realised, it is fitting that the moral evil shall be accompanied by the amount of non-moral evil which *it* deserves.

Trinity College, Cambridge.

GEORGE BERKELEY ON MORAL DEMONSTRATION

By Graham P. Conroy

In the *Philosophical Commentaries*, his personal notebooks, which he was writing while still a student at Trinity College, Dublin, George Berkeley made the entry:

Three sorts of useful knowledge—that of Coexistence, to be treated of in our Principles of Natural Philosophy; that of Relation, in Mathematics; that of Definition, or inclusion, or words (which perhaps differs not from that of relation), in Morality.[1]

Taking his cue from John Locke, whose *Essay Concerning Human Understanding* was being used as a philosophy text in his college classes, the young Berkeley saw an apparent similarity between the methods of proofs in mathematics and in morality, which should be called more properly demonstration than proof; for XVIth- and XVIIth-century philosophers had made a distinction between proofs and demonstrations. For example, Descartes took the experiencing of sense objects by our minds as proof of an external world, inasmuch as this experience was given to us even against our own acts of will or certainly independently of them. This proof did not carry the same measure of certainty for the Cartesians that a demonstration from self-evident rational principles could have given. But this latter was impossible since Descartes' Augustinian voluntarism ruled out a knowledge of God's intentions and acts. Thus any logical necessity or self-evidence in the observations of nature were precluded, for God could at any moment alter the ordered course of nature if he so chose.

Professor Adamson of the University of Glasgow has written in his article "Demonstration" in Baldwin's *Dictionary of Philosophy and Psychology:*

The term demonstration does not appear to have become a current accepted equivalent [of the Aristotelian *apodeixis*] till the period of the Arabic writers on logic, who translated ἀπόδειξις by it. The earlier Latin use, as in Boethius, does not go beyond the etymological sense, of showing, bringing before the mind as if pointed to, which the term still retains even in its specialized acceptation. For it is the peculiarity of demonstration that it claims for the conclusion reached by a mediating process the same simple absolute certainty that we incline to allow, without question, to the direct apprehension of a fact. The fundamental problems regarding demonstration begin in English philosophy with Locke's assignment of relations among abstract ideas of demonstration, and contrast of them with matters of fact....[2]

---

[1] *Philosophical Commentaries*, entry 853, included in vol. I of *Works of George Berkeley Bishop of Cloyne*, ed. by A. A. Luce and T. E. Jessop (London, 1948).

[2] R. Adamson in *Dictionary of Philosophy and Psychology*, ed. by James Mark Baldwin (New York, 1918), I, 268–269.

Although the problem in its use originated with Locke and his particular way of ideas, the demonstration of moral truth had been a distinguishing feature of the XVIIth century. This was particularly true of the Cambridge Platonists. To Henry More and Ralph Cudworth, morality was "immutable and eternal" and its basic precepts were to be discovered *in rerum natura* by a wise employment of reason. In 1731, just one year before Berkeley published his *Alciphron*, Cudworth's *Eternal and Immutable Morality* appeared posthumously. Previously these notions had been treated in More's *Enchiridion Ethicum* and in Cudworth's *True Intellectual System of the Universe*. In fact, almost every XVIIth-century philosopher believed in the mathematical treatment of ethics. Among the earlier examples of the technique had been Spinoza's *Ethica Ordine Geometrico* and Arnold Geulincx's *Ethica*.

The origin and growth of a demonstrative method is in itself instructive. Descartes' influence was still strong as a founder of mathematical sciences and this, coupled with a desire of many moralists to divorce ethics from theological dogmatics, led to the general tendency of XVIIth-century thinkers to seek a mathematical system of ethics. The only alternative which the XVIIIth-century moralist saw open to him were an uncritical acceptance of dogmatic theological pronouncements or a theological utilitarianism such as that espoused by William Paley on the one hand or the adoption of a demonstration of immutable moral precepts on the other. It is this latter type of ethical doctrine which was most influential upon Locke. J. A. Passmore has pointed out the impact of Cudworth's thinking upon Locke,[3] and W. von Leyden, the editor of Locke's *Essays on the Law of Nature*, has shown that of Nathaniel Culverwell and Bishop Cumberland.[4] In addition to the Platonist influence, however, there is that of John Wilkins, Bishop of Chester, Warden of Wadham College, and one of the founders of the Royal Society.

In his *Of the Principles and Duties of Natural Religion* Wilkins distinguished among three kinds of certainty which he named Physical, Mathematical, and Moral Certainty, all else being relegated to the realm of probability. Physical certainty depended upon the evidence of sense, "which is the first and *highest Kind of Evidence* of which human Nature is capable."[5] Mathematical certainty he held as applying to mathematical things primarily without excluding other matters which might be capable of a like certainty, viz. "all such simple abstracted beings as in their own Natures do lie so open, and

[3] See J. A. Passmore's *Ralph Cudworth, An Interpretation* (Cambridge, 1951). Chapter VII, "Cudworth and the British Moralists," 90–106.

[4] See W. von Leyden's *John Locke's Essays on the Law of Nature*, Latin text with tr. (Oxford, 1954), 39 *et seq.*

[5] John Wilkins, *Of the Principles and Duties of Natural Religion* (9th ed., London, 1734), 5.

are so obvious to the Understanding, that every Man's Judgment (though never so much prejudiced) must necessarily assent to them."⁶ Moral certainty is that whose evidence is not of the same kind as of the former, but is such as to necessitate the assent of everyone though there be no natural necessity that such things must be so else a contrary state of affairs involve a contradiction. The mark of their assent is that no one can "admit of any reasonable doubt concerning them."⁷ But to expect demonstrative certainty in moral matters was not possible for Wilkins as it had not been for Aristotle, for *"Moral* things, which being not of such *simple abstracted* Natures, but depending upon *mixed* circumstances, are not therefore capable of such kinds of demonstrative Proofs."⁸ Men must accept a statement or a conclusion as true on its own proper evidence or else nothing will be believed except that which has the highest evidence and all else will be uncertain or doubtful, and hence impossible of being known. Further, it was his belief that all conclusions deduced from first principles established on these grounds would possess the same degree of certainty as in the original principles.

But Locke wanted to go further; there was a basic unresolved tension between his Scholastic training at Oxford and the empirical direction of his thought. For him there was only demonstrative knowledge and intuitive knowledge (such as that of the self), and against this degrees of probability. If ethics was to be a 'science' in the Platonic-Scholastic meaning of 'science,' it must be composed of a body of demonstrably certain propositions. The way to this and over Wilkin's objections was to show that in spite of the mixed circumstances in which moral problems occurred, their demonstration could be rendered simple by illustrating that moral names were framed by men apart from real things and applied to situations, and thus are not signs for unknowable real essences as are the names of substances. The names of substances are the nominal essences men form from the real things but which cannot designate them since we have no knowledge of all the basic atomic, or corpuscularian internal relations of the substances being named. Therefore Locke thinks his way to a 'science of ethics' leads through the identification of real and nominal essence in moral ideas.

Both Locke and Berkeley were for certainty in knowledge and in this sense were heirs to the Platonic and Scholastic tradition while at the same time disavowing it. "Knowledge" was only that which was certain. Probabilities were not real knowledge; they were only "probable truths." Two sciences qualified for Locke as possessing this "certain knowledge." These were mathematics and ethics. Physics only possessed probable truths. Both mathematics and ethics consisted of perfectly demonstrable propositions. Both deal with complex ideas

⁶ *Ibid.,* 6. ⁷ *Ibid.,* 7. ⁸ *Ibid.,* 21.

which *are* their own archetypes rather than with simple ideas which always *point*, as their archetypes, to external objects, that is to say, deal only with those abstract ideas Locke calls "mixed modes and relations." Ethics, treating as it does of abstract ideas only, becomes a purely abstract science; and to the moral philosopher it would make no difference whether or not a just act anywhere or at any time ever existed. Such a view is completely foreign to Berkeley's insistence on the parallels between theory and practice in his ethical writings and alien to his general views on abstract ideas.

Locke had said, "I doubt not but from self-evident propositions by the necessary consequences as incontestable as those in mathematics the measures of right and wrong might be made out" and that such an interpretation as his might place "morality amongst the sciences capable of demonstration."[9]

Berkeley's entries in the *Philosophical Commentaries* show that in ethics as well as in metaphysics he was greatly influenced by Locke. These entries cannot be properly understood without reference to Locke. To appreciate and evaluate the meaning of these entries, it is necessary to have Locke's 'theory' of ethics in mind.

Now Locke had demonstrated, he believed, that mathematics was distinct from natural science and held that certainty was possible in the first case but not in the second since the object of the former was, in his estimation, a mode whose real essence is one with its nominal essence. Mathematics proceeded syntactically; it was a matter of discovering the necessary connections between the terms the exact definitions of which one knew. In like manner, Locke concluded, morality should be constructed as a demonstrative science since its objects—the abstract ideas of justice, right, fortitude, etc.—were also modes whose real and nominal essences coincided. Therefore, truth in both mathematics and morality should be independent of actual experience and to that extent *a priori*. Correspondences in language will have for him a corresponding relationship in the world of reality. "If it be true in speculation, that is, in *idea* that *murder deserves death*, it will also be true of any action that exists conformable to that *idea* of *murder*."[10]

Locke regarded his science of morality more difficult to axiomatize than the science of mathematics because the abstract ideas involved had only words for their symbols, possessing no further sensible signs. Conversely, mathematical questions utilize both since in geometrical demonstrations one may have both the word 'triangle' and the plane figure on paper. Moral concepts, being conveyed by words, only allow a greater possibility of confusion in their use. Nonetheless, if one is careful in applying these more complex notions, an exact science of morals actually can be achieved. Such was Locke's belief.

[9] *Essay Concerning Human Understanding*, IV, III, 18.　　[10] *Ibid.*, IV, 8.

That Berkeley's early view on a science of morality is not dissimilar to that of Locke can be seen from the following entry from the *Commentaries*: "Morality may be Demonstrated as mixt Mathematics."[11] Later entries show Berkeley's position changing. He realizes that this type of demonstration does no more than inform us how people in a society have used words and in a lexicon fashion tell us which words include which.[12] This tells us nothing of the foundations of morality. It can only render an account of how at a given time people do indeed use language.

This is an advance upon his earlier stand in the *Commentaries* when he thought that morality was capable of rigorous demonstration. Ethics on Lockian terms, like mathematics, will be *a priori* and certain, but will be at the same time vacuous or tautologous. If one gives the proper definitions of moral terms, he can never err in deducing moral judgments. This Berkeley apparently believed at first and held that mathematics was easier to demonstrate than morals only because the "words in Metaphisiques & Morality being mostly known to all the definitions of them may chance to be controverted."[13]

Before long, however, Berkeley came to see the absurdity of this kind of extreme rationalism and the "trifling nature of Locke's propositions."[14] Such propositions merely informed one of how a man intended to use moral terms. It has been said that Locke felt he was not dealing with descriptive words that functioned vacuously in purely syntactical contexts, but with actual ideas. His science of morality, nevertheless, even though it be allowed this provision, would fail to provide an empirical 'science of morality' as Locke conceived it. It would not be empirical since there are no ideas of sensation or reflection of the moral terms and non-deductive since empirical reference would have to be made for such a 'science' to be significant. Berkeley delivers a telling blow to this type of demonstration when he says, "fruitless the distinction twixt real and nominal essence."[15]

If this were all one wanted to know and nothing more, then Berkeley's blunt assertion, "To demonstrate morality it seems one need only make a dictionary of words and see which included which,"[16] would spell the end of the matter. But he sees the trifling nature of the whole procedure. All statements that issue from definitions will be vacuous since tautologous; the definitions will tell us how the demonstrator uses words. It is not a "necessary truth" that the logical

---

[11] *Philosophical Commentaries*, entry 755.

[12] *Ibid.*, entry 690. This type of work was attempted prior to Locke by Wilkins, Bishop of Chester, in his book *An Essay Toward a Real Character, and a Philosophical Language* (London, 1668). It was commissioned by the Royal Society (see Sprat's *History*). [13] *Ibid.*, entry 162. [14] *Ibid.*, entry 691.
[15] *Ibid.*, entry 536. [16] *Ibid.*, entry 690.

order and the order of reality must in any way duplicate each other.

Yet in a paper written after the *Essay*, Locke appears to take a position more in keeping with the tone of Berkeley. In this paper, *Of Ethics in General*, Locke deprecates a moral theory that concerns itself merely with the analysis of moral terms, for ethics should consider

species of action in the world, as justice, temperance, and fortitude, drunkenness and theft. But all the knowledge of virtues and vices which a man attained to this way would amount to no more than taking the definitions of the significations to the words of any language, either from men skilled in that language or the common usage of the country, to know how to apply them and call particular actions in that country by their right names, and so in effect would be no more but the skill how to speak properly.... The end and use of morality being to direct our lives and by showing us what actions are good, and what bad, prepare us to do the one and avoid the other; those that pretend to teach morals mistake their business and become only language masters.[17]

It is this type of stigma, that of being a "language master," of manipulating terms and framing meaningless and empty abstract ideas that Berkeley directs against his predecessor. It is probable that the statement in this later paper is not a *volte-face* for Locke, a repudiation of his 'science of morality'; for he had held he wasn't dealing with mere terms but with real ideas as well. Such a possible defense would have been untenable on at least two grounds, however. First, even though they (demonstrations) dealt with ideas, such ideas should be some kind of empirically derived abstractions if his earliest account of language and ideas in the *Essay* is to give him a consistent empiricism. But Locke specifically denies himself this escape by holding moral terms to have no symbols representing them other than names, no other sensible symbols, hence, no ideas—certainly not of sensation and not even of reflection. Second, any reference to empirical grounding of definitions would not properly be within the scope of the 'science of morality' as Locke conceived it.

Thus, Locke's rationalism will prove his undoing. Either Berkeley can reject his intended moral science as a web of empty tautologies which say nothing about the world and the actual habits of human beings; or, if he retreats back into empiricism and holds that moral terms stand for abstract general ideas, he can apply his own critique of abstract ideas to such terms and show them to be devoid of meaning, since they either involve contradiction or apply to no direct empirical referents, for we never meet "justice," but only just acts.

Lockian a priorism is rejected by Berkeley not simply because he

[17] Included in Lord Peter King, *Life and Letters of John Locke* (London, 1858), II, 125–127. Also cf. 129, sect. 9, quoted by R. I. Aaron in *John Locke*, 2nd ed. (Oxford, 1955), 263.

maintains that 'good,' for example, cannot be defined completely apart from all contexts and that it does make a difference that some just acts do really exist; but because, in large measure, of his developing views on the nature of self, or spirit.[18] Several entries on demonstration occur at the same place in the *Commentaries* where we find remarks expressive of Berkeley's completed views on the nature of spirit and there is, no doubt, a connection between the two sets of thoughts. The acts of spirit cannot be known by ideas since ideas are inert and cannot be like active things. These are known by notions. If demonstration can be only of names which represent ideas and ideas of spiritual activity are systematically unknowable and impossible, then moral demonstration is impossible inasmuch as morality is a matter which primarily concerns the will, or volitions. "The opinion," declares Berkeley, "that men had Ideas of Moral actions has render'd the Demonstrating Ethiques very difficult to them."[19] And several entries earlier he also writes:

We have no Ideas of vertues & vices, no Ideas of Moral Actions wherefore it may be Question'd whether we are capable of arriving at Demonstration about them, the morality consisting in the Volition chiefly.[20]

Berkeley's insistence upon morality as a matter of the will, his rejection of the meaningfulness of moral terms such as 'freedom,' 'good,' 'justice,' 'right,' 'obligation,' 'fortitude' and the like when prescinded from all exemplifications of such qualities, and his denial of any *a priori* demonstrability of ethics, by no means can be assumed to be a dismissal of the use of reason in establishing moral precepts. For Berkeley moral acts will have an element of rational calculation within them. The goodness of an act is a quality perceived from the effects of that act in a specific moral situation or context. It is a matter of present or future pleasure felt or to be felt. The rightness of an act, however, is, Berkeley believes, a quality to be ascertained by the "fitness" of that act to a universal rule of reason, and a rule governing actions done, being done, and to be done—acts of basic human significance and import.

Bearing this in mind, the demand for relativism and reality in ethics, it is surprising to know that in 1712 Berkeley composed a treatise which seems to be a direct violation of his stand on demonstration. The question then arises as to whether his rationalist doctrine of the *Passive Obedience* can be reconciled with his sensate eudaemonism. In actuality it cannot. The basic technique of the *Passive Obedience* is that very same demonstrative procedure which

---

[18] The Berkeleian doctrine of spirits makes it increasingly clear that ideas of moral actions are not possible; hence no demonstrability to ethics. Berkeley even comes to question the possibility of the demonstration of ideas themselves.
[19] *Philosophical Commentaries*, entry 683.   [20] *Ibid.*, entry 669.

Berkeley dismissed in the *Philosophical Commentaries* and in the *Principles*. Demonstration is of ideas and there are no positive ideas of moral terms and moral acts strictly speaking. Berkeley had written earlier in the *Commentaries:* "I must not to pretend much of Demonstration, I must cancell all passages that look like that sort of Pride, that raising of Expectation in my Readers." [21] In the face of his many strictures upon demonstration, he then writes a book on a demonstrative theory of ethics whose "eternal rules of action" have "the same immutable universal truth with propositions in geometry." [22]

This change of direction is puzzling. Yet if one realizes that Berkeley is here writing a treatise that is primarily political in nature and only secondarily ethical, one can better understand the particular problems. The ethical notions which Berkeley brings to bear on the question of political loyalty are only extended and developed as far as his immediate purpose required. *Passive Obedience* is not an attempt to work out an ethical system in whole or in brief.

The chief difficulty arising in the questions Berkeley discusses lies in his meaning of 'negative moral precepts.' According to this treatise those statements and precepts admit of no exceptions. In other words, those precepts are such that they admit of no empirical or prudential qualifications to men's unquestioned obedience of them. What kind of propositions then could these be that would possess such a high degree of certainty?

In attempting to find candidates for the appelation of 'negative moral precepts,' one is ultimately driven to consider the Decalogue. Therein we seem to find such candidates. Among these would be such moral imperatives as "thou shalt not to steal," "thou shalt not murder," "thou shalt not commit adultery." If a negative moral precept is defined as one which admits of no exception, then these sentences qualify admirably. The reason why they so qualify is not because, as a matter of fact, to transgress their admonitions would be wrong, but because each is a tautology and says nothing. Each is necessarily true, but true vacuously. 'Steal,' 'adultery,' and 'murder' are all words which contain a built-in moral judgment. Each stands for a type of wrong act. Therefore, when one says, 'one ought not to murder,' he is only saying 'one ought not to engage in immoral killing.' Since what is immoral is always wrong in matters of morals, this is no more than saying 'one ought not to do what one ought not to do.' In these cases it would seem that any validity the sentences have would have to come (according to the demands of certainty) through revelation rather than reason of the sort being used, or must be empirically grounded as ultimately concerning the being and cohesion of some kind of moral order of spirits.

[21] *Ibid.*, entry 858. [22] *Passive Obedience*, in *Works*, VI, 45.

It is significant that Berkeley writes in the *Philosophical Commentaries*: "Reasoning there may be about things or Ideas or Actions but Demonstration can only be verbal." [23] Reasoning for Berkeley can never be abstract reasoning; it is always reasoning-cum-sense. In the last analysis, the moral principles of the *Passive Obedience* are not established by the type of demonstration of Locke nor by the kind of rationalist argument one finds in Kant. His precepts on investigation illustrate themselves to be empirical generalizations upon experience or prudential maxims. He takes into account the feelings and inclinations of men. He starts from these and asks how they can be harmonized with God's purposes which cannot be demonstrated but which must come through revealed pronouncements to the common man, to the philosophical man through an induction of particulars, i.e. through seeing what courses of life, kinds of characters, and what types of acts lead to men's real happiness.

By experience, our own as well as that of others we do see that certain kinds of activities and lives seem to lead to observable consequences and we come to learn that the life of license will not pay off in the long run except in debased coin. Pure ratiocination will not tell us this; observation will give us a clue. As for finding the patterns of conduct that will lead us to "the Happyness of the life to come," [24] that will have to come ultimately through an investigation of natural and revealed religion.[25] It is a measure of Berkeley's realism on moral issues that he realizes men are not won over to the practice of virtue merely by increasing their power of abstract reasoning. He understands that most human beings must be won over to this conduct by persuasion and education.

We may say that Berkeley ultimately abandoned demonstration of moral matters for three reasons: (1) systematic: since morality concerns actions, actions are not given through ideas, and only ideas can be demonstrated (which is itself doubtful),[26] moral truths are incapable of being demonstrated; (2) psychological: the abstract nature of demonstration makes it difficult for the common man and is incapable of providing him with motives for just acts. "In short the dry strigose rigid way will not suffice, he must be more ample &

[23] *Philosophical Commentaries*, entry 804.   [24] *Ibid.*, entry 539.

[25] This will be largely a matter of revelation which will set the larger ends of morality and leave to us the discovery of the means and types of acts necessary to attain them. Revelation will not prescribe all the human duties, much will be left to empirical considerations.

[26] Berkeley eventually comes to hold that only names, rather than ideas strictly, are demonstrable; hence all demonstration is merely verbal. Mathematics (excepting geometry), being only about names or signs, is the demonstrative science par excellence.

copious else his demonstration [27] tho never so exact will not go down wth most"; [28] (3) procedural: Berkeley is unwilling to divorce theory completely from practice in human conduct.

Yet, Berkeley was not the only moralist of his age to abandon the rationalistic and demonstrative approach to ethics in favor of an empirical consideration of its subject matter, the acts of men in concrete situations. In the swing from the Platonic-Scholastic tradition, which found its last great upholder in Locke, he was joined by his theological colleague and fellow bishop, Joseph Butler.

In his *Ethical Sermons* Butler maintained that the subject matter of moral philosophy could be treated in either of two ways: from the abstract relations of things apart from exemplifications in human acts and from a study of the acts as they occur in life situations in which the actor is the central figure for investigation. He also maintained that each method has its advantages and that each leads to the practice of virtue. Butler probably had Samuel Clarke in mind as the chief proponent of the former view and his contemporary the Earl of Shaftesbury as representative of the latter method. His preference for the empirical method over the demonstrative appears to be based on the wider appeal which a discussion of concrete moral situations would have rather than upon any belief that the rationalist method is in any way inadequate to its subject. Butler must be said to have believed each of the two approaches to be valid.[29]

Foreseeing and modern as were Butler's views, George Berkeley went beyond him by completely rejecting demonstration and thereby opened the way for a further reduction of the field of moral propositions, more of which he took simply as matters of fact. This he did in a more thorough and polished way than Butler, Shaftesbury, or Mandeville who are often held up as precursors of David Hume in ethics.[30] Thus Berkeley stands as the transitional figure between XVIIth-century rationalistic ethics and the empirical moral philosophy of the XVIIIth, although his very position as a transitional figure has caused his interest and merit as a moralist to go unacknowledged.

Eastern Washington College.

---

[27] It is possible that Berkeley may occasionally be using demonstration in two different senses: as a technical term and in the common usage of "to show or illustrate." This quotation could be employing the term in the latter way (*Philosophical Commentaries*, entry 163). In this usage of 'demonstration' *Alciphron* would be the "more ample & copious" method of offering proof on moral subjects.

[28] *Philosophical Commentaries*, entry 163.

[29] Joseph Butler, *Analogy of Religion and the Fifteen Sermons* (London, 1893). In Author's Preface to Sermons, 372.

[30] Hume himself names "Mr. *Locke*, my Lord *Shaftsbury*, Dr. *Mandeville*, Mr. *Hutchinson*, Dr. *Butler*," in the Introduction to the *Treatise of Human Nature* as among "some late philosophers in *England*, who have begun to put the science of man on a new footing, and have engaged the attention, and excited the curiosity of the public."

BERKELEY AND THE PROBLEM OF EVIL

BY JACKSON P. HERSHBELL

Almost coincident with Berkeley's major literary activity, beginning in 1709 with the publication of his *Essay Towards a New Theory of Vision* and ending in 1744 with his *Siris: A Chain of Philosophical Reflexions and Inquiries*, several important works appeared in England and on the Continent dealing with the problem of evil. As early as 1702 William King's *De origine mali*, considered by A. O. Lovejoy "the most influential" of eighteenth-century theodicies, appeared.[1] In 1709, a year before the publication of Leibniz's *Théodicée*, the main principles of his optimism had been anticipated by Shaftesbury's work, *The Moralists: A Philosophical Rhapsody*.[2] And Pope's four epistles of the *Essay on Man* were issued between 1733 and 1734, two years before Berkeley's *Alciphron: or the Minute Philosopher*.

Of these works, and there are others which could be cited to illustrate the apparent preoccupation of eighteenth-century writers with the problem of evil, Berkeley was familiar with at least two. In the *Philosophical Commentaries*, a series of notes written by Berkeley between 1707 and 1708, but not intended for publication, there are several entries criticizing King's views concerning the human will and the divine *potentia*. And in his *Treatise concerning the Principles of Human Knowledge* (1710), Berkeley uses King's characteristic title for God, "Active Principle."[3] Berkeley was, of course, familiar with Pope's *Essay*, having advised him to omit an address to the Saviour, patterned after that of Lucretius to Epicurus.[4] He was also familiar

---

[1] Though the original Latin work was not widely read, Edmund Law's English translation was published in 1731, and underwent five editions during his lifetime. For an excellent discussion of King's *De origine mali*, see A. O. Lovejoy, *The Great Chain of Being* (New York, reprint 1965), 212ff.

[2] Commenting on *The Moralists*, Leibniz wrote: "I have found in it almost all of my *Theodicy* before it saw the light of day. . . . If I had seen the work before my *Theodicy* was published, I should have profited as I ought and should have borrowed its great passages." Quoted by S. Grean, in *Shaftesbury's Philosophy of Religion and Ethics* (Ohio, 1967), ix.

[3] LJ (followed by a Roman and an Arabic numeral) = *The Works of George Berkeley Bishop of Cloyne*, edited by A. A. Luce and T. E. Jessop (9 vols., London, 1949-57). References are to volume and page. The present reference is LJ.II.70.. For a summary of the relationship between King and Berkeley, see A. A. Luce, *The Life of George Berkeley Bishop of Cloyne* (London, 1949), 43-44.

[4] Alexander Pope, *An Essay on Man*, ed. Maynard Mack (London, 1947), xxiii. Berkeley and Pope were, of course, personal acquaintances and Pope ascribed "to Berkeley ev'ry virtue under heav'n." See also Luce, *Life of Berkeley*, 59-60.

with Shaftesbury's writings; for example, the *Characteristics*, the ethical theory of which is summarized in Dialogue III, 3 of *Alciphron*.[5]

In view, then, of Berkeley's knowledge of some contemporary works dealing with the problem of evil, to what extent was he himself concerned with the problem? An answer to this question is of interest not only for placing Berkeley's thought in the context of eighteenth-century optimism, but also for understanding his own philosophical system, which was clearly a piece of religious apologetics.[6] At least from the *Principles* onwards, Berkeley was making a reasoned case for those "who are tainted with skepticism, or want a demonstration of the existence and immateriality of God, or the natural immortality of the soul,"[7] and surely as part of his apologetic enterprise, it would seem natural for him to give some account of the ancient problem of evil, this being, according to Edmund Law in his Preface to King's *De origine mali*, "one of the noblest and most important Subjects in Natural Theology."[8] That Berkeley was aware of the problem is clear from two of his early major works, the *Principles* and *Three Dialogues Between Hylas and Philonous* (1713). At the end of the former work, for example, Berkeley is concerned with giving some account of the "blemishes and defects of Nature"[9] and the particular pains of finite spirits which "appear to be *evil*."[10] Berkeley again gives specific attention to evil, imperfection, sin, or wickedness in the *Alciphron* and *Siris*, and there are passages in a number of his other works relevant to the problem. He never undertook, however, a systematic treatment similar, for example, to that of King, and this seems strange, especially since throughout his writings Berkeley emphasizes the orderliness and harmony of a nature which is the product of a "wise, just, and benevolent God."[11] Indeed the visible world is the universal language of the Author of Nature, and if Berkeley's "immaterial hypothesis" with its formulation "*esse* is *percipi* or *percipere* (or *velle*, i.e., *agere*)" is taken seriously, it is clear that *everything*, including what men consider evil, seems to depend for its existence on God.[12]

[5] For a discussion of Shaftesbury and Berkeley, see Jessop's introduction to *Alciphron*, LJ, III, 10ff.

[6] This is clearly demonstrated by T. E. Jessop, "Berkeley as Religious Apologist" in *New Studies in Berkeley's Philosophy*, ed. W. Steinkraus (New York, 1966), 98-110.

[7] From Berkeley's preface to the *Principles*, LJ, II, 23.

[8] William King, *An Essay on the Origin of Evil*, trans. Edmund Law (London, 1731), iii of translator's preface.   [9] LJ, II, 111.   [10] LJ, II, 112. Italics in LJ.

[11] LJ, III, 252. Berkeley's insistence on the goodness and wisdom of God is found, of course, not only in the *Alciphron*, but permeates his early major philosophical work, the *Principles*. See, for example LJ, II, 26, 54, 65, 72, 82.

[12] This formulation of the "immaterial hypothesis" is Berkeley's own and one of the earliest. LJ, I, 53. It forms an important part of the complete hypothesis. See A. A.

Apart from its various philosophical formulations, to which attention will be presently given, the problem of evil is perhaps most severely and commonly encountered in human experience, and under no circumstances can Berkeley be considered to have been oblivious to phenomena such as pestilence, famine, earthquakes, and death. In his earliest writing in 1706, Berkeley described the "vast horrours" and the "dismal solitude, the fearful darkness and vast silence" of the Cave of Dunmore,[13] and in 1717 during his Italian journey he witnessed the eruption of Vesuvius.[14] Surely what drove Berkeley into the field of medicine and speculation on the nature and uses of tar water in the *Siris*, was the "appalling sickness and mortality attending a famine that began in Ireland in 1739."[15] In *Three Letters to Thomas Prior* (1744-47) he talks about bubonic plague as well as

... ulcers, itch, scald-heads, leprosy, King's evil, cancers, the foul diseases, and all foul cases, scurvies of all kinds, disorders of the lungs, stomach and bowels, in rheumatic, gouty and nephritic ailments, megrims, inveterate headaches, epilepsies, pleurisies, peripneumonics. . . .[16]

The description continues, a veritable Pandora's box of human ills. Berkeley was aware of earthquakes as is evident from his essay "On Earthquakes" in the *Gentlemen's Magazine* (April 1750), and in 1751 he was much distressed by the death of his son William, his "pretty gay plaything."[17]

Given, then, Berkeley's personal or experiential acquaintance with the darker phenomena of this world, how did he deal with the philosophical problem of evil, recently given a simple formulation by H. J. Paton as " . . . the problem of reconciling the existence of evil with the goodness of God," presuming God is doing what he can and wants to do about it.[18] Since the traditional division of evils into three classes—evils of imperfection or limitation, natural evils, and moral evils—provided the general scheme of King's argument, it is appropriate to consider Berkeley's own handling of the problem under these three heads.[19]

Luce's excellent discussion, "Berkeley's New Principle Completed" in *New Studies in Berkeley's Philosophy*, ed Steinkraus, 1 12.

[13]Berkeley's *Description of the Cave of Dunmore*, LJ, IV, 257ff.   [14]*Ibid.*, 247 50.
[15]From Jessop's introduction to the *Siris*, LJ, V, vi.   [16]LJ, V, 179.
[17]Berkeley's letter to Bishop Benson, quoted in Luce, *Life of Berkeley*, 208.
[18]H. J. Paton, *The Modern Predicament* (New York, 1958), 357. There are, of course, a number of other formulations of the problem, but Paton's is perhaps the simplest and best.
[19]King, *Concerning the Origin of Evil*, 73: "Whatever, therefore, is incommodious or inconvenient to itself, or anything else; whatever becomes troublesome, or frustrates an *Appetite* implanted by God; whatever forces any person to do or suffer what he would not, that is *Evil*.

II. Now these Inconveniences appear to be of three kinds, those of Imperfection,

For Berkeley, God is a being of "infinite perfection" who needs no instrument such as matter in order to produce "ideas" in finite beings. God's will is "no sooner exerted than executed."[20] Since matter as "an unextended, thinking, active being which is the cause of our ideas" is, therefore, according to Berkeley, an unnecessary and indeed a contradictory hypothesis in explaining the world,[21] it can no longer be accounted the principle of evil understood as privation or defect. And yet it is clear from Berkeley's thought that things ("ideas") and finite spirits are not perfect as God is perfect: "God is a thinking intelligent being in the same sense with other spirits, *though not in the same imperfect manner and degree.*"[22] Moreover, created beings among themselves are not all equally perfect. Somewhat later in *Alciphron*, for example, Euphranor finds it reasonable to conclude that

> ... there are innumerable orders of intelligent beings more happy and more perfect than man, whose life is but a span, and whose place is but a point, in respect of the whole system of God's grandeur.[23]

This world with its sinners, bears, in fact, "no greater proportion to the universe of intelligences than a dungeon doth to a kingdom."[24]

The term "perfect" has, of course, various meanings such as complete, flawless, or exact, and as a result Berkeley used the word "perfect" in different ways. For example, assuming Euphranor represents Berkeley's own position in *Alciphron*, he asserts in two different contexts (a discussion of the nature of beauty and the literary merits of Scripture) that "a thing is said to be perfect in its kind when it answers for the end for which it was made."[25] A thing's perfection cannot, however, according to Berkeley, be determined wholly by the senses; reason is required to ascertain its end or use. Moreover, what may be a defect in one thing is not so in another; the uses of a razor and axe are different, and both do not require the same degree of sharpness. In the sense, then, of subservient to an end or use, Berkeley can affirm that everything is perfect. In the sense of exactness, however, not everything is perfect. Regular exactness "or scrupulous attention to what men call the 'rules of Art'" is not observed in nature. Hence, lakes, rivers, oceans are not bounded by straight lines, and hills and mountains are not exact cones or pyramids.[26]

Natural, and Moral ones. By the Evil of Imperfection, I understand the Absence of those Perfections or Advantages which exist elsewhere, as in other Beings: By Natural Evil, Pains, Uneasinesses, Inconveniences and Disappointments of Appetites, arising from Natural Motions: By Moral, vicious Elections, that is, such as are hurtful to ourselves, or others."

In the *Théodicée*, Leibniz also recognized these three classes of evils. Indeed, the classification is a traditional one, probably going back to Proclus (*De mal. subst.*, 240).

[20]LJ, II, 219.   [21]*Ibid.*, 216.   [22]LJ, III, 171.
[23]*Ibid.*, 172.   [24]*Ibid.*   [25]*Ibid.*, 124 and 233.   [26]*Ibid.*, 227-28.

Some of Berkeley's views in the *Alciphron* on perfection are, of course, anticipated in the *Principles;* many of the same arguments again appearing in the *Siris,* his last major work. In the *Principles,* he argues that

> ... the very blemishes and defects of Nature are not without their use, in that they make an agreeable sort of variety, and augment the beauty of the rest of the creation, as shades in a picture serve to set off the brighter and more enlightened parts.[27]

Similarly, in the *Siris* Berkeley affirms:

> Natural productions, it is true, are not all equally perfect. But neither doth it suit with the order of things, the structure of the universe, or the ends of Providence that they should be so....[28]

And somewhat later, when discussing Plotinus with apparent approval, Berkeley remarks:

> ... that same Philosopher observes that, it may be, the governing Reason produceth and ordaineth all those things; and, not intending that all parts should be equally good, maketh some worse than others by design. As all parts in an animal are not eyes; and in a city, comedy, or picture, all ranks, characters, and colours are not equal or like; even so excesses, defects, and contrary qualities conspire to the beauty and harmony of the world.[29]

Though Berkeley does not use the analogy himself, just as an artist makes harmony out of contrasting or opposing elements, so does God, the Author of Nature. And could men but "see" the big picture, it would become clear despite the unequal perfection of things, i.e., their having different uses or not being complete, exact, or self-sufficient, the universe as a whole is perfect or manifests the harmonious design of a God who is wise and good. It would seem, then, that evil as defect does not exist for Berkeley: the defects or blemishes only result from our limited perspectives.

Insofar as Berkeley gave attention, then, to imperfection, his views do not differ substantially from those of King, Shaftesbury, or Pope. For Shaftesbury, there are no real flaws in a perfect universe, and for King and later, Pope, the evils of imperfection are explained by the principle of plenitude, the gist of the argument being that nothing created can be perfect, but that everything created is as perfect as it need be. The "fullness" of the universe depends, in fact, on the infinite differentiation of things, and there is a Great Chain of Being running through the universe with "no manner of chasm or void, no link deficient."[30] Similarly, in Berkeley's *Siris,* guiding his ruminations,

[27] LJ, II, 111.   [28] LJ, V, 121.   [29] LJ, V, 123-24.
[30] Lovejoy discusses this principle in *Great Chain of Being* 208-26. The quotation is part of Law's comment on King's thought, cited by Lovejoy, 215.

there is the theory that "there runs a chain throughout the whole system of beings" connecting them and preserving them "ever well adjusted and in good order."[31]

Moreover, since God enjoys "all possible perfection," it is clear that He does not act for his own good, but for that of His creatures. Yet so far as men's natural state is concerned, God does not favor individuals, and the general design of Providence

> ... is not therefore the private good of this or that man, nation, or age, but the general well-being of all men, of all nations, of all ages of the world, which God designs should be procured by the concurring actions of each individual.[32]

Both individual pains and natural blemishes, then, must be seen in terms of a total world structure created and sustained by a perfect Deity.

As already seen, Berkeley was not oblivious to such phenomena as earthquake, famine, and plague. In fact, he himself raises the objection in the *Principles* that

> ... monsters, untimely births, fruits blasted in the blossom, rains falling in desert places, miseries incident to human life are so many arguments that the whole frame of Nature is not immediately actuated and superintended by a spirit of infinite wisdom and goodness.[33]

His answer to this objection is simply that there are "certain general laws that run through the whole chain of natural effects,"[34] and although God can and does occasionally interrupt the orderly processes of nature, as in the case of miracles, His action is in accord with fixed laws

> ... which He will not transgress upon the account of accidental evils arising from them. Suppose a prince on whose life the welfare of a kingdom depends to fall down a precipice: we have no reason to think that the universal law of gravitation would be suspended in that case.[35]

Indeed, this operation according to general and stated laws is indicative of God's providence and is "so necessary for our guidance in the affairs of life, and letting us into the secret of Nature, that without it ... all human sagacity and design could serve to no manner of purpose."[36] Moreover, it is important for man to co-operate with God's designs, for:

> In religion, as in nature, God doth somewhat, and somewhat is to be done on

---

[31] LJ, V, 133. For an interesting discussion of the Great Chain of Being in Berkeley's thought, see A. D. Ritchie, "George Berkeley's *Siris:* The Philosophy of the Great Chain of Being and the Alchemist Theory," *Proceedings of the British Academy for the Promotion of Historical, Philosophical, and Philological Studies*, 40 (1954), 41-55.
[32] LJ, VI, 21.   [33] LJ, II, 110.   [34] *Ibid.*, 67.   [35] LJ, VI, 32.
[36] LJ, II, 111.

the part of man. He causes the earth to bring forth materials for food and raiment; but human industry must improve, prepare, and properly apply both the one and the other, or mankind may perish with cold and hunger.[37]

Berkeley, then, seems to recognize that natural evils exist, but they are "accidental" or simply arise out of the workings of the laws of nature which are evidence of a wise and good God. Were nature, on the contrary, random and without general laws, then there would be reason to deny God's goodness. Man, moreover, bears a certain responsibility for his actions, and there is a tendency on Berkeley's part to view natural evils as being partly deserved. In response to Alciphron's assertion that "the spoiling of the Egyptians, and the extirpation of the Canaanites" were cruel and unjust acts "unworthy of God,"[38] Crito replies that the Egyptians and Canaanites, in effect, deserved what they got, and though man, being imperfect, has no such right over his fellow-creature, God, who is "holy, omniscient, impassive," does.[39] Similarly, in a third letter to Thomas Prior prefaced by the text, "They provoked Him to anger with their own inventions, and the plague broke in upon them," Berkeley recommends tar-water against bubonic plague in the event "it shall please the same Providence yet further to visit us for our sins with the third and greatest of human woes."[40]

The problem of pain is again handled by Berkeley as being the result of general laws, and though a particular pain be accounted as *evil*, when considered "as linked with the whole system of beings," it is good.[41] Pains only appear to be evil. In general, Berkeley's response to natural evil is similar to that of Pope whose " . . . first Almighty Cause acts not by partial, but by gen'ral laws: th'exceptions few."[42] Indeed, there is little reason to doubt that Berkeley agreed:

> All Nature is but Art, unknown to thee;
> All Chance, Direction, which thou canst not see;
> All Discord, Harmony, not understood;
> All partial Evil, universal Good.[43]

Berkeley differed, however, from his contemporaries in regarding Nature or natural laws and events as being the language of God.[44] If one understands "language" to mean, not written or spoken words, but an arbitrary use of sensible "signs" having no resemblance or necessary connection with the things signified, and yet capable of

---

[37] LJ, VI, 212. [38] LJ, II, 250. [39] *Ibid.*, 251.
[40] LJ, V, 193. Ireland was ravaged by famine in 1739, and then by the Jacobite rebellion in 1745-46. [41] LJ, II, 112.
[42] Pope, *Essay on Man* (Mack edition), 33. [43] *Ibid.*, 50-51.
[44] See M. Guéroult's excellent article, "Dieu et la Grammaire de la Nature selon George Berkeley," *Revue de Théologie et de Philosophie* 5 (1953), 161-71.

suggesting to us an infinite variety of things, not only those near and actual, but also those distant and future, it is, according to Berkeley, evident that God speaks to us. The proper objects of vision, for example,

> ... constitute an universal language of the Author of Nature, whereby we are instructed how to regulate our actions in order to attain those things that are necessary to the preservation and well-being of our bodies, as also to avoid whatever may be harmful or destructive of them.[45]

Hence, the great variety of this visual language, the perfect adaptation of its signs with the infinite variety of things signified and the regularity which prevails in the functioning of this language, show not only that a spirit or mind, but a spirit wise and good governs the world with our interests and preservation in view.

When not employing the language metaphor, Berkeley views nature as being "nothing else but a series of free actions, produced by the best and wisest Agent."[46] But though God's actions are free, they are not capricious; He sustains the laws of nature without variance and change. Ultimately these laws of Nature form a system of "such rules or precepts as that, if they be all of them, at all times, in all places, and by all men observed they will necessarily promote the well-being of mankind."[47] Included within this system are not only natural laws but also moral laws. Both kinds are called "laws of nature" by Berkeley, though he does distinguish them. What is usually called a "natural law" is "any general rule which we observe to obtain in the works of nature, independent of the wills of men."[48] Such a law does not imply a duty. On the other hand, a moral law is also a law of nature or "a rule or precept for the direction of the voluntary actions of reasonable agents."[49] These laws of nature do involve duties. Thus the moral and natural worlds become for Berkeley partly, though not wholly, coincident. And as God is responsible for maintaining natural laws, so man is responsible for maintaining moral laws. From God's steady observance of the natural laws, which He will not change for the benefit of a particular individual or group, natural calamities sometimes result. Similarly, man's observance of moral laws, such as that of obedience to government, may result in human miseries. In either case, the accidental consequences of a law have "no intrinsic natural connexion with, nor do they strictly speaking flow from, its observation. . . . And these accidental consequences of a very good law may nevertheless be very bad. . . ."[50] Similarly the bad accidental consequences do not show a defect of wisdom or goodness in God's law. In the case of moral laws, they show only a defect of men's righteousness, and in the case of natural laws, they show only a defect of men's

[45] LJ, I, 231. [46] LJ, VI, 24. [47] Ibid.
[48] Ibid., 35. [49] Ibid. [50] Ibid., 38–39.

knowledge. Both kinds of laws are framed for the general good of mankind.

But the possibility of a defect in men's righteousness and the accidental bad consequences of a moral law, raise the problem of moral evil. How does Berkeley explain this?

Berkeley had intended to write a second part to the *Principles*, dealing with such topics as ethics, the human will, and God's reasons for the creation of the world. The manuscript, however, was lost during his Italian journey, and he never reworked it. Consequently, Berkeley's thoughts on these subjects are not fully known. In his extant writings, moreover, there are not many sections which deal with moral evil or the question of why God permits men to do evil, especially in such a way that the innocent often suffer more than the guilty. The usual theistic response is to claim that the Creator made men free, and that freedom to do good is somehow meaningless without freedom to do evil.

The problem of free will is raised in Dialogue VII of the *Alciphron*, where Alciphron argues against the possibility of human freedom and maintains as a consequence of the impossibility of human freedom that the whole system of rewards and punishments, "which suppose merits and demerits, actions good and evil," becomes meaningless. For, according to Alciphron, man is basically a machine such that:

Corporeal objects strike on the organs of sense whence ensues a vibration in the nerves, which, being communicated to the soul or animal spirit in the brain or root of the nerves, produce therein that motion called volition: and this produceth a new determination in the spirits, causing them to flow into such nerves as must necessarily by the laws of mechanism produce such certain actions.[51]

Euphranor replies that if the soul is corporeal, he would have to agree. But since the soul is incorporeal, the argument does not hold. To admit this would be to admit that motion and volition are one and the same. Moreover, it could be added, Alciphron's position attributes causal properties to an otherwise passive material substance, the existence of which seems contradictory to Berkeley.

Alciphron offers further objections against human freedom, none of which seem to receive very serious attention. For example, the claim that since God knows all things in advance, they must be pre-determined is briefly countered by Euphranor's saying that this makes no difference for, "If it is foreseen that such an action shall be done, may it not also be foreseen that it shall be an effect of human choice and liberty?"[52] In general, however, Berkeley's argument for free will

[51]LJ, III, 309-310.

stands on much the same ground as his argument for immaterialism: trust your senses, and be wary of too fine a reasoning. "It is," he says,

> self-evident that there is such a thing as motion; and yet there have been found philosophers who, by refined reasoning, would undertake to prove there was no such thing. Walking before them was thought the proper way to confute those ingenious men. It is no less evident that man is a free agent: and though, by abstracted reasonings, you should puzzle me, and seem to prove the contrary, yet, so long as I am conscious of my own actions, this inward evidence of plain fact will bear me up against all your reasonings, however subtle and refined.[53]

It is quite clear, then, that Berkeley considers men free agents, but how is God related to their actions? Is not the obvious conclusion either that God is ineffectual or that He chooses not to stop man's choice of evil? There are two instances where Berkeley discusses the relationship between man as agent and God as agent. They are in the *Dialogues between Hylas and Philonous*, and in his correspondence with the American philosopher, Samuel Johnson.

In the *Dialogues*, after establishing that the world consists only of ideas and spirits, things perceived and spirits perceiving, Hylas asks Philonous if this is not an admission that all causality is immediately attributable to spirits. Philonous agrees and alludes to the Scriptures wherein "God is represented as the sole and immediate Author of all those effects which some heathens and philosophers are wont to ascribe to Nature, matter, Fate, or the like unthinking principle."[54] Hylas then accuses him of making " . . . God the immediate Author . . . of murder, sacrilege, adultery, and the like heinous sins."[55] Philonous' answer is threefold. First, he claims that even if matter is used as an instrument by God, God is still guilty. Second, moral responsibility lies in the motive, not in the deed. Many men must kill in self-defense and therefore do not sin. We cannot judge God's motives by seeing His actions. Finally, Philonous claims that although, according to his immaterialist hypothesis, spirit is the cause of all things, he has

> . . . no where said that God is the only agent who produces all the motions in bodies. It is true, I have denied there are any other agents besides spirits; but this is very consistent with allowing to thinking rational beings, in the production of motions, the use of limited powers, ultimately indeed derived from God, but immediately under the direction of their own wills. . . .[56]

In a letter of September 10, 1729, Samuel Johnson presses the case harder, using the instance of the "habitual sinner":

> . . . if in an habitual sinner, every object and motion be but an idea, and every wicked appetite the effect of such a set of ideas, and these ideas, the immedi-

[53]*Ibid.*   [54]*LJ*, II, 236.   [55]*Ibid.*   [56]*Ibid.*, 237.

ate effect of the Almighty upon his mind; it seems to follow, that the immediate cause of such ideas must be the cause of those immoral appetites and actions; because he is borne down before them seemingly, even in spite of himself. . . . When therefore a person is under the power of a vicious habit, and it can't but be foreseen that the suggestion of such and such ideas will unavoidably produce those immoralities, how can it consist with the holiness of God to suggest them?[57]

To this question Berkeley reiterates the argument of the *Dialogues* that immediacy versus instrumentality is irrelevant, and reminds Johnson that since ideas are inert and passive, guilt can be located only in the will:

As to guilt, it is the same thing whether I kill a man with my hands or an instrument; whether I do it myself or make use of a ruffian. The imputation therefore upon the sanctity of God is equal, whether we suppose our sensations to be produced immediately by God, or by the mediation of instruments and subordinate causes, all which are His creatures, and moved by His laws. This theological consideration, therefore, may be waived, as leading beside the question; for such I hold all points to be which bear equally hard on both sides of it. Difficulties about the principle of moral actions will cease, if we consider that all guilt is in the will, and that our ideas, from whatever cause they are produced, are alike inert.[58]

According to Berkeley, then, men are responsible for their actions, the morality of these depending chiefly on the volition. Men can be blamed or praised only for those actions which are consequences of their volition. Thus a man ought not to be blamed or praised for his congenital abilities or capacities, since "we are only to be praised for those things which are our own, or of our own Doing, Natural Abilitys are not consequences of Our Volitions."[59] And though Berkeley never considered specifically the problem posed by lunatics, idiots, and those acting under psychological compulsion, his answer would perhaps be that such individuals cannot be considered free since their actions are not their own, that is, not the consequences of their volition. In any case, the majority of men are responsible for their actions; in fact, some of the greatest ills or evils afflicting mankind, are wrought by man himself, it being, for example, from man's lack of charity that "whole provinces are laid waste, cities, palaces and churches, the work of many . . . are in an instant demolished," and that "after an infinity of rapes, murders, rapines, sacrileges, when fire and sword have spent their rage . . . the dreadful scene often ends in Plague or Famine as the natural consequences of War."[60]

Berkeley never attempted to account for moral evil other than as the result of a "carnal and irregular" will[61] not always subordinate to the divine will which decrees the laws of nature and the laws of morality for the "common good of all men."[62] Unlike King, or Pope, Berkeley never argues that God manipulates the evil which men do on behalf of the common good. That God, who is good, uses wicked men to good purpose, is an argument that has no place in Berkeley's scheme.

In general, Berkeley's treatment of the problem of evil does not differ greatly from that of his contemporaries. Though he was certainly aware of the blemishes and evils of the created world, there was a tendency on his part to minimize them. Whether he would have agreed with Pope's famous saying, "Whatever is, is right," is not certain, though he could perhaps be classed with those *"philosophes trompés"* proclaiming *"tout est bien,"* against whom Voltaire was to protest in his poem on the Lisbon earthquake and again, in *Candide*. Despite the novelty of his "immaterialist hypothesis," Berkeley was very much the child of his age. To be sure, he differed from the deists in seeing Nature as the language or free acts of a God "in whom we live, move and have our being." And though man's powers to cause motion and to choose were significant, they depended on God not withdrawing them or choosing to confute them at any instant. But in making nature dependent for its existence on the infinite mind of God, indeed God being the only efficient cause, all other causes in nature being only occasional, did not Berkeley's philosophy demand, perhaps more so than others, a considered and systematic response to the problem of evil? Perhaps such an inquiry was unpalatable to Berkeley owing to his distrust of metaphysical speculation. Or perhaps he saw the futility of it. After all, Berkeley could find a partial solution to the problem of evil in the traditional Christian teaching of an afterlife; for "that natural appetite of immortality, which is so generally and so deeply rooted in mankind, we cannot suppose implanted in us by the author of our beings, merely to be frustrated."[63]

University of North Dakota.

[61] *Ibid.*, 135.   [62] *Ibid.*, 130.   [63] *Ibid.*, 108.

BERKELEY'S *QUERIST* AND ITS PLACE IN THE ECONOMIC THOUGHT OF THE EIGHTEENTH CENTURY[1]

T. W. HUTCHISON

I

IN 1734, when Berkeley returned to Ireland as Bishop of Cloyne, that island had for some time been sunk deep in a combination of conditions which economists would today distinguish as those of a depressed economy, a distressed area, an under-developed country, and an exploited colony. Straightaway, Fraser tells us, ' the social condition of Ireland, especially of the aboriginal population, began to engage Berkeley's thoughts '.[2] He set out to combat the economic distress around him both by practical measures in his own diocese (one in which it was then unusual for the Bishop even to reside),[3] and by composing a plan of, and summons to, national action in his pamphlet *The Querist*, published in three instalments in 1735, 1736 and 1737, as well as in a London edition at about the same time. Bishop Berkeley defended his concern with economic problems in his foreword to the second edition : ' I anticipate the same censure on this, that I incurred upon another occasion, for meddling out of my profession. Though to feed the hungry and clothe the naked, by promoting an honest industry, will, perhaps, be deemed no improper

---

[1] I am very grateful to Dr J. O. Wisdom of the London School of Economics for advising me about, and actually lending me copies of, a number of writings on Berkeley, including some most helpful unpublished work of his own.

[2] Fraser, *Works of George Berkeley*, Oxford, vol. 4, p. 242

[3] Vide E. D. Leyburn, ' Bishop Berkeley : " The Querist " ', *Proceedings of the Royal Irish Academy, Dec. 1937,* who quotes a letter of Berkeley's of 1737 : ' Our spinning school is in a thriving way. The children begin to find a pleasure in being paid in hard money ; which I understand they will not give to their parents, but keep it to buy clothes for themselves. Indeed I found it difficult and tedious to bring them to this ; but I believe it will now do. I am building a workhouse for sturdy vagrants, and design to raise about two acre of hemp for employing them. Can you put me in a way of getting hempseed ; or does your Society distribute any ? It is hoped your flax-seed will come in time. . . .' (Vide Fraser, op. cit., vol. 4, pp. 247-248).

52

employment for a clergyman, who still thinks himself a member of the Commonwealth.'

In its original form *The Querist* consisted of nearly 900 'queries' arranged with an apparently extreme and provocative haphazardness.[1] Altogether the pamphlet presents a thoroughly consistently-reasoned and comprehensive policy to raise the Irish economy and the standard of life of the people from their depressed and dependent state. But the first aim of *The Querist* was to stimulate thought and discussion and to 'make his countrymen think'—as he puts it—rather than to lay down a rigid programme : 'The Querist, indeed, only puts questions, and offers hints, not presuming to direct the wisdom of the legislature.' (Introduction to *Queries Relating to a National Bank, Extracted from the Querist*, 1737.) Berkeley was hopeful that thought and public discussion could lead to enlightened government action which would radically improve economic conditions and, above all, 'feed the hungry and clothe the naked'.

Although the result is consistent and well-knit, Berkeley's programme is rather built upwards out of particular practical proposals suggested by the closely-observed problems around him, than deduced downwards from a set of formulae or generalisations. Berkeley did not have at his disposal or seek to construct an organised orthodox set of definitions, assumptions, or 'tools of thought'. He simply brought to bear his great mind and deep sympathies on a set of practical commonsense proposals, introducing almost as a by-product the minimum of theory and analysis necessary for supporting and explaining his programme. Today *The Querist* must be read (as must, of course, most eighteenth-century and earlier economic writings) in the spirit in which Berkeley himself had asked that even his profounder philosophical arguments should be approached : 'I wish . . . our opinions were fairly stated and submitted to the judgment of men who had plain common sense, without the prejudices of a learned education.'[2] This invocation of 'plain common sense' might well have appealed to the main Scottish architects of classical political

---

[1] I have used Hollander's reprint of the first (1735-37) edition except in one or two (specified) places. A second edition was published in 1750 omitting many of the queries of the first edition, mainly the sharper and more sarcastically worded ones. The second edition added only a few queries not in the first. The differences in the two editions are important for Berkeley's character in his later years but have no significance for his economic arguments.

[2] Fraser, op. cit., vol. I, p. 332 (The Third Dialogue between Hylas and Philonous)

53

economy, Hutcheson, Smith, and, to some extent, Hume. But, unlike Hutcheson and Smith, Berkeley addressed himself to a particular practical problem and did not approach political economy as one department of a comprehensive 'philosophical' system of moral studies. On the other hand, though going straight for topical, practical issues, Berkeley was incomparably freer from the business, financial, or party-political interests which pervaded so many of the economic pamphleteers of that (and many another) period. Few economic writers can ever have combined to a higher extent the virtues of immediate practical relevance and profound intellectual disinterestedness.

There is little or nothing in the way of specific references by Berkeley to the background of writings and ideas on political economy which may have helped him in building up the programme of *The Querist*. But however much or little Berkeley may have read and marked the writings of his contemporaries and recent predecessors, most of his leading ideas are to be found in the English economic thought of the previous half-century, in particular in the works of Petty (1662 et seq.), Barbon (1690), North (1691), and John Law (1705). The rather staccato interrogative procedure of *The Querist* may have been suggested by Petty's monetary tract *Quantulumcunque* (1682). There had also been one or two noteworthy pamphlets dealing specifically with Irish monetary problems.[1] It is clear, too, that in the course of his European and American travels, Berkeley had studied closely the details of banking institutions and the acute contemporary monetary problems in different countries. He had obviously followed with deep interest the course of John Law's experiment in Paris (1716-20) with his government-controlled Banque Royale and its paper currency, but had not allowed its disastrous practical conclusion to distract him from the theoretical penetration and soundness contained in some of Law's ideas.

Apart from *The Querist*, the only other of Berkeley's works bearing at all on political economy is his short *Essay towards preventing the Ruine of Great Britain* (1721). His message here is mainly a moral one, directed against the misuse of economic freedom which had produced the South Sea Bubble. But his economic proposals for

---

[1] For example, Thomas Prior, a close friend of Berkeley, had published his *Observations on Coin* in 1729, and there had been Isaac Newton's *Representation* of 1712. Both these were republished by McCulloch in his *Old and Scarce Tracts on Money*.

BERKELEY'S 'QUERIST'

Britain, though very briefly stated, are, in general outline, very similar to those later proposed for Ireland in *The Querist*, and we shall make some quotations from the *Essay* as well as from *The Querist*.

2

The main features of Irish economic conditions with which Berkeley was confronted, and which he sought to remedy, can be gathered from the suggestions of *The Querist*, as one goes through it. Monetary conditions were primitive, defective, and confused in the extreme.[1] Moreover, the currency change of 1701 had had the effect of discouraging exports, already hard hit by English policy, notably by the prohibition on Irish woollen exports in 1699, 'one of the most infamous statutes that ever disgraced a legislature', as Arthur Young subsequently described it.[2] Apart from these particular aggravations there was much in the conditions Berkeley contemplated in Ireland in the 1730s which seems closely similar in general outline to those assumed by many seventeenth- and eighteenth-century economists elsewhere, both in Britain and France. In addition to facing primitive monetary difficulties, and sharp but persistent strains on the balance of payments in conditions of intense national rivalry, Berkeley was, above all, confronted with chronic and heavy unemployment. It certainly did not occur to Berkeley, in Ireland in 1735, as coming within the bounds of practical policy, to consider the setting up and supervision of institutional arrangements which could conceivably render self-regulating at satisfactory levels, both the internal level of aggregate demand, supply and employment, and, externally, the balance of payments. Only, it seemed to Berkeley, by a comprehensive and complex programme of State action combining labour legislation with fiscal, monetary, and public-works policies, could a high level of employment and external solvency be secured for Ireland.

There is one further condition facing Berkeley and seventeenth- and eighteenth-century economists generally, which marks another vital difference between his assumptions and those which later became more orthodox. From his close knowledge of labour conditions he had to assume that generally the supply of labour was very inelastic

[1] Cf. J. Johnston, 'Commercial Restriction and Monetary Deflation in 18th Century Ireland', *Hermathena*, 1939, 28, 79 ff.
[2] Cf. Lipson, *Economic History of England*, London, 1931, vol. 2, p. 204

55

once a certain traditional and very low standard of living had been earned, scraped, or begged. More moralistically, one might say—as contemporaries often did—that the Irish people were bone idle, preferring as much leisure as possible to regular work, or that any rise in their daily wage-rates was likely to be taken out in higher absenteeism per week. This is how Berkeley put it: 'Whether the bulk of our Irish natives are not kept from thriving by that cynical content in dirt and beggary which they possess to a degree beyond any other people in Christendom?' (i. 19)

'The oddity of Ireland is Berkeley's favourite theme in *The Querist*', an Irish biographer has stated.[1] But on this point, at any rate, it would be quite unnecessary to invoke any special Irish oddity. A few years later Dean Tucker was complaining that *English* labourers 'are as bad as can be described; who become more vicious, more indigent and idle in proportion to the advance of wages and the cheapness of provisions. . . . This is the ruin of all our trade, too many there are who will not accept work one part of the week but on such terms as will enable them to live in vice and idleness the rest.' Stripped of all moralising, this bare fact about the prevalent shape of the supply curve of labour, whether Irish or British, is asserted by one well-informed observer after another in the seventeenth and eighteenth centuries, from Petty and Defoe to Arthur Young and Sir James Steuart, and of course it can be met with in many parts of the world today not yet penetrated with the urban-industrial gospel of regular work, and not stimulated in its appetites by capitalist advertising or government propaganda and compulsion.[2]

[1] cf. J. M. Hone and M. M. Rossi, *Bishop Berkeley*, London, 1931, p. 200

[2] This problem is extensively discussed and documented in the remarkable study, *The Position of the Laborer in a System of Nationalism*, by E. S. Furniss, Boston, 1920, pp. 234-235: 'This tendency, represented by the "back-turning supply curve" for labor, is recognized by all students of economics, but in *laissez-faire* doctrine it is recognized only as the exception and not as the rule. . . . We find a widespread agreement among the writers of Mercantilist England . . . That the effect of increased prosperity among the English laborers was not a better, but an inferior, quality of industry, not more, but less, labor we must conclude from the almost unanimous testimony of contemporary writers. . . . The wants of the average individual to-day are but loosely restricted by custom and tradition . . . Among traditionalistic peoples, on the contrary, where a rigid standard of living, embracing not much more than the necessaries of physical subsistence, obtains, any increase in wages will result in an immediate diminution in labor hours.' Cf. also Cunningham, *Growth of English Industry and Commerce, The Mercantile System*, 5th ed., Cambridge, 1925-27, p. 566, who refers to 'the repeated charges of idleness . . . brought

56

This stubborn fact of a 'perverse' supply curve of labour is an extremely obstructive and irritating one for those anxious to promote a programme of economic development and expansion, whatever their political assumptions. Many of the seemingly odd 'interventionist' suggestions, sometimes harsh, sometimes optimistic, to be found in seventeenth- and eighteenth-century writings, arise from this general fact about the supply curve of labour—that an increase in wage-rates will be followed by a *fall* in the quantity of labour forthcoming per week—a fact which the classical economists later treated mainly as an exception in their theorising, though some of the details of the Poor Law Reform may have been attributable to it. It may well be that by the beginning of the nineteenth century the disciplines of urban industrialism, aided by the removal of possibilities for self-employment, had twisted the more rigid 'perversity' out of the general labour supply curve. Anyhow, in the classical system it seems generally to have been assumed that a rise in wages would be followed by an increase in the supply of labour, and vice versa, and finally we have Marshall laying it down:[1] 'Subject to ... qualifications, it is broadly true that the exertions which any set of workers will make rise or fall with a rise or fall in the remuneration which is

against the poor', and quotes Defoe: 'I make no difficulty to promise on a short summons to produce above a thousand families in England, within my particular knowledge, who go in rags and their children wanting bread, whose fathers can earn their 15 to 25 shillings per week but will not work, who may have work enough but are too idle to seek after it, and hardly vouchsafe to earn anything but bare subsistence and spending money for themselves.' See also Heckscher, *Mercantilism*, London, 1935, vol. 2, p. 165, who, discussing what he describes as the doctrine of 'the economy of low wages', cites as an upholder Sir William Petty, 'who had no private interests to bias him in favour of employers, and who had a better scientific culture than most writers of the Restoration period'. Heckscher concludes that 'according to the statements of many mercantilist writers the more people were paid, the less they worked'. Frances Hutcheson agreed with these 'mercantilists' in holding that 'if a people have not acquired an habit of industry, the cheapness of all necessaries of life rather encourages sloth' (*System of Moral Philosophy*, 1755, vol. 1, p. 318). But his pupil Adam Smith significantly altered the emphasis, laying it down that 'the liberal reward of labour' increases both the numbers and the industry of the common people: 'Some workmen, indeed, when they can earn in four days what will maintain them through the week, will be idle the other three. This, however, is by no means the case with the greater part.' (*Wealth of Nations*, Everyman ed., p. 73) Hume is non-committal, but notes the phenomenon of more labour being forthcoming in years of scarcity than in those of plenty (see *Essay on Taxes*).

[1] *Principles*, 8th ed., p. 142

offered to them.' It is also important that for the construction of self-adjusting models it is, *purely theoretically*, much more convenient to assume that a rise (or fall) in wages increases (or decreases) the supply of labour, rather than the reverse, which seemed the more realistic (though both theoretically and practically the far more awkward) assumption, for many seventeenth- and eighteenth-century economists.[1]

3

We may look, then, at *The Querist* as a programme for building up and maintaining a high and stable level of employment, and for raising the standard of living of the mass of the people, in the face of chronic unemployment, a 'perverse' supply curve of labour, vast inequalities in the distribution of wealth, and catastrophically primitive monetary arrangements. In spite of the great differences in assumptions, Berkeley's programme falls very easily under the three heads

[1] Furniss, op. cit., mentions many devices used or recommended for combating the 'perverse' labour supply curve in the eighteenth century. In 1946-47, post-war shortages and rigidities produced for a time a similar temporary perversity at a critical point of the British economy, in the coal-mining industry. It encourages one to believe in the hypothesis of regularities in economic behaviour when one notices how closely all the eighteenth-century measures were followed in various proposals, some rather pathetic, discussed at the time (except for the proposal of a direct cut in money wages institutionally impossible in 1946-47): Berkeley's and North's idea of stimulating new wants (p. 178) was revived in proposals to rush special supplies of 'incentive goods' such as nylons and tinned pineapple to the shop-windows of mining towns: Tucker's proposed immigration of foreign protestants (p. 35) was repeated in the proposed importation of masses of Italians: the same purpose of reducing real wages by taxing food, discussed by John Law, and with reservations by Hume (p. 136), was to be achieved at the later date by reducing food subsidies: the suppression of fairs, festivals and distractions from regular work (p. 150) had the milder equivalent of cutting down midweek soccer and racing. But in the twentieth century this 'perversity' could be only a temporary *curiosum* soon dissolving before the massive long-run disciplines of modern advertising, government propaganda and the emulative spirit, undeveloped, of course, in the eighteenth century. (The page references indicate where Furniss discusses the eighteenth century policies.) As regards pure theoretical convenience, the devoted attachment shown in recent years to the idea of the *interest* rate as an effective and satisfactory (if not optimal) equilibrator of the demand and supply of the other main contractually-rewarded factor of production, indicates (whether or not the attachment is justified) how convenient has been the assumption, impossible in the eighteenth century, that the *wage* rate was a smooth instrument of satisfactory equilibration in an expanding economy.

58

under which any such modern programme could conveniently be considered:

(a) the supply curve of labour and the labour market;
(b) fiscal policy and problems of the balance of payments;
(c) monetary institutions and policy.

(a) *The labour market*: Human wants are the driving force behind an active and prosperous economy, and the most liberal way of countering a 'perverse' supply curve of labour is to stimulate the desire for a higher standard of living and for new commodities (or 'incentive goods') not entering into the traditionally-accepted very low consumption habits, say a pair of shoes, rather better housing, and perhaps even a little soap or sugar:

> Whether the creating of wants be not the likeliest way to produce industry in a people? And whether if our peasants were accustomed to eat beef and wear shoes they would not be more industrious? (I. 20)

At very low traditional levels there is a vicious circle of poverty and idleness which has to be broken through if the standard of living of the people and the wealth of the country is to be increased:

> Whether nastiness and beggary do not, on the contrary, extinguish all such ambition, making men listless, helpless and slothful? (I. 66) Whether comfortable living doth not produce wants, and wants industry, and industry wealth? (I. 113)[1]

Whatever the possibilities of raising wants and standards without the blessed weapons of modern commercial advertising and

---

[1] Cf. Furniss, op. cit., p. 178: 'There was one small group of writers who took a more advanced position in regard to the standard of living than that attained by the mass of social observers. ... This group comprised Dudley North, George Berkeley, and David Hume.' Furniss quotes North (*Discourses*, 1691, p. 27) as follows: 'The main spur to trade or rather to industry and ingenuity is the exorbitant appetites of men which they will take pains to gratify, and so be disposed to work, when nothing else will incline them to it; for did men content themselves with bare necessities, we should have a poor world' (cf. Mandeville). Hume wrote: 'It is a violent method and in most cases impracticable to oblige the labourer to toil in order to raise from the soil more than what subsists himself and family. Furnish him with manufactures and commodities and he will do it for himself.' Furniss might have added Sir James Steuart to this group: 'Steuart's idea is that normally the primitive man would not work, unless forced, to produce anything beyond his barest necessities; but once his taste for luxuries developed, he became willing to work hard to produce a surplus with which to purchase luxuries.' See S. Sen, *Economica*, 1947, vol. 21, on 'Sir James Steuart's General Theory of Employment, Interest and Money'.

59

government propaganda, Berkeley (like Petty, Steuart, and many other seventeenth- and eighteenth-century economists) holds it to be the inescapable duty of the State to make sure that there is employment for all those ready and eager to take it, an objective which will not otherwise be sufficiently attained by any automatic self-adjusting mechanism. Berkeley does not lay down the frontier line, so importantly administratively but so difficult to draw precisely, between voluntary and involuntary idleness, and he does not elucidate the condition which subsequently came to be described as 'genuinely seeking work'. But he is perfectly clear that there is vast and chronic *involuntary* unemployment, and he is incensed by the paradox of poverty and unemployment side by side :

> Whether there can be a greater reproach, on the leading men and patriots of a country, than that the people should want employment? (II. 194)
>
> Whether it be not a new spectacle under the sun, to behold in such a climate, and such a soil, after so long a peace, and under such a gentle government, so many roads untrodden, fields untilled, houses desolate, and hands unemployed ? (III. 2)
>
> Whether we are not in fact the only people who may be said to starve in the midst of plenty ? (III. 101)

Local machinery should be set up for getting statistics of unemployment, and organising public works accordingly, on roads, bridges, drainage, public buildings and manufactures :

> Whether it may not be right to appoint censors in every parish to observe and make returns of the idle hands ? (II. 197)
>
> Whether a register or history of the idleness and industry of a people would be an useless thing ? (II. 198)
>
> Whether we are apprized of all the uses that may be made of political arithmetic ? (II. 199)
>
> Whether it would be a great hardship if every parish were obliged to find work for their poor ? (II. 200)

Berkeley proposed that it should be impossible to beg a living, or live on public relief without working, and he was prepared to advocate compulsory labour, which he bluntly described as 'temporary slavery' (not as a 'National Labour Corps', or as a 'Corrective Labour Service', to cite some typical neologisms). His proposal was intended for beggars and for common criminals (in the old-fashioned sense of 'criminal' which excludes 'political unreliability', 'thought-crime', etc.):

60

Whether it would be a hardship on people destitute of all things, if the public furnished them with necessaries which they should be obliged to earn by their labour? (II. 213)
Whether temporary servitude would not be the best cure for idleness and beggary? (II. 215)
Whether the public hath not the right to employ those who can not, or who will not, find employment for themselves? (II. 216)

Of course, in judging these proposals one must try, as best one can, to imagine the condition of the Irish poor at this time, and bear in mind the awkward but seemingly indubitable fact of the 'perverse' supply curve of labour, as well as what eventually became the alternatives of starvation or the workhouse in nineteenth century Britain, and prison or the slave-labour camp in the twentieth-century industrialisation of some other parts of the world. Anyhow, we agree with Sampson that Berkeley's 'advocacy of temporary slavery for beggars is not really so startling as might at first appear'.[1] The great ancestor of economic liberalism, Frances Hutcheson himself, laid it down at this period that 'sloth should be punished by temporary servitude at least'.

(b) *Fiscal policy and the balance of payments*: Berkeley's fiscal proposals were aimed at reducing extreme inequalities, helping employment at home, and eliminating the main source of strain on the Irish balance of payments. He completely agreed with Mandeville's argument—expressed also by many other seventeenth- and eighteenth-century economists—that it was the expenditure of the rich that employed the mass of the people:

Whether the industry of the lower part of our people doth not much depend on the expense of the upper? (II. 229)

[1] See Sampson, *Works of Berkeley*, vol. 3, p. 112. In his unrevised and posthumously published book, *The Dilemma of Our Times*, London, 1952, Harold Laski wrote: 'From the ruthless attack on almsgiving, and the equally ruthless promotion of enclosures, it was easy to move to a position where even a man like Bishop Berkeley could propose that the sturdy beggar be taught the habits of industry by undergoing a term of enslavement' (p. 93). Without any further reference to the element of humane equalitarianism in Berkeley's policies this quotation might be very seriously misleading, and we venture to believe that the author would have wanted to revise it before publication. We also venture to believe that Berkeley would have emphatically condemned the heavy gaol sentences for absenteeism and unpunctuality imposed by the labour legislation of certain contemporary governments so oddly supposed to be operating in the interests of the working class. See also Hutcheson, op. cit., p. 319.

But Berkeley, being morally opposed to luxury and to gross inequalities, did not agree with the conclusion which, with rather forced cynicism, Mandeville had suggested as following from this proposition, to the effect that it was therefore inevitably beneficent that the extravagance of the rich and the grossest inequalities of fortune should be given free rein:

> Whether necessity is not to be hearkened to before convenience and convenience before luxury? (I. 63)
> Whether to provide plentifully for the poor, be not feeding the root the substance whereof will shoot upwards into the branches, and cause the top to flourish? (I. 64)
> Whether as seed equally scattered produces a goodly harvest, even so an equal distribution of wealth doth not cause a nation to flourish? (2nd ed., I. 220)

Moreover, luxury goods made up a very large part of Irish imports while several of her main export markets had been prohibited outright by English restrictions. Berkeley did not propose to leave the balance of payments to take its course, but proposed combining sumptuary laws against luxuries with import duties protective of Ireland's solvency:

> Whether as our exports are lessened, we ought not to lessen our imports? And whether these will not be lessened as our demands and these as our wants, and these as our customs or fashions? (I. 105)
> What the nation gains from those who live in Ireland upon the produce of foreign countries? (I. 107)
> Whether those, who drink foreign liquors and deck themselves and their families with foreign ornaments, are not so far forth to be reckon'd absentees? (I. 110)
> Whether the dirt, and famine, and nakedness of the bulk of our people might not be remedied even though we had no foreign trade? And whether this should not be our first care, and whether, if this were once provided for the conveniences of the rich would not soon follow? (I. 112)

The expenditure of the rich could and should be so canalised as to give employment at home (for example, on houses and furniture), and solvency externally:

> What would be the consequences, if our gentry affected to distinguish themselves by fine houses rather than fine clothes? (II. 230) [1]

---

[1] Barbon had made a similar point as to the beneficence of expenditure by the rich on building 'since the erection of houses employs a greater number of people than feeding and clothing'. See Furniss, op. cit., p. 57, and Barbon, *Discourse*, 1690, p. 62.

62

Whether building would not peculiarly encourage all other arts in this kingdom? (II. 232)

Whether by these means much of that sustenance and wealth of this nation which now goes to foreigners would not be kept at home and nourish and circulate among our own people? (II. 236)

Whether as industry produced good living, the number of hands and mouths would not be increased, and in proportion thereunto, whether there would not be every day more occasion for agriculture? And whether this article alone would not employ a world of people? (II. 237)

The putting in hand of desirable public works could and should be used to raise and maintain the level of employment at home:

Whether it would not be of use and ornament, if the towns throughout this kingdom were provided with decent churches, town-houses, workhouses, market-places and paved streets, with some order taken for cleanliness? (II. 248)

Elsewhere in *The Querist*, and in his *Essay* of 1721, Berkeley proposes, for the central governments of both Britain and Ireland, large schemes of public expenditure, which might, or might not, be met out of taxation, and which would make up, or if necessary more than make up, for the cutting down of private luxury expenditure at home. He mentions education, learned academies, public buildings ('adorning them with paintings and statues'), and, exactly like Petty, 'triumphal arches, columns, statues, inscriptions, and the like monuments of public services'.[1] However, unlike Petty and Steuart, Berkeley does not attempt to analyse how the government can affect the level of aggregate activity by what are now called budget deficits or surpluses. Perhaps this is partly because he laid his main emphasis on monetary policy.

(c) *Monetary institutions and policy:* Berkeley's main attention and emphasis are not on his labour and fiscal policies, important though these are to his programme. His main, central, proposals are those for a national bank and a paper currency. Similarly, his remarks on the nature and functions of money, with which he supports his central

---

[1] cf. Berkeley, *Essay*, 1721, in Fraser, *Works*, vol. 3, p. 205. Sir W. Petty, also concerned with chronic unemployment, favoured government spending on 'entertainments, magnificent shews, triumphal arches' since this government expenditure is 'a refunding the said money to the tradesmen who work upon these things' (See *Economic Writings*, ed. Hull, vol. 1, p. 33.)

63

proposals, are analytically the most interesting contribution of *The Querist*. Both Berkeley's practical proposals and his analysis are very similar to those of John Law, and may be said to follow the school of thought which Heckscher describes as 'Paper-Money Mercantilism'.[1]

The principal aim of monetary institutions and policy must be to maintain a high level of economic activity and above all to prevent the paradox of poverty and unemployed resources existing side by side. In his *Essay* of 1721 Berkeley had written: 'Money is so far useful to the public as it promoteth industry, and credit having the same effect is of the same value with money'. *The Querist* asks:

> Whether money be not only so far useful, as it stirreth up industry, enabling men mutually to participate the fruits of each other's labour? (I. 5)
> Whether money circulating be not the life of industry; and whether the want thereof doth not render a state gouty and inactive? (III. 8)
> Whether all regulations of coin should not be made, with a view to encourage industry, and a circulation of commerce, throughout the kingdom? (III. 140)
> Whether facilitating and quickening the circulation of power to supply wants be not the promoting of wealth and industry among the lower people? (III. 186)

The function of money is to convert a lively 'natural' or 'real' demand into a *monetary* demand adequate to give that high level of employment which is morally and economically desirable. Money has been described as 'coined liberty'; Berkeley would have described it as 'coined power' and insisted that this power should be rightly distributed and circulated:

> Whether the real end and aim of men be not power? And whether he who could have every thing else at his wish or will, would value money? (I. 7)
> Whether the public aim in every well-governed State be not, that each member, according to his just pretensions and industry, should have power? (I. 8)

No one has ever exposed more repeatedly and fundamentally, even to the point of exaggeration, the error (attributed since Adam Smith to a somewhat indiscriminate body of his predecessors known as 'Mercantilists') that the precious metals are, in some sense, the

---

[1] On what he calls 'Paper Money Mercantilism', see Heckscher, *Mercantilism*, vol. 2, pp. 231 ff.

64

ultimate form of wealth, the accumulation of which should be the ultimate end of all economic policy. For example:

> What makes a wealthy people? And whether mines of gold and silver are capable of doing this? (I. 31)
>
> Whether there be any virtue in gold or silver, other than as they set people at work, or create industry? (I. 32)

In spite of the strong prejudices attaching to gold and silver, money is essentially a 'ticket', and, as things are, through the reliance on an uncertain supply of the precious metals, tickets of convenient denominations are simply not available. Hence the circulation of payments, which it is the essential function of these tickets to facilitate, is slowed down:

> Whether the prejudices about gold and silver are not strong, but whether they are not still prejudices? (III. 88)
>
> Whether it doth not much import to have a right conception of money? And whether its true and just idea be not that of a ticket, entitling to power and fitted to record and transfer such power? (III. 89)
>
> Money being a ticket, which entitles to power and records the title, whether such power avails otherwise than as it is exerted into act? (III. 176)
>
> Whether business at fairs and markets is not often at a stand, and often hindered, even though the seller hath his commodities at hand, and the purchaser his gold, yet for want of change? (III. 179)
>
> Whether beside that value of money which is rated by weight, there be not also another value consisting in its aptness to circulate? (III. 180)
>
> As wealth is really power, and coin a ticket conveying power, whether those tickets which are the fittest for that use, ought not to be preferred? (III. 181)

Such being the essential functions of money, it is clear that a supply of paper money can be much more conveniently regulated than can the supply of the precious metals, as had been shown, Berkeley claimed, in America:

> Whether it be not agreed that paper hath, in many respects, the advantage above coin, as being of more dispatch in payments, more easily transferred, preserved, and recovered when lost? (I. 207)
>
> Whether there are not to be seen in America fair towns, wherein the people are well lodged, fed, and clothed, without a beggar in their streets, although there be not one grain of gold or silver current among them? (I. 284)
>
> Whether paper doth not by its stamp and signature acquire a local value, and become as precious and scarce as gold? (III. 87)

Paper money is for Berkeley the highest stage in the development of exchange economies, and he sees no important distinction between money and credit (as he had already indicated in his *Essay* of 1721):

> Whether in the rude original of society, the first step was not the exchanging of commodities, the next a substituting of metals by weight as the common medium of circulation, after this the making use of coin, lastly a further refinement by the use of paper with proper marks and signatures? And whether this, as it is the last, so it be not the greatest improvement? (III. 100)
> Whether all circulation be not alike a circulation of credit, whatsoever *medium* (metal or paper) is employed, and whether gold be any more than credit for so much power? (III. 10)

To issue and regulate the paper currency a National Bank should be set up. Such banks, Berkeley claimed, were already operating successfully in Venice, Amsterdam, and Hamburg, and one had in fact already been under discussion for Ireland:

> Whether all things considered, a national bank be not the more practicable, sure and speedy method to mend our affairs, and cause industry to flourish among us? (II. 129)
> Whether a national bank would not at once secure our properties, put an end to usury, facilitate commerce, supply the want of coin, and produce ready payments in all parts of the kingdom? (II. 12)

It was vital that the National Bank should be publicly owned and controlled. The power to issue and regulate the supply of money was much too important to be left in private hands, Berkeley considered:

> Whether a bank in private hands might not even overturn a government? And whether this was not the case of the bank of St. George in Genoa? (I. 214)
> Whether by a *national bank*, be not properly understood a bank, not only established by public authority as the Bank of England, but a bank in the hands of the public, wherein there are no shares: whereof the public alone is proprietor, and reaps all the benefit? (I. 222)

Berkeley went into much detail in his proposals for a National Bank.[1]

---

[1] 'Letter on the Project of a National Bank,' *Works*, ed. Luce and Jessop, London and Edinburgh, vol. IV, 1951, pp. 185 sqq. His main points were that there should be no private shareholders, and that the directors should not themselves be members of the government or parliament, but should be appointed and periodically inspected by a committee, composed of members of the government and parliament, which would regularly be changing its membership.

66

BERKELEY'S 'QUERIST'

But he insisted that any scheme must be treated as experimental and that his own proposals admitted of many variations. He was well aware of the crucial importance of wooing public confidence discretely and cautiously:

> Whether there should not be great discretion in the uttering of bank notes, and whether the attempting to do things *per saltum* be not often the way to undo them? (II. 138)
>
> Whether the main art be not by slow degrees and cautious measures to reconcile the bank to the public, to wind it insensibly into the affections of men, and interweave it with the constitution? (II. 139)

Berkeley, also, could hardly have been unaware of the dangers of inflation and speculation, of which there had, comparatively recently, been such monstrous examples in London and Paris. Berkeley attributed these disasters to undisciplined private appetites which a publicly regulated monetary authority should be able to control. In any case, it was a chronically depressed economy that he was most concerned with:

> Whether we may not easily prevent the ill effects of such a bank, as Mr. Law proposed for Scotland, which was faulty in not limiting the quantum of bills, and permitting all persons to take out what bills they pleased, upon the mortgage of lands, whence, by a glut of paper, the price of things must rise? (I. 25)
>
> Whether the public aim ought not to be that men's industry should supply their present wants, and the overplus be converted into a stock of power? (II. 120)
>
> Whether money, more than is expedient for these purposes, be not upon the whole hurtful rather than beneficial to a state? (II. 122)
>
> Whether therefore bank-bills should at any time be multiplied, but as trade and business were also multiplied? (II. 124)

The supreme aim of the monetary authority must be a high level of production and employment:

> Whether the promoting of industry should not be always in view, as the true and sole end, the rule and measure of a National Bank? And whether all deviations from that object should not be carefully avoided?

Finally, a right understanding of the nature and functions of money, followed by appropriate government action could do very much to raise the standard of living of the Irish people:

> Whether that which employs and exerts the force of a community deserves not to be well considered, and well understood? (III. 317)

67

Whether the immediate moves, the blood and spirits, be not money, paper or metal ? (III. 318)
Whose fault is it if poor Ireland still continues poor ? (III. 324)

4

There does not appear to have been any immediate practical success attributable to *The Querist*, though according to Fraser 'there was an appreciable amendment in the circumstances of Ireland towards the middle of the last (eighteenth) century' which he somewhat vaguely connects with Berkeley's work.[1] A responsible national banking institution was eventually set up in 1783. But the body of 'employment' analysis and policy, finely represented by *The Querist* (though in its main outlines, if not in terminology, the same as what became accepted by the majority of economists almost exactly two centuries later) foundered, in its own day, on two main difficulties. First, there was not the statistical information, or the government administration, to work the analytically sound policies. Secondly, the 'perverse' supply curve of labour was a persistent obstacle, so that the earlier optimistic proposals—like Berkeley's—for guaranteeing the right to work, eventually petered out, later on in the century, in the negative disciplines of the workhouse (originally often intended as a form of public works, as by Berkeley himself).[2]

But even if *The Querist* was no more than normally successful in 'making his countrymen think' (and act) successfully, what of its longer-term contribution in helping subsequent economists to think ? Here the success of *The Querist* has certainly been quite undeservedly patchy and slight. Adam Smith presumably must have known Berkeley's pamphlet, but does not show any sign of the influence of some of its most important arguments. Subsequent economists of the classical period could hardly find much of value in *The Querist* if they took at all seriously the Mill-Say analysis of markets, or based their study of a monetary economy on such a proposition as Adam Smith's that 'money can serve no other purpose besides purchasing goods', and 'therefore, necessarily runs after goods', and were thence led to assume that the analysis of a barter economy could be applied without essential modification to a monetary economy. Berkeley would have considered it much rather misleading than helpful to

[1] Cf. Fraser, op. cit., vol. 4, p. 243
[2] Cf. Furniss, op. cit. ch. 5, 'The Enforcement of the Duty to Labor'.

proclaim with Smith that 'we trust with perfect security that the freedom of trade, without any attention of government, will always supply us ... with all the gold and silver we can afford to purchase or to employ, either in circulating our commodities, or in other uses'. But it was such assumptions as these of the 'Smithian revolution', driven dogmatically home by James Mill and Ricardo, which coloured, at least to a dangerously significant extent, a majority of the more orthodox and influential nineteenth-century writings.

It is hardly surprising that, when Maria Edgeworth commended *The Querist* to Ricardo in the warmest terms, she got no reply on the subject from that quarter.[1] *The Querist* was reprinted in 1829, but the only notice taken of it seems to have come from Sir James Mackintosh, the philosophical opponent of James Mill, who remarked: 'Perhaps *The Querist* contains more hints, then original, still [1829] unapplied in legislation and political economy, than are to be found in any equal space'.[2]

In 1871 Fraser's great edition of Berkeley appeared, and it was reviewed by John Stuart Mill in what must have been one of his last essays.[3] Mill's remarks on *The Querist* are too brief for any sure interpretation. But they convey at least a strong unconfirmed suggestion that Mill was still not clear of the typical orthodox misunderstandings of seventeenth- and eighteenth-century economic thought, exemplified in his wholesale youthful condemnations (1829) of all his predecessors of 'the last two centuries' (presumably excluding Adam Smith).[4] Mill praises Berkeley for considering 'luxurious expenditure a detriment', and for his perception 'that money is not in itself wealth, but a set of counters'—which perception, Mill very questionably claims, places Berkeley much in advance of his age. But Mill's praise of Berkeley for his condemnation of luxury requires some essential qualifications which it is doubtful whether Mill would have accepted.

One might perhaps assume from Mill's praise, that Berkeley, with his strong disapproval of luxury, was much nearer as an economist to Adam Smith, with his unconditional eulogy of 'parsimony', than he was to Mandeville, who cynically defended the public beneficence

---

[1] See Ricardo's *Works*, ed. Sraffa, vol. 9, p. 231
[2] J. Mackintosh, *Dissertation on the Progress of Ethical Philosophy*, 1829, p. 211
[3] See J. S. Mill, *Dissertations and Discussions*, vol. 4
[4] See J. S. Mill, *Essays on Some Unsettled Questions of Political Economy*, pp. 47-48, and p. 73

of. 'vicious' luxury expenditure. To make such an assumption would, however, be to make a complete mis-classification and misunderstanding of Berkeley's economics. It is, of course, true that *purely morally*—and Berkeley did not separate his moral and his economic doctrines—he considered luxury expenditure ' a detriment' and was a severe critic of Mandeville. But if one separates out Berkeley's economic analysis there can be no question that here he was on the same side of the fence as Mandeville, along with Petty, Barbon, Steuart and countless lesser writers; and that he would have rejected the economic analysis of saving and investment (or that saving *is* investment) on which Adam Smith based his eulogy of parsimony (however much *morally* Berkeley would have approved). We entirely agree with Professor Johnston that Berkeley, on the *economic* issue 'shared Mandeville's opinion' that there was an important problem in maintaining a high level of aggregate demand.[1] Berkeley condemned Mandeville's cynical reliance on luxury expenditure in the midst of mass poverty, but laid as much emphasis as he could on a high level of government expenditure (on roads, bridges, drainage, public buildings and works of art) and on raising the standard of living of the poor. Berkeley emphatically did not believe that the level of aggregate effective demand could be left to settle itself, and that incomes not spent in one way would inevitably get spent in another, and therefore that 'parsimony', private and public, is unconditionally beneficial.

It is worth lingering on this point because to the period of Berkeley's *Querist* (1735-50), and to the morally similar, but economically deeply contrasting, criticisms of Mandeville by two great philosophers at that time, may well be traced the parting of the ways for more than a century and a half of British economic thought. Berkeley and Hutcheson (Adam Smith's revered teacher in Glasgow) were both morally incensed by Mandeville.[2] Berkeley's point of view we

[1] J. Johnston, 'The Monetary Theories of Berkeley,' *Economic History*, 1938, pp. 21-24.

[2] In the inspiring penultimate chapter of the *General Theory*, where Keynes discusses Mandeville and other forerunners of his ideas, he puts forward a very odd generalisation to the effect that after Mandeville the doctrine *critical of* ' the utmost thrift and economy both by the individual and the state ... did not reappear in respectable circles for another century, until in the later phase of Malthus the notion of the insufficiency of effective demand takes a definite place as a scientific explanation of unemployment'. (*General Theory*, p. 362.) This is simply to wipe out the best part of a century of British and French economic thought. Malthus on this

70

have described as the most complete moral opposition, but with every implication of agreement on pure economic analysis or the relevant economic assumptions. Hutcheson's criticism of Mandeville is based less on moral and political grounds and more on a fundamentally contrasting *economic* analysis, as far as this goes. For Hutcheson, income not spent in one way will be spent in another, and if not wasted in luxury will be devoted to prudent useful purposes. Until everyone in the world has attained to the necessaries of life, aggregate demand can be, and (it seems inevitably to be assumed) *will* be, at an adequate level, or even a 'maximum' level, without any 'vicious' luxury expenditure.[1] Hutcheson's simple sentences,

subject was a not-always-consistent conservative, trying to cling on to some of the seventeenth- and eighteenth-century ideas against the ardent revolutionary dogmatists of the New Political Economy. Moreover, to say, as Keynes did (*Eugenics Review*, 1937, vol. I, p. 16) that 'Malthus first told us' about 'the devil of unemployment' is historically unfounded. Unemployment had been a central preoccupation of British and French economists for at least 150 years before Malthus, as is clear from the writings of such leaders as Petty, Boisguillebert, Berkeley, and Steuart, and from Furniss's book which summarises much of the rank-and-file opinion—a book written in 1920 which it is now most illuminating to read through Keynesian spectacles. Though calling attention to what seem to be some important gaps in Keynes' brief pioneer sketch of this phase in the history of economic thought, we would reject entirely the treatment of Keynes' chapter on this subject by some of his most enthusiastic disciples. Mr. Harrod, for example, has written (*Life of J. M. Keynes*, London, 1951, p. 460): 'In Keynes' handling of the mercantilists, he appears to me to have seized on isolated passages to find wisdom that was not really there. "Roy strongly objects to Chapter 26" he wrote to Mrs. Robinson, "as a tendentious attempt to glorify imbeciles."' It is not quite clear who is calling whom an imbecile. But if, by chance, this term was really being applied to Petty, Mandeville, Berkeley, and Steuart, it would certainly only be in the tradition of the classical treatment of their predecessors, as exemplified, in particular, by J. S. Mill and Fawcett.

[1] Cf. Hutcheson, *Remarks upon the Fable of the Bees* (Glasgow, 1750, first published c. 1727): 'Unless therefore all mankind are fully provided not only with all necessaries, but all innocent conveniences and pleasures of life, it is still possible without any vice, by an honest care of families, relations, or some worthy persons in distress, to make the greatest consumption' (p. 63). Hutcheson then seizes upon one of the most far-fetched examples of Mandeville, his argument that robbers are good for trade as they stimulate production by locksmiths: 'Who needs be surprised that luxury or pride are made necessary to public good, when even theft and robbery are supposed by the same author to be subservient to it, by employing locksmiths? ... Were there no occasion for locks, had all children and servants discretion never to go into chambers unseasonably, this would make no diminution of manufactures; *the money saved to the housekeeper would afford either better dress, or other conveniences*

71

in themselves apparently harmlessly general, led on, in the work of his great pupil, to the new analysis of saving and investing, the assumption that income not spent in one way is always spent in another, since no one wants to hold money for its own sake, and so, in due course, with the aid of Tucker and Turgot, and later J. B. Say, and J. Mill, to the 'classical' analysis of markets, the doctrine of 'the impossibility of general overproduction', to the Ricardo-Treasury view that public works will not diminish unemployment, and to the orthodox dismissal of all 'under-consumptionist' arguments.

At a vital juncture in the second quarter of the eighteenth century Hutcheson pointed to the high-road of nineteenth-century orthodoxy, while Berkeley, like most of his contemporaries and predecessors, kept along the low road, which, for almost a century and a half from Adam Smith to Keynes, was in Britain followed only by a minority of unorthodox 'cranks'. The roads have now joined up again, and fortunately we do not have to enquire here how drastically those following the orthodox high-road had to change their direction, how

---

to a family, which would equally support artificers: even smiths themselves might have equal employment. Unless all men be already so well provided with all sorts of convenient utensils, or furniture, that nothing can be added, a necessity or constant usefulness of robbers can never be pretended, any more than the public advantages of shipwrecks and fires, which are not a little admired by the author of the fable' (pp. 64-65, italics supplied). It may well be very reasonable, in some contexts, to assume that all income-receivers will spend their money on one thing (household 'utensils') if they don't have to spend it on another (padlocks), but the development of Hutcheson's notion into a universal axiom had serious consequences in some lines of economic investigation. A hundred and fifty years later Alfred and Mary Marshall, with the same degree of significance, advanced the same assumption that income and resources not used in one way will be used in another: 'It is not good for trade to have dresses made of material which wears out quickly. For if people did not spend their means on buying new dresses they would spend them on giving employment to labour in some other way.' (*Economics of Industry*, 1879, p. 17.) Keynes went so far as to hold, in 1936, that 'contemporary thought is still deeply steeped in the notion that if people do not spend their money in one way they will spend it in another.' (*General Theory etc.*, p. 20.) We suggest that the decisive injection of this simplificatory but questionable assumption into the orthodox body of economic thought comes from Adam Smith's teacher Hutcheson.

It may be noted that though Adam Smith built wholeheartedly on Hutcheson's assumptions, the perfectly-balanced Hume, like Berkeley, accepted Mandeville's economic argument. See his essay on *Refinement in Arts*, which puts him in the opposite camp to Hutcheson and Smith. On how very much Smith's economic theory owed to Hutcheson see G. Bryson, *Man and Society*, etc., Princeton, 1945, p. 215.

...ich (if any) of the orthodox intellectual equipment had to be jettisoned in the change of course, and how much was lost by the long neglect of the sort of ideas of which Berkeley was such a distinguished expositor.

One thing, however, which we suggest might be finally discarded—if it does still survive—is the view of eighteenth-century economic thought (including Berkeley) held by such orthodox authorities as J. S. Mill, Henry Fawcett, Leslie Stephen, and Marshall; and along with their views might go that liberalist-progressivist interpretation of eighteenth-century economic thought according to which the more sweepingly a political economist introduced and generalised the assumption of a satisfactorily self-equilibrating mechanism throughout most of the economic universe, the more advanced, enlightened, and correct he inevitably was.

J. S. Mill, for example, goes on in his review to suggest that if Berkeley had 'followed up his ideas further he might have anticipated the work of Adam Smith' as though this must be the sole, the highest, and the most inevitable criterion of intellectual achievement for economic writers before 1776. Marshall was expressing a similar view of eighteenth-century history when he wrote of Adam Smith: 'Whenever he differs from his predecessors he is more nearly right than they; while there is scarcely any economic truth now known of which he did not get some glimpse.'[1] On the contrary, it seems clear

---

[1] See Marshall, *Principles*, 8th ed., p. 757. Marshall's predecessor at Cambridge, Henry Fawcett, in generalising about eighteenth-century (and earlier) effective demand theories had not even omitted Adam Smith from his generalisations. In his much-studied *Manual of Political Economy*, 6th edn., 1883, he writes (pp. 472-473): 'All political economists who preceded James Mill and Ricardo, and many who have succeeded them, seem to anticipate a general over-production of commodities as a possible or even probable contingency.' And Fawcett goes on to explain that by over-production he is assuming that all these economists meant *absolute* over-production irrespective of price, i.e. 'a greater quantity of all commodities may be produced than people really want'.

The influential and distinguished Leslie Stephen unfortunately took his political economy straight from Fawcett. It is therefore hardly surprising to find him not even mentioning Berkeley's *Querist* in his *History of English Thought in the Eighteenth Century*. Stephen must have included *The Querist* in that 'incoherent mass of empirical maxims' which 'for the first time ... was codified into a definite system and elevated to the dignity of a science' by Adam Smith: 'The English economists before the appearance of the *Wealth of Nations*, claimed only to be adepts in the mysteries of commercial accounts. After it, they began to regard themselves as investigators of a new science *capable of determining the conditions and the*

73

to us that a large part of Berkeley's achievement is his lucid practical statement of an economic truth of which Adam Smith showed strangely little sign of having glimpsed, and which it was a main consequence of Smith's doctrines, and those of his more dogmatic successors, largely to conceal and even to suppress in Britain for a very long time. This particular economic truth is, of course, that an inadequate level of employment and effective demand may be a serious problem which state action by fiscal, monetary, and other policies can and ought to deal with.[1] Unless one believes that Adam Smith was 'more nearly right' on this subject than, say, Lord Keynes, or the British White Paper on *Employment Policy* of 1944, then one cannot hold that Smith was more nearly right than Berkeley (or Petty or Steuart). In fact, the main assumptions, analysis, and programme of Berkeley's *Querist* are very closely similar in essential outline to those which Keynes argued for in the inter-war years: that is much more centralised monetary management, public works, and tariffs if necessary to protect the balance of payments, all with the objective of raising the level of employment and productivity above its depressed level. One can readily imagine Berkeley agreeing, for the Ireland and Britain of his day, with Keynes' generalisation about

---

limits of human progress.' (op. cit., vol. 2, p. 283 ; my italics.) There is clearly much truth in Stephen's generalisations, but unfortunately 'codification' meant over-simplification, and the omission of much that had been important to Smith's predecessors in the eighteenth century, and was to be so again to his successors in the twentieth century.

[1] Professor Viner holds that in Bentham's time 'it was too early for proposals to stabilise employment through monetary or fiscal measures' (*American Economic Review*, 1949, p. 362). As we see it, it was definitely not too early for such proposals in 1662, for example, when Petty wrote his *Treatise*, or in 1735 when Berkeley wrote his *Querist*, or in 1767 when Steuart wrote his *Principles*—to take three leading examples only. On the contrary, by Bentham's time it was *too late* for such proposals, which had been superseded by Smith's analysis of saving, investing and the holding of money, which was to be developed by some of Bentham's own closest associates into the classical theory of markets and the Ricardo-Treasury 'view' on public works. Further, we are not quite clear how the existence of Berkeley's *Querist* is compatible with the generalisation that 'there was not until the very last moments of the century either a single major political debate which turned on the economic conditions of the poor or *a single major writer* who had important suggestions as to how to improve them, with the sole exception of Adam Smith's plea for freedom of trade'. (Viner, op. cit., p. 361, my italics.) It may be that Berkeley is not to be classified as a 'major writer' simply because he was not a forerunner or disciple of Adam Smith.

the British inter-war economy, that 'the outstanding faults of the economic society in which we live are its failure to provide for full employment and its arbitrary and inequitable distribution of wealth and incomes' (*General Theory, etc.*, p. 372). Of course, one may take the view that the Keynesian theory was 'largely an emotional and hysterical reaction to crisis conditions, a "depression psychosis" ... based more on temperament and bad temper than on sober appraisal and objective judgement.'[1] Of course, an historian of thought who takes such a view of Keynes' theory is not likely to see much significance in the writings of Berkeley, or Petty, or Mandeville, or Steuart. If it seems that Keynes (and others) had to fight a hard battle of rediscovery this can only have been necessary because of the triumphantly successful intellectual aggression of the over-simplifiers of the early nineteenth century. The line of thought to which Berkeley was such a distinguished contributor—though only one of many in eighteenth-century economic thought—*could* have continued uninterrupted through the nineteenth century, whatever the policies which had or had not been found appropriate from decade to decade. After the 'Keynesian Revolution' there are still many people left who can read Marshall and Walras with comprehension. After the 'Jevonian Revolution' the doctrines on value of J. S. Mill and even Ricardo were still met with wide and orthodox sympathy. But after the 'Smithian Revolution', as dogmatically driven home by J. Mill and Ricardo, the doctrines on effective demand, and on macroeconomic analysis generally, of Petty, Berkeley, Steuart, Boisguillebert, Quesnay, and many lesser writers, passed completely beyond the pale of orthodox comprehension, until finally we have the extraordinary spectacle of the Professor of Political Economy at Cambridge proclaiming unchallenged in a best-selling textbook. that all political economists who preceded James Mill and Ricardo anticipated as a probable contingency that more commodities may be produced than people will really want at any price.

It is the force and distinction of *The Querist's* exposition, rather than any great originality or subtlety of analysis, which places it along with the writings of Petty and Steuart, as one of the leading pre-classical statements of macroeconomic analysis and policy, before *The Wealth of Nations* initiated the 'classical' approach based to a considerable extent on the assumption that the main aggregates of

---

[1] J. Viner, *International Trade and Economic Development*, Oxford, 1953, pp. 9-10.

75

demand and supply tended—apart from periodic frictions—to be, on the whole, satisfactorily self-regulating.

It might perhaps be said of Berkeley, as Sidgwick said of Mill, that his main achievement was to have ' brought a higher degree of philosophical reflection to bear upon the exposition of the common doctrines' (of political economy such as they were in 1735). With Berkeley this 'higher degree of philosophical reflection' worked to heighten his reliance on a practical imprecise common sense, rather than in the direction of a clear-cut formulation and 'codification' (which in the social sciences has usually in fact meant over-simplification, and much more over-simplification than has usually been first realised at the time). Such analytical generalisations as Berkeley uses (on value, or on the quantity theory of money) [1] are thrown out *ad hoc*, the practical problem shaping and determining the 'tools of thought', as economists call them, rather than the other way round.

Was Berkeley a liberal or a socialist? The question is anachronistic and, of course, rather absurd. In his epoch he was one of the greatest (perhaps *the* greatest) of philosophers and Christians on the side of intellectual and religious liberalism. But ' *economic* liberalism' seems to be a separate and often much narrower concept. Anyhow, it seems difficult to describe as an ' economic liberal' in any sense of this rather unsatisfactory term, one who advocated *some* measure of compulsory labour, sumptuary laws, extensive public works, control of speculation, and the principle of economic planning.[2] On the other hand, though Berkeley was certainly very much of a paternalist, we would completely disagree with a French description of *The Querist* as 'a defence of economic authoritarianism'.[3] For Berkeley was essentially a middle-of-the-road moderate, and a man of empirical and not *a priori* maxims. Writing on the morrow of the South Sea Bubble, and surrounded by the paradox of chronic unemployment and poverty, Berkeley stood for a great deal of control and direction, and

[1] ' Whether the value or price of things, be not a compounded proportion, directly as the demand, and reciprocally as the plenty ' (I. 24).
' Whether, *ceteris paribus*, it be not true that the price of things increase, as the quantity of money increaseth, and are diminished as that is diminished ' (III. 157).
[2] ' Whether if a man builds a house he doth not in the first place provide a plan which governs his work? And shall the public act without an end, a view, a plan? ' (I. 53).
[3] See A. V. Espinas, ' La troisième phase et la dissolution du mercantilisme ', *Revue internat. de sociologie*, 1902, 10, 179.

did not consider as within the scope of practical politics the devising and setting up of self-adjusting individualist price-mechanisms. He could hardly have been unreservedly enthusiastic about some of the manifestations of the new economic liberalism of his day, especially in the field of speculation. Nor did he regard economic liberty as an end in itself. Here is a final quotation indicative of his general position: 'Liberty is the greatest human blessing that a virtuous man can possess and is very consistent with the duties of a good subject and a good Christian. But the present age aboundeth with injudicious patrons of liberty. . . . It hath been always observed of weak men, that they know not how to avoid one extreme without running into another.'[1]

[1] Berkeley, *Works*, vol. 3, ed. Fraser, p. 195

The London School of Economics and Political Science
Houghton Street, Aldwych, London, WC2

THE DEVELOPMENT OF BERKELEY'S ETHICAL THEORY.

THOUGH Berekeley wrote no systematic ethical treatise, it is clear from the *Commonplace Book* that he at one time intended to write in detail on morals. In the sanguine pages of the *Commonplace Book*, the "new principle" is destined to solve all problems and simplify all sciences. All previous thinkers had been "embrangled in words," and Berkeley regards it as his God-appointed task "to remove the mist and veil of words."[1] It was his hope that the exposition of the new principle would do this, and enable men to see things as they really are. Even in the *Principles* his claims for his new doctrine are as insistent as ever. His principles "abridge the labor of study and make human sciences more clear, compendious, and attainable than they were before."[2] After making this claim, he goes on to state some of the consequences in mathematics and natural philosophy. But as to the consequences in ethics only a few hints are given. "If the principle be applied to morals, errors of dangerous consequence to morality may be cleared, and truth appear plain, uniform, and consistent." "But," says Berkeley, "the difficulties arising on this head demand a more particular disquisition than suits with the design of this treatise."[3] It is a sign that Berkeley regarded this as tantamount to a promise to deal specially with ethics that in the second edition of the *Principles*, published in 1734, when he had abandoned the project of this special dissertation, this sentence is omitted. Again, in the *Commonplace Book* he remarks that there are three kinds of truth—natural, mathematical, and moral.[4] These three kinds of truth are to be found in the three departments of useful knowledge, natural philosophy, mathematics and ethics. He

---
[1] *Commonplace Book*, I, p. 33. All references are to the Oxford edition (1901) of the *Works*.
[2] *Principles*, I, p. 334.
[3] *Ibid.*, I, p. 339.
[4] *Commonplace Book*, I, p. 37.

419

intended to treat of all these in detail, but in no case was that intention carried out, though we know from the closing sections of the *Principles* the general lines on which he would have handled the problems of mathematics and physics. And we have several tracts dealing with these sciences, e. g., *Arithmetica, Miscellanea Mathematica, De Motu, The Analyst,* and *A Defence of Free Thinking in Mathematics.* It was Berkeley's purpose to deal with ethics in Part II of the *Principles.* He set to work on this undertaking after Part I (what we know as the *Principles*) was completed, but never finished it. The unfinished manuscript was lost during his travels in Italy and he never attempted to re-write it.[1]

But though accident has deprived us of this specifically ethical treatise, yet scattered up and down Berkeley's work there is a fair amount of writing on ethical subjects. It is enough not merely to enable us to reconstruct the main outlines of Berkeley's system, but also to trace the development of his views. The *Commonplace Book* teems with suggestive remarks, which probably give some idea of the argument of the lost Part II of the *Principles.* In addition, three of the dialogues in *Alciphron* are mainly ethical, and there is much valuable matter in *Passive Obedience.*

Berkeley's jottings in the *Commonplace Book* show that in ethics, as in other departments of philosophy, he was deeply influenced by Locke. Such isolated entries as "Morality may be demonstrated as mixt Mathematics," cannot be understood without reference to Locke. Most of Berkeley's memoranda in the *Commonplace Book* have Locke in view; and in order to appreciate their meaning it is necessary to have in mind Locke's theory of ethics.

Ethics, for Locke, is a perfectly demonstrable science, because

---

[1] In the *Commonplace Book* (I, p. 19) Berkeley speaks of "The two great principles of morality . . . to be handled at the beginning of the Second Book." There can be no doubt that "the Second Book" refers to the projected Part II of the *Principles.* In the *Commonplace Book* he frequently speaks of "the First Book" and comparison of the points mentioned with the *Principles* (Part I) shows that "the First Book" always means the *Principles* (Part I). In a letter to the American Samuel Johnson, Berkeley says that he had made considerable progress with the Second Part, but lost the manuscript during his journeys in Italy.

in ethics we have "real knowledge." He gives two examples of sciences in which we have this "real knowledge," (i) mathematics, (ii) ethics. Both these sciences consist of perfectly demonstrable propositions. Both are concerned, not with simple ideas, which always imply as their archetypes external things, but with complex ideas, which are their own archetypes. Both deal with those abstract ideas which Locke calls "mixed modes and relations." The mathematician considers the properties of the triangle as abstract ideas. The idea of a triangle is so framed as to make it possible that a 'real' concrete triangle should conform to it. But whether such a 'real' triangle exists is irrelevant to the mathematician. Similarly, in ethics we deal only with abstract ideas. Ethics is a purely abstract science. To the moral philosopher it is of no moment whether a concrete just act anywhere exists.[1] Mathematics and ethics are both demonstrated on the basis of certain definitions and axioms. Between moral ideas there are the same necessary relations as hold between mathematical ideas. "I doubt not but from self-evident propositions by necessary consequences as incontestable as those in mathematics the measures of right and wrong might be made out."[2]

Locke never altogether abandoned his belief in a mathematically demonstrated science of ethics,[3] though he came to feel less and less able to demonstrate it himself. This is clear both from the changes which he introduced in the fourth edition of the *Essay*,[4] and from his correspondence with Molyneux. Molyneux repeatedly requested him "to oblige the world with a treatise of morals . . . according to the mathematical method." Locke replied (September 20, 1692) expressing distrust in his own ability for the task; but promising to consider it. Nearly four years later he finally declined to undertake it.

It is thus not strange that Berkeley, already keenly interested in mathematics, should have felt that the mathematical demon-

---

[1] Cf. *Essay*, III, p. 12 and IV, iv, p. 8.
[2] *Ibid.*, IV, iii, 18. Cf. III, xi, 16, and IV, xii, 8.
[3] The examples which Locke gives (IV, iii, 18) are justly said by Berkeley to be "trifling propositions." (*Commonplace Book*, I, p. 39).
[4] Compare the fourth edition with the first at IV, ii, 9.

stration of ethics was a task ready-laid to his hand. Locke had given one hint of the precise way in which the mathematical method might be applied. For Locke, "Certainty is but the agreement or disagreement of our ideas, and demonstration nothing but the perception of such agreement by the intervention of other ideas or mediums."[1] Now in mathematics algebra had been of use in supplying these intermediate ideas, and Locke thinks that by applying a kind of algebra in ethics a demonstrably certain system will be produced. Berkeley was not slow to fasten on this hint. "N. B." he says in the *Commonplace Book*, "to consider well what Locke saith concerning Algebra—that it supplies intermediate ideas. Also to think of a method affording the same use in morals, etc., that this doth in mathematics."[2] Berkeley was keenly interested in algebra (cf. the many references in the *Commonplace Book*, and the article "De Ludo Algebraico" (1707) in *Miscellanea Mathematica*). Algebra is itself a department of pure mathematics, for algebra deals with signs abstracted from the things signified. But the algebra of ethics would be a branch of applied mathematics. Thus "Morality may be demonstrated as mixt Mathematics."[3]

Berkeley never worked out his algebra of ethics.[4] But he

[1] *Essay*, IV, iv, 7.
[2] *Commonplace Book*, I, p. 40.
[3] *Ibid.*, I, p. 46.
[4] It is noteworthy that nearly every philosopher of the seventeenth century believed in a mathematical treatment of ethics. There is, of course, Spinoza's *Ethica Ordine Geometrico Demonstrata*. In the *Ethica* of Geulincx there are many suggestions of the applicability of mathematics to morals. And Leibniz also holds that it may be convenient to treat ethics by the geometrical method. (*Nouveaux Essais*, III, xi, 17 and IV, xii, 8). In England, as Professor Gibson has pointed out (*Mind*, 1896), Cumberland, in addition to Locke, held this view. It is also present in Hobbes. There are probably two main reasons for the prevalence of the view at the time:—(1) So long as Scholasticism held the field, the validity of ethical criteria rested ultimately on the authority of the Church. But with the coming of the Renaissance and the Reformation, the problem of the authority of the moral standard became a very real one. How was moral heterodoxy to be met? To this question there were two answers. Ethics must again become theological. Or ethics must become mathematical. These were the only alternatives. Therefore those who, for any reason, disliked the idea of a theological ethics, or considered it philosophically inadequate, were driven to attempt to demonstrate ethics mathematically. For the philosophers of the seventeenth century as a whole, science means nothing but mathematics and mathematical physics. When the seventeenth

said enough to show that his system would have diverged widely from Locke's. The difference between their systems of ethics would have been identical with that between their theories of mathematics. For Locke, geometry is a pure science, dealing only with relations of universal ideas, abstracted from all concrete experience. On the other hand Berkeley holds that geometry is essentially practical. The *Principles* cut away the speculative parts of mathematics, leaving only what is practical and useful.[1] Geometry deals throughout with concrete existence. In a precisely similar way Berkeley's theory of ethics differs from Locke's. Ethics is for Locke a pure science which omits all question of the realization of abstract ideas in the concrete matter-of-fact of moral experience. But Berkeley's view is very different. Ethics is an applied or practical science. It does not consider relations of ideas by means of intervening ideas.[2] Berkeley holds that ethics is a demonstrative science which, like mathematics, deals with words or signs and not with ideas. We can have no certainty about ideas, as Locke supposed.[3] It is possible to reason about ideas, but demonstration can be only verbal.[4] "To demonstrate morality it seems one need only make a dictionary of words, and see which included which."[5] Words are signs and the reason why demonstration is possible and easy with regard to signs is that they are arbitrary. Hence the demonstrability of mathematics, which deals solely with signs.[6] Further, Berkeley believed that Locke's abstract ideas do not exist either in mathematics or in ethics. An abstract idea of triangle is impossible. Equally impossible is an abstract idea of justice. On Berkeley's theory, we reason always about a particular, which stands for all other particulars of the same kind.

century attempts to treat ethics on the mathematical method, it is simply feeling after a scientific system of ethics. (ii) It was partly due to Descartes that mathematics came to be the science of the day, and Descartes' influence was largely responsible for the unanimity with which the seventeenth century endeavored to reach a mathematical system of ethics.

[1] *Principles*, I, p. 326; I, p. 331.
[2] *Commonplace Book*, I, p. 40; I, p. 43.
[3] *Ibid.*, I, p. 43.
[4] *Ibid.*, I, p. 50.
[5] *Ibid.*, I, p. 39. Cf. I, p. 37 and I, p. 55.
[6] *Ibid.*, I, pp. 45–47.

We take this or that just act, ignore all irrelevant features, and make it stand for and represent all other just acts.

The only difficulty in the way of such a system of ethics which Berkeley mentions is the practical difficulty of reaching agreement with regard to its definitions. The definitions which mathematics employs are not questioned, because the learner comes to them with no preconceived ideas. He is willing to take them on trust. But in ethics it is otherwise. Men approach the subject with presuppositions of their own. They cling to these primitive convictions, and refuse to come to any agreement in the definition of terms.

One very real difficulty which Locke had mentioned is denied by Berkeley. Locke had pointed out that the complexity of moral ideas increases the difficulty of dealing with them by the mathematical method. But Berkeley sees nothing in this.[1] Yet if 'complexity' be extended to include the relations and context of moral ideas, Locke's point becomes a very real one. On Berkeley's theory, if we take a particular triangle it is possible to abstract what is irrelevant to its triangularity, and the particular may be taken to stand for all particulars of the same kind. And, as we have seen, Berkeley thinks the same thing may be done in ethics. But it is not thus possible to isolate a just act. If it be cut loose from its context, it may be no longer a just act. Its justice may consist precisely in the complex relations in which it stands to its environment. But though Berkeley was certainly not aware of this difficulty in the days of the *Commonplace Book*, it is clear from *Alciphron* that he appreciated it later. This may well have been one of the reasons why he abandoned the project of writing a mathematical science of ethics.

But probably another reason weighed with Berkeley. If ethics be a science demonstrable in the same way as mathematics, why has God allowed so much diversity of opinion with regard to its definitions and propositions? There is universal agreement that $2 + 2 = 4$. This agreement Berkeley attributes to God: God brings it about, arbitrarily but not capriciously,

---

[1] *Commonplace Book*, I, p. 51.

that all men should agree that 2 + 2 = 4. But there is no similar agreement with regard to such a proposition as 'Polygamy is wrong.' Now why could not God have secured that all men should agree on moral matters? Locke, indeed, had suggested that God had laid down in the Gospels "so perfect a body of Ethics that reason may be excused from the enquiry."[1] But Berkeley saw that the ethical ideas of the Gospels were accepted by a portion only, and as he feared, by a diminishing portion, of mankind. If God had intended ethics to be as demonstrable a science as mathematics, he would have arranged that the definitions of ethics should be recognized by all men to be as eternal and immutable as those of mathematics. But God has not done this, therefore it cannot be his will that there should be a demonstrable science of ethics.

In Berkeley's works subsequent to the *Principles* no mention is made of a possible mathematical science of ethics. The writings of his middle and later periods, in so far as they are concerned with ethics, are largely controversial. Perhaps the most systematic account of his views is to be found in the *Discourse on Passive Obedience*, where he makes "some enquiry into the origin, nature and obligation of moral duties in general, and the criterions by which they may be known."[2] He takes it for granted that there are moral rules or laws of nature, which carry with them an eternal obligation. He holds that these natural principles of morality have three characteristics:—

(i) Natural principles of morality are also rational. In saying that moral rules are natural laws we interpret nature in the highest sense. The best moral principles are those which may be rationally deduced by the maturest reason. These natural-rational principles "grow from the most excellent and peculiar part of human nature."[3] They are laws of nature, but they are also eternal rules of reason, because they necessarily result from the nature of things and may be demonstrated by the infallible deductions of reason.[4]

[1] Letter to Molyneux, March 30, 1696.
[2] II, p. 104.
[3] *Alciphron*, II, p. 61.
[4] *Passive Obedience*, IV, p. 108.

(ii) Natural-rational principles are also divine. This follows from the whole course of Berkeley's philosophy. Nature consists of divine symbols, and its general laws are simply the arbitrary but not capricious volitions of God. "Nature is nothing but a series of free actions, produced by the best and wisest agent."[1]

(iii) Nature with its laws constitutes a system. "The Law of Nature is a system of such laws and precepts as that if they be all of them at all times in all places and by all men observed, they will necessarily promote the well-being of mankind."[2] Now moral rules are natural laws, and all the characteristics of natural laws belong to moral laws. Hence the same order and regularity which we perceive in the natural world exists also in the moral realm. But the moral and natural spheres are only partly coincident. The moral realm is necessarily natural, but the natural world is not necessarily moral. Vegetable existence possesses all the attributes of the natural, but we cannot predicate morality of it. But the moral world, as we find it existing among self-conscious beings, is a realm of ends, in which man living according to nature considers himself not as an isolated and independent individual, but as "a part of a whole, to the common good of which he ought to conspire."[3]

Tendency to promote or thwart happiness is the criterion of good and evil. It is a natural principle that we consider things in the light of happiness. Good is that which augments happiness, and evil that which impairs it. The *summum bonum* consists in happiness, and duty lies in the effort to attain the good and avoid the evil. It is the will of God that men should seek, not private pleasure merely, but the happiness of mankind as a whole. Berkeley draws a sharp distinction between pleasures of sense and pleasures of reason, but his view of the relative value of these undergoes a marked change between his earlier and his middle period. In the *Commonplace Book* (1705–1708), he does not recognize pleasures of reason at all. "Sensual

---

[1] *Op. cit.*, IV, p. 110.
[2] *Ibid.*, IV, p. 111.
[3] *Alciphron*, II, p. 67.

pleasure is the summum bonum.'"[1] In the Essays in the *Guardian* (1713), pleasures of reason and pleasures of sense are placed on the same level, so long as they are natural and not 'fantastical.' But in *Alciphron* (1732), pleasures of sense are degraded. The view that these constitute the *summum bonum* is strongly attacked. Sense-pleasure is natural only to brutes. Reason is the highest and most characteristic element in human nature, and rational pleasures are natural to man. It is interesting to note in Berkeley's theory of knowledge a similar growing recognition of the importance of reason.

For Berkeley, as for all other British moralists, the problem of the relation of egoism and altruism is urgent. But in Berkeley's ethical, as in his metaphysical philosophy, God solves many difficulties. This problem, among many others, would remain unresolved apart from God. Self-love remains the supreme principle in morality, but it is only at a low stage of moral development that self-love bids a man seek his own happiness only. Rational self-love seeks to regard the world *sub specie aeternitatis*. Self-love advocates only those kinds of actions that are supposed to be in accordance with the will of God. No purely selfish action can be conformable to the will of God. The Hobbist position of undiluted egoism is stated by Berkeley, but only to be refuted by the same arguments as Butler used.

The *summum bonum* cannot be mere temporal happiness. It cannot be confined within the conditions of time. It consists in eternal happiness. Now eternal happiness can be guaranteed only by God. Hence self-love lays down the rule that we act always in conformity with the will of God. The existence of God is required by morality as it is by knowledge. Berkeley's general metaphysical position implies that apart from the existence of God to guarantee the regularity and invariability of our sense-impressions knowledge would be impossible. And so in ethics the supreme moral end would be impossible apart from God. But it is worth noting that Berkeley does not, as Kant does, attempt to base a practical proof of God's existence on his indispensability for morality.

[1] *Commonplace Book*, I, p. 47.

The resemblance both in general and in detail between this theory and that of the other philosopher-bishop of the time is close and striking. Butler's moral philosophy is more systematically developed than Berkeley's; but almost every feature which has contributed to make Butler's work the greatest product of British ethical thought is present in Berkeley's scattered remarks. For Berkeley, as for Butler, reason is ultimately the basis of moral obligation, and the general happiness the *summum bonum*. For both, moral rules are also laws of nature, and action in accorance with nature leads to the attainment of the moral end. They take precisely the same view of nature, as a divinely organized system of ends. Both emphasize, in language strangely similar, the moral importance of the disposition to social life existing in mankind; and both are animated by the same principles of practical social idealism. Only in their view of the interrelation of the 'principles of human nature' do they diverge. Or, it would be truer to say that while Butler's chief originality lies in his moral psychology, Berkeley has almost entirely omitted to make any psychological analysis. But all in all, the similarities are so notable as to suggest the possibility that one was directly influenced by the other. But such a suspicion is really gratuitous. It is indeed just possible, so far as the dates of publication of their works are concerned, that each was indebted to the other. Butler's *Sermons* were first published in 1726. Berkeley's *Passive Obedience* appeared in 1712, and *Alciphron* in 1732. But there is no internal evidence whatever that *Passive Obedience* influenced the *Sermons*, or the *Sermons, Alciphron*. The resemblance may be quite sufficiently accounted for by the antipathy to Hobbes felt by both thinkers, and the similarity of the attitude adopted by them towards the tendencies of ethical thought represented on the one hand by the so-called Cambridge Platonists, and on the other hand by such men of the world as Mandeville and Shaftesbury. To Hobbism both Berkeley and Butler were fundamentally opposed, though Berkeley at least was influenced by the Hobbist doctrine that moral rules are natural laws. From the Cambridge Platonists both learned something—the immutability of moral principles and the rational ground of moral obligation. Both regarded Mandeville's dicta as subversive of all morality. Towards Shaftesbury alone their attitudes diverged somewhat. Butler was more willing than Berkeley to admit that there was something in what Shaftesbury had to say. It is a serious misreading of Butler to class him, as many historians do, with the moral sense school; but at the same time, he is far more ready than Berkeley to learn from Shaftesbury. Berkeley's attitude to Shaftesbury, as we see it in *Alciphron*, is that of a man whose prejudices make him incapable of appreciating whatever truth may exist in the opinions of another with whom he does not see eye to eye.

When we consider the originality of Berkeley's metaphysics, it may seem strange that his writings on ethics make so small a contribution to that branch of philosophy. But it must be remembered that we have only fragments of Berkeley's thought on the problems of morality. What would we think of his metaphysics, if the *Principles* and the *Three Dialogues* had been lost? It may be argued that if Berkeley's ethical treatise had been preserved, it might have paved the way for as great an advance in ethics as his systematic works do in metaphysics. One thing at least may be said with certainty. It is clear from the scattered remarks which we do possess that Berkeley's ethical works would have shown the same two characteristics that assured his success in his metaphysical ventures. As Mr. Balfour has pointed out, two qualities are essential for the philosopher who is going to carry forward his science. He must have philosophical aptitude, and be mentally capable of speculation on the ultimate problems of life and knowledge. But in addition, he must possess the peculiar gift of being able to locate the exact point at which the next philosophical movement may best be made. It was for want of this special acumen that Clarke and Malebranche, in spite of their philosophical ability, were left in a philosophical backwater. But Berkeley had the faculty of noticing just where the next advance could be made. Hence his position in the main current of English philosophy.

It is clear that he did not at first perceive the point at which the next forward step in ethics could be taken. The reason for this was that the main line of ethical thought did not pass through Locke. Berkeley's intuition was not at fault in believing that the main metaphysical advance lay through Locke; and he was enabled to do his own good work by putting his finger unerringly on the spot from which that advance might best begin. His initial mistake in ethics lay in thinking that progress might be made in that branch of philosophy also by observing and correcting Locke's suggestions towards a mathematical treatment of ethics. But Berkeley soon perceived that the path marked out by Locke led into a *cul-de-sac;* and he therefore abandoned the attempt to construct a mathematical system of ethics. In his later ethical work he makes suggestions which do place him right in the center of the line of ethical advance in England. That line led through Hume to Utilitarianism. Berkeley believes, as we have seen, that the *summum bonum* is not private pleasure but the happiness and general good of all. And he draws a sharp distinction between different kinds of pleasure. So far as we can tell from Berkeley's scattered remarks, he did not appreciate the problems which Utilitarianism has to face. As it is, it is an anachronism to call him, as Professor Campbell Fraser does, a theological Utilitarian. But he was moving in that direction, and if he had given to the question the thought necessary to produce a systematic work, he might have been the first Utilitarian.

G. A. JOHNSTON.

GLASGOW UNIVERSITY.

A SYNOPSIS OF BERKELEY'S MONETARY PHILOSOPHY.

BERKELEY had a social as well as a monetary philosophy, and it might seem desirable that one should give a separate account of each. In fact, the two are incapable of separation. It is impossible to give a coherent account of his monetary philosophy without bringing in the essential principles of his social philosophy. As it is convenient in this essay to give prominence to the monetary point of view, the emphasis will be placed on his monetary philosophy. But it must be stated, here and now, that Berkeley developed a philosophy of money only because he was a social idealist, and that he regarded money, rightly understood and used, as a necessary instrument of social welfare.

"Whether money be not only so far useful, as it stirreth up industry, enabling men mutually to participate the fruits of each other's labour" (page 23, No. 5, Hone's Edition).

The real aim and end of men is power—i.e., power to command the industry of others (page 24, No. 7; page 27, No. 37). Such power constitutes real wealth. He who could have everything else at his wish or will would not value money (page 24, No. 7). In the circumstances in which society finds itself it is not practicable to exercise this power except through the medium of money. People in general may not hope to acquire purchasing power except in proportion as they produce goods and services which are in demand by others. Money is only so far useful as it "stirreth up industry," and the discovery of "the richest gold mine that ever was" would only impoverish a kingdom if it rendered its people "lazy, proud, and dastardly" (page 61, No. 18 and No. 20).

The good life (he does not use this actual term) requires that every member of society should have the fullest opportunity of realising his individuality, and this he can only do in an exchange economy when the institution of money makes possible the mutual participation of the fruits of each other's labour (page 23, No. 5). The public aim in every well governed state should be that each member, according to his just pretensions and industry, should have power (page 24, No. 8). This power to stir up the industry of others in our service, which money is the means of "conveying and recording" (page 27, No. 37), avails not otherwise than as it is exerted into act (page 105, No. 177). Consequently it is the interest of every State that its money should rather circulate than stagnate (page 105, No. 178).

Power is referred to action and action follows appetite and will (page 24, No. 9). Fashion creates appetites, the prevailing will of a nation is the fashion, and on this fashion depends the current of industry and commerce (page 24, Nos. 10 and 11). Consequently the wisdom of the legislature should seek to influence the making of fashion, or as we would say, "economic demand" (page 24, No. 13).

To create wants is the likeliest way of producing industry in a people, and, if economic demand is to receive a necessary stimulus, national income must be redistributed in such a way that our peasants may be enabled to eat beef and wear shoes, and the labouring ox be no longer muzzled (page 25, No. 20; page 78, No. 194).

Other things such as climate and soil being given, the wealth of a community is in proportion to its industry, "and this to the circulation of credit, be the credit circulated or transferred by what marks or tokens soever" (page 25, No. 21). It makes no difference to the community whether it has less money swiftly circulating or more money slowly circulating (page 25, No. 22). Money as such has no "intrinsic value." The true idea of money, as such, is altogether that of a ticket or counter (page 25, No. 23), conveying and recording generalized command over the services of others in proportion to the money incomes of individuals and the prices of such services. The value or price of things is a "proportion, directly as the demand, and reciprocally as the plenty" (page 25, No. 24). The terms crown, livre, pound, etc., are merely exponents or denominations of such proportion. A monetary system could exist without any bullion at all. "The denominations being retained, although the bullion were gone, things might nevertheless be rated, bought, and sold, industry promoted, and a circulation of commerce maintained" (page 25, No. 26).

Thus money is a proportion relating to the prices of things, which from one point of view constitute income and from another expenditure. For all commerce is ultimately a "commerce of industry," that is, an exchange of services priced in money for services priced in money (page 27, No. 38).

Money is the cement of economic society and all money is credit. For, in its essence, money is only a means of conveying and recording power to command the industry of others, and others will not give their services in exchange for it unless they have confidence that they in turn can get what they want in exchange for money. "Whether all circulation be not like a circulation of credit, whatsoever medium (metal or paper) is employed, and whether gold be any more than credit for so much power"? (page 87, No. 10).

The material basis of this credit is the superfluity which its producer seeks to exchange for the various things of which he has greater need. If a ship's crew be cast away on a desert island they will immediately set to work, specialising on various tasks and sharing the fruits of their common labour. When one man has provided more than he can consume he will exchange his superfluities to supply his wants, and certain tokens or counters will soon be agreed on to facilitate the conveyance, recording and circulating of the credit thus originating (page 28, No. 49). Thus credit is logically antecedent to the institution of the things called money, and is an essential element in every exchange economy.

The psychological basis of credit is the confidence, already referred to, that the monetary tokens for which a man sells will enable him also to buy.

The superfluities of specialised producers are, doubtless, the material basis of credit, but such superfluities would have no value unless they corresponded to the wants of others, and unless these others were willing and able to give money in exchange for them. Thus credit is based not only on superfluities but on wants, not only on Production but on Consumer Demand. Credit depends on a happy coincidence between reciprocal wants and superfluities in a society of specialised Producers.

That credit is in a true sense based on consumption and Economic Demand is part of the essence of Berkeley's thoughts: " Whether comfortable living doth not produce wants, and wants industry, and industry wealth" (page 35, No. 113). Money is useless unless by its circulation it stirs up industry, and a peasantry deprived of its fair share of the national income cannot by its expenditure encourage the industry of others, and has no motive to exert itself in its own (page 78, No. 194).

Consequently for Berkeley no amount of gold or silver could constitute an adequate "basis of credit" in the absence of this all-important adjustment between an equitable Consumption Economy and its appropriate Production Economy. It would be a "monstrous folly" to import nothing but gold and silver, supposing we might do it (page 116, No. 278); and foolish also to think "an inward commerce cannot enrich a state, because it doth not increase its quantity of gold and silver." A country must thrive while wants are supplied and business goes on (page 114, No. 260).

As population increases, wants increase, but so too do the means of satisfying them more effectively by means of the more efficient organisation and co-operation that become possible. Such an increase must be regarded as broadening the basis of the national credit. As industry produced good living the number of hands and mouths would be increased, and in proportion thereto there would be more employment in agriculture; but, granted an equitable distribution of national income, there was no danger of population outrunning subsistence, though, in the absence of that necessary condition, half of the population was in Berkeley's time starving (page 83, No. 251, and page 40, No. 149).

Since money is credit and credit depends on the exchange of superfluities for superfluities, the production of wealth can only attain a maximum in proportion as money incomes are equalised and consuming power expanded. "Whether as seed equally scattered produces a goodly harvest, even so an equal distribution of wealth doth not cause a nation to flourish" (page 47, No. 220).

Berkeley clearly was of the opinion that the impoverishment of the masses in his day was undermining the true foundations of the nation's credit, and diminishing its real wealth. But he does not really contemplate or desire a society in which the money incomes of all would be absolutely equal. He wanted a less unequal distribution of national income, and he considered that the privileged classes stood to gain rather than lose by a policy which should unmuzzle the labouring ox. He queries whether "facilitating and quickening the circulation of power to supply wants be not the promoting of wealth and industry among the lower people. And whether upon this the wealth of the great doth not depend?" (page 106, No. 187).

To provide plentifully for the poor is feeding the root the substance whereof will shoot upwards into the branches and cause the top to flourish (page 30, No. 64). Yet "when the root yieldeth insufficient nourishment men top the tree to make the lower branches thrive" (page 41, No. 164).

A redistribution of national income he considered necessary in order to promote an economic demand at home for the expanded production of food, clothing, and housing, things which the natural resources of the country rendered it well able to produce. The free circulation of money depends on a right distribution of income. In turn, money freely circulating creates incomes, and their expenditure gives rise to industry, and increases wealth.

Berkeley, reviving an Aristotelian distinction, considered that there was a limit to the natural appetites which demand satisfaction from the current output of wealth. "The best institutions may be made subservient to bad ends" (page 70, No. 113), and money is an outstanding example of this.

Artificial appetites are indeed infinite, and men seek gratification for themselves by speculation and other forms of passing money from hand to hand without industry. A wise government will rigorously suppress such activities, and will not allow money to be considered as an end in itself. The ends of money itself are bounded, and it was mistaking the means for the end which was the fundamental error in the French councils at the time of John Law's scheme (page 70, Nos. 117 and 118).

A progressive increase in the national wealth requires the provision of a flexible supply of money to constitute income. "Whether counters be not referred to other things, which, so long as they keep pace and proportion with the counters, it must be owned the counters are useful" (page 71, No. 122). Even if we had a perfect system of coinage, with an adequate supply of coins of small denominations, it would be more economical and convenient to make this provision through the machinery of a national Bank—i.e., a nationally owned banking system—and such a bank should be established. It should be owned absolutely by the State, and managed entirely in the public interest (page 99, No. 124; page 73, No. 143). It would be fatal to engraft trade on a national bank or propose dividends on its stock. All profits must go to the State (page 69, No. 108; page 52, No. 273).

The question for Berkeley was not one of money *versus* credit, for all money is credit. The question was whether credit institutions should be publicly or privately owned— between public credit and private credit. All banks, whatever their form, exercise public functions in fact; for they bring into existence and cause to circulate obligations which represent a claim on the economic substance of the general public. The control of monetary policy is a concentrated form of social power, and such power cannot safely be entrusted to private hands. It cannot be expected that private persons will have more regard to the public than the public itself; and he queries "if power followeth money whether this can be anywhere more properly and securely placed, than in the same hands wherein the supreme power is already placed" (page 87, No. 16; page 88, No. 20). Private interests are all too ready to subordinate public interests to their own, and have an intrinsic bias which incapacitates them from being sound judges of public interests when their own are in conflict with them. Not only traders should be consulted about trade or bankers about money (page 56, No. 308).

It is of the utmost public importance to ensure that bank money is only put in circulation in association with the rendering of economic services. Bank bills should only be multiplied as trade and business is multiplied (page 71, No. 127). The circulation of paper without industry is ruinous (page 70, No. 116). Private bankers are all too ready to finance such wasteful speculation; and, in seeking a quick financial profit from such loans, ignore the true basis of credit and set in motion forces which lead to inflation and collapse (page 68, No. 102). Only if the banking system as a whole is owned and controlled by the public in the public interest can its prostitution to speculative ends be prevented; but the organisation of the national credit by means of a national bank would strengthen the position of such existing private banks as are willing to fall in with public policy (page 91, No. 48, and page 68, No. 102).

A national bank would put an end to usury—i.e., reduce the rate of interest, facilitate commerce, supply the want of coin, and produce ready payments in all parts of the kingdom (page 61, No. 12). It would mobilise the private credit of individuals, known only to their intimates and to it, and turn it into a means of payment readily acceptable to all because endorsed with the guarantee of such a bank. The credit of such a bank would not be bounded by its capital stock, or limited by the fluidity of its assets, since behind it would be the taxing power of the State. In fact, the whole wealth of the nation would in truth constitute the stock of such a bank (page 94, No. 84; page 99, Nos. 121-123).

Money lent to the rich by such a bank would circulate among the poor, and extend their money incomes, thus increasing wealth while making its distribution less unequal. For no one borrows except with intent to circulate (page 96, No. 95).

There is no worse sign of a country's economic condition than the flight of its unoccupied workers to earn their bread in foreign lands (page 112, No. 245; page 97, No. 104). The money, even if it be gold and silver, which emigrants remit to the land of their birth is only a palliative of an evil economic condition, the true remedy for which is to oil the wheels of commerce and native industry by an organisation of the national credit, which creates the monetary conditions of full employment for all willing workers (page 101, No. 143; page 55, No. 295). That country is in a flourishing condition which is enabled not only to provide employment for an expanding native population, but to attract immigrants to work in its fields and workshops (page 113, No. 248). Such immigrants should be welcomed, not excluded, for their coming enriches the country of their adoption.

Commerce enriches by the multiplication of specialised services for exchange, and domestic commerce is as fertile a source of wealth as foreign commerce, more accessible, and more amenable to control and encouragement by wise public policy (page 114, No. 260).

Our foreign credit really depends on domestic industry, not on the possession of abundant supplies of gold (page 107, No. 201; page 97, No. 110). If our national economy is on a sound basis we shall obtain all the foreign commerce we need, whether we seek it or not (page 38, No. 134). The object of foreign trade is to get, by way of import, the goods we cannot conveniently produce at home. A foreign commerce which brings in gold and silver has misled our judgments about what really constitutes the public weal (page 117, No. 283). Only a wrong-headed patriot or politician (? like Dean Swift, page 116, No. 280) imagines that a country is enriched by drawing gold and silver into it and keeping it there.

Even Berkeley, for all his genius, might not have penetrated to the core of monetary theory if he had not lived in a country having the unique currency conditions outlined in a former Essay in this series. In addition to the monetary problem, there was the distracting problem of the commercial restrictions, which oppressed men's

G

minds like a nightmare, paralysing thought and action. Berkeley argued, quite sensibly, that the correct procedure was to adjust the national economy to the objective facts of commerce, and, by means of a truly national monetary policy, to orient investment activities and redistribute national income in such a way that the domestic consumption of those things would be expanded which the country was best fitted to produce. He sought to secure such an adjustment between the national production economy and the national consumption economy that every kind of consumption would be encouraged which was both economically possible and socially desirable. So far from curtailing "supply" and restricting consumption the latter must be expanded, only its pattern being altered. He argued that money must play a part of overwhelming importance in the dynamics of such a national policy, and that the correct reaction to an externally imposed necessity for economic adjustment was, before all else, a monetary one.

It might be asked at this stage whether Berkeley made any adequate distinction between money and purchasing power. All the time he seems to place the emphasis on the need for supplying an adequate amount of monetary medium, whatever its form, and to have assumed that this would incidentally bring about an increase of purchasing power. The problem of hoarding or "idle balances" did not present itself as one that required serious consideration. Money could only be put in circulation if enterprise could be induced to borrow, but "no one borrows except with intent to circulate." The circulation of money, lent in the first instance to the rich, would soon expand the incomes, and therefore the purchasing power, of the poor (page 96, No. 95). In Berkeley's time the monetary economy had by no means permeated every vein of the nation's economic life. Large strata of economic exchanges were still being carried on on a barter basis of goods for goods or services for land. Public policy, and the pressure of a cruel land system, were compelling increasing payments, in money, of taxes and rents at a time when external commerce was strangled and internal commerce was confronted with difficulties of transport as well as the subtler obstacles for which he advocated a monetary remedy. All the time the circumstances of the East India Trade were depleting the silver constituents of the monetary medium, and a diminishing amount of metallic money was being set the task of effecting an increasing proportion of the exchanges that were being effected. A public policy that requires from the peasant population increasing payments in money is an indirect compulsion to abandon the barter in favour of the monetary economy. All history shows that, if this pressure is accompanied by a growing scarcity of money, the result is oppression and a harsh exploitation, especially of the peasant classes.

In these circumstances, so far as the practical problem was concerned, it was safe to assume that to increase money in any acceptable form would automatically increase purchasing power. In our own day, when money permeates all economic relations, it is quite possible to increase the quantity of money without increasing the quantity of purchasing power, and the distinction between them is of far more than theoretical interest.

Yet a scrutiny of Berkeley's language suggests that he was aware of the distinction though he did not stress it. Wealth is "power to command the industry of others," but it can only exercise this power when transformed into money, which is the means of transferring and recording such power—the transmission gear, so to speak, and not the engine. What is this wealth so mobilised other than what we call purchasing-power? The origin of wealth is industry (page 27, No. 40), and therefore industry is the ultimate cause and origin of purchasing power, provided, of course, that industry is adjusted to the wants of others, and that these wants become effective in economic demand. This again requires such a distribution of income as will enable mass consumption to absorb the products of what may here be called mass production.

Consequently, for Berkeley purchasing power was a result of a "commerce of industry" and of a quick circulation of money "oiling the wheels of commerce." Can modern analysis go farther?

It would also appear that Berkeley failed to distinguish between money and credit. In fact, he deliberately asserts that the essence of all money, whatever its form, is credit. He was, however, aware of the important part played by gold and silver as a means of foreign remittance. There are "two things which might draw silver out of the bank, when its credit was once well established, to wit, foreign demands and small payments at home" (page 54, No. 294). There should be a constant care to keep bank bills at par, but this will be assured if bank bills are multiplied only as trade and business are also multiplied (page 71, Nos. 126 and 127). The right use of the precious metals is to keep them at home or send them abroad "just as it most serves to promote industry" (page 117, No. 288). A country such as ours, having no gold mines "nor a free trade," cannot support for any time the sending out of specie; but, in fact, our payments are made by bills, and our foreign credit really depends on our domestic industry, and our bills on that credit (page 107, Nos. 200 and 201). Consequently, he maintained that "we may maintain a much greater inward and outward commerce, and be five times richer than we are, nay, and our bills abroad be of far greater credit, though we had not an ounce of gold or silver in the whole island"? (page 97, No. 110).

Clearly Berkeley would have allowed the precious metals to play their accustomed part in the maintenance of exchange parity, and would not have worried overmuch if the last ounce of gold and silver had to be exported in this cause. Such gold and silver as was available he would associate with the national money at the current parity, and freely send it out of the country if it was necessary to humour the foreigner, but he regarded it in no real sense as the basis of the nation's credit or as a necessary support for the purchasing power of its money.

In these days, when legal tender paper, or the right to acquire it, is so important a part of the cash reserve of commercial banks, the distinction between money and credit is largely a distinction between the credit of privately owned commercial banks and the national credit associated with legal tender paper. It is important to distinguish between the purchasing medium (bank credit) which represents the *debt* of a privately owned commercial banking system, and the legal tender money which the system *owns* and looks on as its cash reserve. Berkeley, writing at a time when private banking was in its infancy, wanted to bring about the establishment of a publicly owned commercial banking system. The circulating medium constituting the liabilities of such a system would, of course, be legal tender, in fact, if not in name; and even if it was convenient for certain purposes to distinguish between its notes outstanding and its deposits, the distinction would be one of form rather than substance.

Even as things are the ordinary individual makes no distinction between money in the form of bank-notes or deposits and money in the form of legal tender, but uses each in the way which is most convenient for his purposes. Both money and credit are to him a means of acquiring goods or services offered in exchange—"credit for so much power." The point of view of the ordinary individual is Berkeleyan, and it is quite possible that the modern theory of money and credit would have followed Berkeleyan lines more closely if it had not been for the historical fact that modern banking systems have grown up under a system of private ownership, which makes the distinction between money and credit of great importance, both from the practical banking point of view and the point of view of public policy.

The modern financier lives and moves in a stratosphere in which money debts are liquidated when an equal amount of money, whatever its origin, is repaid, but to Berkeley's mind monetary obligations could only be finally liquidated when transformed into (solid) goods and services. He cared not at all for what we would call the technical or financial basis of credit, but considered that monetary transactions which were a condition of the multiplication and exchange of services gave no occasion for alarm, while his national banking system would frown on all transactions which aimed only at a financial profit by "exchanging money without industry," and in any case would be under no temptation to encourage them.

The idealist philosopher who disbelieved in the independent reality of matter was before all else a realist in his economic thinking.

JOSEPH JOHNSTON.

VARIÉTÉS

UNIVERSALIZATION IN BERKELEY'S RULE — UTILITARIANISM

by Joseph KUPFER

One need only remark the title of a recent article (¹) on Berkeley's ethics to realize the thinness and piecemeal nature of the scholarship in this sphere of Berkeley's philosophy. Commentators have been content for the most part to point out features of utilitarianism, Deism, egoism, deontology and eudemonism but no where is to be found a unified account of Berkeley's ethics.

A precursor to both Kant and British rule-utilitarianism Berkeley's emphasis on universalization in morality has gone especially unnoticed. This is unfortunate because he writes on a subject of both contemporary and historical importance with his usual clarity and insight. He employs the criterion of universalization in two distinct and distinctive ways: to determine a fundamental moral principle, and to test for genuine moral rules. After establishing that the basic principle in morality concerns the welfare of mankind, Berkeley employs a universalization procedure in arguing against both act-utilitarianism and reliance upon a "moral sentiment" (Shaftesbury) as the means for securing the summum bonum. He concludes that only by adopting rule-utilitarianism as our moral principle will we meliorate man's condition.

In order for rule-utilitarianism to have content, of course, there must be rules whose utility has been ascertained. The canon of universalization again emerges. Berkeley maintains that those rules which if universally practiced would lead to the general good (happiness) are those we ought to obey. Like Kant, Berkeley concludes, for example, that "we ought not lie" is a moral rule. Berkeley exhibits his British

---

(1) Paul OLSCAMP, "Does Berkeley Have an Ethical Theory"; *Berkeley : Principles of Human Knowledge*, Ed. Turbayne (Indianapolis : Bobbs-Merrill, 1970), pp. 182-200.

heritage (²) by filling in the formal Kantian test with utilitarian content. This fleshing out is not, of course, compatible with Kant's basic deontological stance.

Some moral rules, moreover, are *never* justifiably disobeyed; although they oblige "categorically", because Berkeley does not speak in this idiom we shall refer to the obligation simply as "universal". These are *pro*scriptions, rules enjoining us not to act in specific ways and are distinguished from *pre*scriptions by meeting a universalized version of the Kantian formula: "'ought' implies 'can'". Universal ability to conform to a moral law is therefore a necessary though not sufficient condition for the universal obligation to conform to that moral law.

What fellows is an exegesis revealing Berkeley's rule-utilitarianism as informed by the concept of universalization. The justification for rule-utilitarianism and the procedure for distinguishing the genuine from the spurious in moral law both devolve upon this notion. The distinction between *pro*scriptions and *pre*scriptions which enables Berkeley to claim universal obligation for some moral laws also turns upon universalization — a universalized form of "ought" implies "can". But before we can begin to grasp fully the extent of the concept's significance in Berkeley's ethics we must first turn to a consideration of his understanding of the purpose of morality and action.

I

Berkeley is concerned with working out a rational means for deciding among alternative moral actions. He believes that the telos of moral conduct provides us indirectly with a standard for such decision. He offers a variety of arguments for what I shall call the Greatest Goodness Principle: We ought to act so as to produce the greatest goodness of the greatest number. His principal argument is theistic and deductive in character, but its interest lies in the way that it is independent of appeal to God, odd as that may at first sound, and upon an implicit conception of justice and universality. The conception emerges negatively: we cannot know what constitues a moral action until we ascertain a moral standard; until we have such a standard we have no means of dif-

---

(2) Bishop Richard Cumberland (1631-1718) espoused a version of utilitarianism involving moral laws; Samuel Clarke's (1675-1729) mathematically modelled intuitionism concerned the discovery of moral law; and even Shaftesbury's (1671-1713) moral sense theory subscribes to the proposition that the public good is the end of morality.

ferentiating morally among men ; therefore, without such a principle of differentiation, we must weigh the good of each man equally in deciding upon the moral standard of action. In order to see that this is indeed the epistemological substance of the argument, however, we must first scrutinize its theistic face, and then see to what extent its gaze is limited.

Now as God is a being of infinite goodness, it is plain the end He proposes is good. But, God enjoying in Himself all possible perfection, it follows that it is not His own good, but that of His creatures. Again, the moral actions of men are entirely terminated within themselves, so as to have no influence on the other orders of intelligences or reasonable creatures ; the end therefore to be procured by them can be no other than the good of men. But, as nothing in a natural state can entitle one man more than another to the favour of God, except only moral goodness ; which, consisting in a conformity to the laws of God, doth presuppose the being of such laws, and law ever supposing an end, to which it guides our actions ; it follows that, antecedent to the end proposed by God, no distinction can be conceived between men ; that end therefore itself, or general design of Providence, is not determined or limited by any respect of persons. It is not therefore the private good of this or that man, nation, or age, but the general well-being of all men, of all nations, of all ages of the world, which God designs should be procured by the concurring actions of each individual (*PO* 7) (³).

This demonstration can be laid out in the following way :

              1. God is infinitely good.
therefore   2. The end He proposes must be good.
              3. God is perfect.
therefore   4. The end He proposes cannot be his own good, but that of his rational creatures — man in particular (not angels).
              5. All men are equal in the eyes of God, save with respect to moral goodness.

(3) All occurrences of abbreviations in this essay refer to Luce and Jessop's *The Works of George Berkeley*, London : Thomas Nelson and Sons, 1948. "*PO*" refers to *Passive Obedience* ; Volume VI ; "*Alciphron*" refers to *Alciphron, or The Minute Philosopher*, Volume III ; "*GE*" refers to *Essays in the Guardian*, Volume VII ; "*SER*" refers to *Sermons*, Volume VII.

6. Moral goodness consists in conformity to the criterion of moral goodness (assumed to be the laws of God).
7. A criterion (Law) (by definition) supposes an end or purpose to which it guides our action.

therefore 8. Prior (logically) to knowledge of God's purpose or end, all men must be considered equal in His eyes (since there can be no moral goodness without a moral criterion (law), and no criterion without purpose or end).

therefore 9. The public good of all men of all times must be taken to be the end of the moral order.

therefore 10. Since we ought to conform our will to God's purposes, we ought to promote the public good.

Although Berkeley's metaphysical ground of the Greatest Goodness Principle is God, its epistemological primacy is established from the *lack* of a principle of moral individuation. Instead of speaking of God's purposes and laws let us consider the logic of determining moral criteria itself.

1. A criterion for moral action consists in directing action so as to promote the good of some or all men;
2. if a criterion for moral action consists in directing action so as to promote the good of some men only then a principle of moral differentiation is necessary;
3. prior to the ascertainment of the criterion, however, no such principle exists;

therefore 4. the criterion of moral action consists in directing action so as to promote the good of all men.

The deductive theistic argument thus rests on the recognition of the absence of a principle of moral differentiation prior to the determination of a moral criterion for action. In working out our moral criterion, therefore, *justice as universality functions as an epistemological principle*. It should be noted that in this argument, law is presupposed as the form of the criterion of moral action. In his analogical argument from the order and purpose of the natural world Berkeley tries to substantiate this presupposition (⁴).

---

(4) In *Alciphron* I, 16, Berkeley concludes that we ought to "infer the same union, order, and regularity in the moral world that we perceive to be in the natural", because the "pattern of order" in the natural world is "worthy the imitation of rational agents". In the earlier *Passive Obedience* 14, he remarks that the good of the natural world (for which we

Berkeley's arguments for the necessity of obeying moral law will be analyzed shortly, but this seems as good a time as any to distinguish between the two sorts of law in Berkeley's overall metaphysics. The two sorts of law are both considered by Berkeley to be "Laws of Nature", but one is scientific, concerning the physical, while the other is moral. The former more or less circumscribe the patterns of ideas which are generated in our experience by God, while the latter direct the voluntary action of free agents. As Berkeley indicates, only the latter imply an obligation:

> For we ought to distinguish between a twofold signification of the terms *law of nature*, which words do either denote a rule or precept for the direction of the voluntary actions of reasonable agents, and in that sense they imply a duty; or else they are used to signify any general rule which we observe to obtain in the works of nature, independent of the wills of men, in which sense no duty is implied (*PO* 33).

Corresponding to the operation of each sort of law is a good appropriate to it. The operation of natural physical laws accounts for the pleasure we experience. Pleasure is pretty much what Berkeley means by happiness — a natural, non-moral good. Broad has this to say about Berkeley's view of the non-moral nature of happiness:

> God's ultimate end for mankind is an *eternal* state of affairs in which non-moral good and evil (i.e., happiness and unhappiness) are distributed among men in accordance with their moral desert. This moral desert arises solely from obedience or disobedience to rules of conduct which are enjoined by God as a means to men's *temporal* happiness without regard to desert. Presumably, then, Berkeley recognizes a purely non-moral value and disvalue in happiness and unhappiness respectively, and a purely moral value and disvalue in obedience and disobedience respectively to God's command [5].

---

can propose no "nobler pattern" for our own conduct) is brought about by conformity to natural laws:

"... it is evident that those actions (which constitue nature) are not adapted to particular views, but all conformed to certain general rules ... And these indeed are excellently suited to promote the general well-being of the creation ...".

[5] C. D. Broad, "Berkeley's Theory of Morals", *Revue Internationale de Philosophie*, 23-24 (1953), p. 85.

Distinguishing between the two sorts of law enables us to take into account the two sorts of natural good : the non-moral (happiness) and the moral (the result of acting *from* the moral law, not merely *in accordance* with it) (⁶). Berkeley hereby presages Kant's requirement that the moral good be autonomous from happiness.

In employing the Greatest Goodness Principle, therefore, we have in mind only non-moral goodness — happiness. This must be so because until we have the fruits of the applications of this Principle (laws, rules) we can have no notion of *moral* goodness. The telos of the moral universe is the aggregate of each man's natural, non-moral good, counting equally. As we saw above, we must consider each man's good equally because we lack a means of differentiating among men until after (in the order of knowing) we employ our Greatest Goodness Principle (⁷).

The question now facing Berkeley is : how do we implement this supreme moral principle? For we must answer this question before we see the need to answer the epistemological question dormant in Berkeley's presupposition about law : how do we ascertain moral law? Let us turn now to Berkeley's justification for rule-utilitarianism, for why we should rely on laws to promote the public good.

II

Berkeley assumes that obeying the principle "We ought to promote the public good", is too important to be left to chance :

> Having thus discovered the great end to which all moral obligations are subordinate, it remains that we inquire what methods are necessary for the obtaining that end (*PO* 7).

---

(6) This is not the time to elaborate on Berkeley's conception of moral worth. It should be remarked, however, that there is considerable evidence in *Sermon* II, *Guardian Essay* IX, and *PO* 13, that the motive of furthering the public good through obedience to moral law is requisite for moral goodness.

(7) It strikes me that this sort of reasoning lies at the root of one traditional argument levied against ethical egoism as a principle or theory. The argument holds that 'It is in my interest to do A_1," (where A_1 is an act believed by the speaker to be in his interest) is not a moral reason for acting because anyone can urge isomorphically that it is in his interest to perform some such act (A_1). This objection to ethical egoism amounts to pointing out that "in my interest" is not a principle of moral differentiation.

This reveals a meta-ethical assumption of rationalist character. The Greatest Goodness Principle requires method, a reasoned implementation.

Berkeley proceeds to the derivation of rule-utilitarianism as the method by which to secure the common weal: we ought to determine the rightness and wrongness of particular acts by reference to rules which, when observed, necessarily promote the public good. What Berkeley means by "necessarily promote the public good" will be discussed later.

Berkeley succinctly states what have come to be considered the general features of rule-utilitarianism in this passage from *Passive Obedience* 31:

> In framing the general laws of nature, it is granted we must be entirely guided by the public good of mankind, but not in the ordinary moral actions of our lives ... The rule is framed with respect to the good of mankind; but our practice must be always shaped immediately by the rule.

Berkeley here draws the distinction between using the promotion of the public good as the criterion for testing a candidate for a moral *rule* and using the public good directly as the criterion for the rightness or wrongness of a particular act. The former method is employed when we adopt rule-utilitarianism as our second basic principle; the latter method is employed when we adopt act-utilitarianism as our second basic principle. Berkeley sees the difference between rule-utilitarianism and act-utilitarianism as the difference between mediating the application of the utility principle by applying rules in the former case, and applying the utility principle directly in the latter.

The form of Berkeley's main argument for rule-utilitarianism is to propose what Broad([8]) calls "prima facie" alternative ways of producing the public good, but which seem to be for Berkeley, on the face of his expression, logically exhaustive alternatives:

> The well-being of mankind must necessarily be carried on one of these two ways. Either, first, without the injunction of any certain universal rules of morality, only by obliging every one upon each particular occasion to consult the public good, and always to do that which to him shall seem, in the present time and cir-

---

(8) BROAD, p. 76.

cumstances, most to conduce to it [act-utilitarianism]. Or, secondly, by enjoining the observation of some determinate, established laws, which, if universally practised, have, from the nature of things, an essential fitness to procure the well-being of mankind [rule-utilitarianism] (*PO* 8, my italics).

Berkeley nowhere purports to deduce, from anything else he has said (either about God or the public good) that these are the only alternatives. Accordingly, it seems that the "necessity" of the choice follows from Barkeley's claim that these two ways exhaust the logical possibilities. They obviously do not exhaust all the plausible alternatives for promoting the public good, let alone all the logical possibilities of means for such promotion. Berkeley himself, in fact, adds a third alternative to these two. When he writes *Alciphron* ([9]), he adds a detailed discussion of this third method : dependence on the "moral sense" for the choice of action which will best promote the public good. Even in *Passive Obedience*, however, he gives this alternative passing, albeit dishonorable mention,

> Tenderness and benevolence of temper are often motive to the best and greatest actions ; but we must not make them the sole rule of our actions ... (*PO* 13).

Since Berkeley himself adds this third method of securing the aim of morality, Broad's interpretation of the first two as "prima facie" alternatives is more charitable than the view that Berkeley simply overstates the case by using language that suggests a logical claim where he meant only to make a psychological one. Berkeley's *strategy*, taking *Passive Obedience* and *Alciphron* together, is to consider the three rival means for promoting the public good : rule-utilitarianism, act-utilitarianism, and the moral sense or passions. What Broad fails to notice, however, is much more significant, viz., that Berkeley employs a species of universalization argument in his examination of the methods for meliorating the condition of mankind. He disposes of act-utilitarianism and reliance upon the moral sentiment as second order moral principles by drawing out the dangers of the general adoption of each.

---

(9) *Alciphron* III, 5.

A

If we were to adopt act-utilitarianism as our second basic principle we should not promote the public good for a variety of considerations Berkeley advances. We could never be certain that the consequences of a particular act would be in the public interest:

> First, it will thence follow that the best men, for want of judgment, and the wisest, for want of knowing all the hidden circumstances and consequences of an action, may very often be at a loss how to behave themselves (*PO* 9).

We could never be certain, therefore, that our moral judgment is correct. Moreover, because of the complexity of the judgment required if we were to adopt act-utilitarianism as our principle, and because of the amount of information we should need to make such a decision, we should often simply not know what to do. The purpose of normative ethics for Berkeley is to provide a theory which is practical, which can in fact aid men in making their moral decisions. Thus, he rejects act-utilitarianism on practical grounds.

To estimate all the consequences of an act, if possible, would be an impractical task: "In short, to calculate the events of each particular action is impossible; and, though it were not would yet take up too much time to be of use in the affairs of life" (*PO* 9).

A more important objection is Berkeley's claim that if we were to employ this principle ubiquitously we should have no objective standard by which to judge actions, our own or others. This is because we should have to make decisions upon the rightness and wrongness of actions on the basis of the calculated consequences of the act. Each of us, however, calculates differently:

> For, since the measure and rule of every good man's actions is supposed to be nothing else but his own private disinterested opinion of what makes most for the public good at that juncture; and since this opinion must unavoidably in different men, from their particular views and circumstances, be very different: it is impossible to know whether any one instance of parricide or perjury, for example, be criminal (*PO* 9).

The principle of act-utilitarianism, then, aside from being impractical, can not provide us with an objective standard or measure by which to judge actions. When we envision the world in which act-utilitarianism is adopted we realize the dangers we run with such a principle.

B

Berkeley engages in ethical psychology when he describes the content of moral experience per se and the morally relevant features of human nature. In *Alciphron*, as well as in *Guardian Essay XII* he shows his awareness of the importance of those sentiments, feelings, instincts which often direct one toward the right sort of behavior :

> That men have certain instinctive sensations or passions from nature, which make them amiable and useful to each other, I am clearly convinced. Such are a fellow-feeling with the distressed, tenderness for our offspring, and affection towards our friends, our neighbours, and our country, an indignation against things base, cruel, or unjust (*Alciphron* III, 5).

Even in *Passive Obedience*, as we have seen, Berkeley mentions natural feelings which influence behavior towards the morally right. Such feelings, however, ought not be taken as our criterion or guideline in making moral decisions and judgments.

The first objection against adopting as a principle something like "One ought to let one's moral sentiment determine one's choice of action", is that, like all passions, those often associated with morally laudable behavior can lead us to rash action, the consequences of which are far from contributing to the public welfare :

> ... but we must not make them [sympathy, tenderness, *et al.*] the sole rule of our actions ; they are passions rooted in our nature, and, like all other passions, must be restrained and kept under, otherwise they may possibly betray us into as great enormities as any other unbridled lust (*PO* 13).

A second objection to reliance on the moral sense or feelings is that antipathy and attraction to actions and their consequences are often acquired, and impossible to distinguish from the natural antipathies and attractions which, on this suggestion, are supposed to be our moral guide-lines :

> ... it is true, there are certain natural antipathies implanted in the soul, which are ever the most lasting and insurmountable ; but as custom is a second nature, whatever aversions are from our early childhood continually infused into the mind give it so deep a stain as is scarce to be distinguished from natural complexion. And as it

doth hence follow, that to make all the inward horrors of soul pass for infallible marks of sin were the way to establish error and superstition in the world ; so, on the other hand, to suppose all actions lawful which are unattended with those starts of nature would prove of the last dangerous consequences to virtue and morality (*PO* 21).

We should not take as a rule of behavior, then, either the presence or absence of inclination toward or away from a practice. It is often impossible to tell whether such inclination is natural, hence to be relied upon, or learned. It is also impossible to depend upon our natural morally relevant feelings prevailing over other natural or acquired feelings which are less noble. The morally relevant feelings or sentiments may be insufficiently strong to direct us toward the right :

> These passions [morally relevant] are implanted in the human soul, with several other fears and appetites, aversions and desires, some of which are strongest and uppermost in one mind, others in another. Should it not therefore seem a very uncertain guide in morals, for a man to follow his passion or inward feeling? And would not this rule infallibly lead different men different ways, according to the prevalency of this or that appetite or passion (*Alciphron* III, 5)?

This variation in strength of passion is also possible for any one individual over a period of time or in differing circumstances. Basing our moral decisions on "moral sentiment", therefore, fails as a universal normative guideline.

If, on the other hand, we were to adopt rule-utilitarianism as our second principle we should not have to face the problems which attend the adoption of these two alternatives. There would be no lack of certainty in making moral judgments and decisions : "... it being far more easy to judge with certainty, whether such or such an action be a transgression of this or that precept, then whether it will be attended with more good or ill consequences" (*PO* 9). There would be an objective standard to which to appeal (moral rules) rather than the subjective calculation of each man. There would be no dependency upon feelings which might vary from one individual to the next and within one individual from one time to the next. What is required, however, is a way of determining genuine moral laws. To this question we now turn our attention.

III

Two things are of importance in Berkeley's justification for obeying moral rules. The first is his implicit reliance on a universalization argument: what are the consequences of universalizing the several methods of making moral decisions. As we have seen, rule-utilitarianism is the only credible method for Berkeley. Directly involved in this is the second matter: the rules we are to follow have a "necessary connection" with the public good. Indeed, it is this connection which buttresses the observation of moral law as the best method of decision making. It is no wonder then that we find these two matters, universalization and necessary connection, in Berkeley's answer to the question: how do we ascertain moral law?

Berkeley proposes that we test candidates for moral law by a universalization procedure. We are to universalize a practice or rule-observation. The colloquial expression of this line of reasoning, one which most of us employ at one time or another is: "What if everyone did that?"

Berkeley's universalization argument runs: If (1) the consequences of everyone behaving in a certain way would undermine the public interest, then (2) no one ought to behave in that way [10]. It follows from this that we are obliged to obey the rule which forbids this sort of action (e.g. Thou shalt not steal).

It is interesting to note in passing that Berkeley avoids an error which Singer claims has been committed by some of Berkeley's successors (Broad is a notable example). This is the error of thinking that if the consequences of everyone's doing X (or following a rule) are bad then the consequences of anyone's doing X are bad; and, equally as fallacious, thinking that if the consequences of everyone's not doing X (or not following a rule) are good, then the consequences of anyone's not doing X are good. Berkeley takes great pains to show that *although* the sort of reasoning given above in fallacious, moral laws are nevertheless universally binding.

> And, notwithstanding that these rules are too often, either by the unhappy concurrence of events, or more especially by the wicked-

---

[10] See Marcus SINGER, *Generalization in Ethics* (New York: Knopf, 1961). He refers to it as a "generalization argument": "If the consequences of everyone's acting or being treated in a certain way would be undesirable, then no one ought to act or be treated in that way (*without a reason*) ..." (pp. 67-8).

ness of perverse men who will not conform to them, made accidental causes of misery to those good men who do, yet this doth not vacate their obligation : they are ever to be esteemed the fixed unalterable standards of moral good and evil (*PO* 13).

Berkeley is considering "everyone" independent of particular circumstances, circumstances which might, in a particular case, help produce consequences the contrary of those resulting from *everyone* acting in the described way. The consequences of a particular act performed by a particular man ("anyone") may be good ; nevertheless, the act is prohibited if and only if it is a member of a class of acts whose universal performance is destructive of the public good.

The laws which pass the universalization test are those which a reasonable agent *would* choose to obey if he were perfectly fair and not biased. This is intimated by Berkeley when he says that we are to compare an action with the "eternal law of reason" in trying to determine the rightness or wrongness of an action (*PO* 13) and when he assures us that "in general conclusions, drawn from an equal and enlarged view of things ; it is not possible there should be so great, if any, disagreement at all amongst candid rational inquirers after truth" (*PO* 29). The sort of law referred to by Berkeley seems to be one which perfectly rational agents would in fact naturally conform to :

> [let us] suppose indeed a society of rational agents acting under the eye of Providence, concurring in one design to promote the common benefit of the whole, and conforming their actions to the established laws and order of the divine parental wisdom ... (*Alciphron* III, 10).

The moral rules are rational in nature, and are therefore the precepts of the fully rational, informed man. Berkeley implies that there is in substance no difference between the Ideal Spectator and Rule-Utilitarian Principles. Berkeley assumes empirical knowledge of the purpose of civil government. But this is also a metaphysical purpose. Man is *by nature* social for Berkeley, and the function or purpose of civil society and civil law is man's well-being :

> ... there is implanted in mankind a natural tendency or disposition to a social life ... the peculiar wants, appetites, faculties, and capacities of man being exactly calculated and framed for such a state, insomuch that without it it is impossible he should live in a condition in any degree suitable to his nature. And since the bond and cement of society is a submission to its laws, it plainly follows

that this duty hath an equal right with any other to be thought a law of nature (*PO* 25).

It is also revealing that Berkeley begins his argument for "passive obedience", as a moral law with the following statement, "The miseries inseparable from a state of anarchy are easily *imagined*" (*PO* 16, my italics). His first step is to summon up the horrors of not taking for our rule "passive obedience".

Compare this to what Paton notes about the categorical imperative as a Law of Nature :

> The best, if not the only, way to make such a law vivid in our imagination is to picture to ourselves a world in which everybody in fact acted in accordance with it. This is the eminently sensible procedure which Kant now commends to us ... The duty of fire-watching, for example, was sometimes pressed home by the question 'What would happen if everybody refused to do it?' ([11])

Berkeley is here arguing for the necessary connection between (the universal observation of) the rule of passive obedience and the promotion of the public good on the basis of the universalization procedure : if the consequences of everyone's disobeying civil law would be detrimental to mankind, then no one ought to disobey civil law. He concludes from this that the public good "of necessity" will not be promoted by this practice of civil disobedience.

Berkeley is considering the state of "anarchy", that state which obtains when no one obeys the civil law. Thus, when he counsels us to imagine a state of anarchy, he is asking us to imagine the realization of the antecedent : (1) "if no one obeyed the civil law". The consequences of everyone behaving in this way, he tells us, would be horrendous. He is stating the consequences which must follow upon everyone's disobeying the civil law — confusion, disorder, and misery. From which he concludes that (2) "we ought not disobey civil laws". Berkeley sees himself as providing the substance for the imaginary test, for in this opening section of his discussion about the rule of passive obedience, after claiming that the miseries *inseparable* from a state of anarchy are easily imagined, he says :

> Without this [civil law] there is no politeness, no order, no peace, among men, but the world is one great heap of misery and con-

---

(11) H. J. Paton, *The Categorical Imperative* (London : Hutchinson and Co., 1947), p. 152.
(12) *Ibid.*, Paton, p. 146.

fusion; the strong as well as the weak, the wise as well as the foolish, standing on all sides exposed to all those calamities which man can be liable to in a state where he has no other security than the not being possessed of anything which may raise envy or desire in another — ... *From which it plainly follows*, that loyalty, or submission to the supreme civil authority, hath, if universally practised in conjunction with all other virtues, a *necessary connexion* with the well-being of the whole sum of mankind (*PO* 16, my italics).

We arrive at the necessary connection between the rule of civil obedience and the welfare of humanity in a negative way — by imagining a world in which none obey the rule. The purpose of the institution of civil law, not particular civil laws, is identical with the telos of society, government, or social life, to wit — the well-being of mankind. Now Berkeley obviously has some metaphysical-empirical presupposition of what man in a state of nature is or would be like, otherwise he would not and could not claim that without civil law misery would be man's daily diet. He offers the existence of social instincts as partial evidence for this natural sociability. His belief that God has constituted man so as to flourish in a civil setting leads to the conclusion that social life and civil law are *necessary* conditions for the good of mankind (*PO* 25).

This assertion is supported by empirical observation, but remains a metaphysical claim about the nature of man and the *essential* purpose of social life and civil law. Berkeley's application of the universalization procedure to the rule of passive obedience rests on this presupposition, since if one questions the claim that *the* "purpose" of civil law is to enable man to fulfill his own nature, then it is questionable whether civil law is a necessary condition for the public good. Berkeley's conclusion that the necessary consequences of obeying the rule of passive obedience are in the public interest would be also disputable. If one maintains that the state in which there is no civil law is peaceful and pleasant, then surely one would not agree that the purpose of civil law is the public good and that civil law is necessary for the public good. *A fortiori* the claim that "passive obedience", if universally practiced, has a necessary connection with the public good would be found unwarranted.

Berkeley's difficulty, one not shared by Kant, results from his need to make metaphysical claims about the telos of various institutions, practices, or rules. The purpose is identified with that for which the rule or practice is a necessary condition and that for which the rule's observation is a necessary condition is the necessary or essential consequence of the rule's observation. Consider our example of the rule of passive obedience. Civil law is a *necessary condition* for the welfare of mankind ; therefore, the observation of the rule "we ought not disobey the civil law" has a *necessary connection* with the public good ; therefore, we ought not disobey this rule. This line of reasoning rests on Berkeley's hidden metaphysical presupposition : man's nature is such that civil law is a necessary condition for the public good.

By applying the universalization test we "see" the consequences of a general practice or its absence. Berkeley does this much as Kant does to show that without the institution of genuine promise-making particular human purposes, or the purpose of getting out of financial straits, would not be attained. In contrast to Kant, though, Berkeley's universalization formula has utilitarian flesh.

The universalization argument is a definition of what it is to be a moral law.

> Such a rule [moral law], if universally observed, hath, from the nature of things, a necessary fitness to promote the general well-being of mankind : therefore it is a law of nature (PO 31).

Its ultimate warrant is found in the belief that God wills laws for the good of all men. "What is right for one man is right for all" is a proposition grounded in God's nature and will, Berkeley's *arguments* for moral equality notwithstanding. Propositions of this form, however, as Singer amply illustrates, are endemic to most moral reasoning or accounts of such reasoning. Regardless of his justification of it, Berkeley seems on firm moral terrain when he employs the universalization argument in testing for moral rules.

Because the success of the Berkeleian universalization procedure depends upon certain metaphysical claims, and because the "necessary connection" must be something weaker than a *logically* necessary connection, yet stronger than an inductive relationship, it is appropriate if not altogether translucent to refer to it as a "metaphysical" connection.

We have already seen that Berkeley distinguishes between two sorts of natural law : physical and moral. Within the latter class he further distinguishes between "negative" and "positive" rules. I shall refer to negative rules, such as "no one ought to lie", as "*proscriptions*", and positive precepts such as "everyone ought to support the needy", as "*prescriptions*". Only the former entail a universal duty ; the latter "admit of limitation" and require the exercise of human "prudence" and "discretion". Only *proscriptions*, therefore, are always binding, never to be broken. Berkeley expresses this "categorical" nature :

... 'Thou shalt not commit adultery', 'Thou shalt not steal', are so many unalterable moral rules, which to violate in the least degree is vice or sin ... the least breach whereof hath the inherent stain of moral turpitude (PO 15).

Does Berkeley have a reason for claiming that only *pro*scriptions entail universal duties? And what is the principle upon which the distinction between *pro*scription and *pre*scription rests?

The argument which reveals the ground of this distinction is found in PO 26. What is crucial in this argument is that it rests upon the Kantian proposition that "ought" implies "can".

The "Kantian" statement that "ought" implies "can" ([13]) means that it is never our duty to do that which we cannot physically do. Berkeley attempts to reconcile two fundamental desiderata of his moral theory: some rules are universally binding, and "'ought' implies 'can'". His articulation of *pro*scriptive law represents the fruit of this undertaking.

Berkeley believes that only those rules which *always can* be obeyed demand universal obedience. He is implicitly generalizing the "'ought' implies 'can'" formula to "'always ought' implies 'always can'". Thus, a necessary condition for claiming that we always ought to obey rule R is that we always can obey rule R. "Universal obligation" implies "universal performability". Berkeley believes that *pro*scriptions can satisfy this condition and therefore carry universal obligation.

Of course, "universal performability" is not a sufficient condition for universal obligation. As we saw above, as rule must pass the universalization test in order to qualify as a moral rule in the first place. Passing this test together with universal performability then constitute necessary and jointly sufficient conditions for universal obligation. *Pre*scriptions satisfy only the former condition and not the latter, and are therefore moral laws, but are not universally binding.

Berkeley maintains that everyone is always able to "not-do" anything. This does not mean that everyone is able to omit doing anything *all the time*, i.e., never perform a physical action. It means, rather, that

---

(13) In A Commentary on Kant's *Critique of Practical Reason* (Chicago : The University of Chicago Press, 1960) L. W. Beck remarks in a footnote, p. 200, "One of Kant's most famous 'statements' — 'Thou canst because thou shouldst' — does not exist in his writings in this neat form (cf. David Baumgardt, 'Legendary Quotations and the Lack of References', *Journal of the History of Ideas*, VIII (1947), 116). But statements that express this inference less succinctly abound, e.g., *Critique of Practical Reason*, 30 (118-19) ; *Critique of Pure Reason*, A 807-B 835 ; etc.

everyone, at any given time is able to not-do any physical act. Nothing empirical, in principle, can stand in the way of not-doing. Everyone is able, moreover, to refrain from doing many things simultaneously. Thus, everyone is always able to conform to the *proscriptive* subclass of moral laws. PO 26 is the link between the universalized Kantian proposition "'always ought' implies 'always can'" which seems to be a meta-ethical proposition, and Berkeley's more explicit position that only *pro*scriptions demand universal obligation.

> ... I shall explain the reason of distinguishing between positive and negative precepts, the latter only included in this general proposition [nothing can justify the 'least violation of them'].
>
> Now, the ground of that distinction may be resolved into this, namely, that very often, either through the difficulty or number of moral actions, or their inconsistency with each other, it is not possible [empirically with regard to 'difficulty', logically with regard to 'inconsistency'] for one man to perform several of them at the same time; whereas it is plainly consistent and possible that any man should, at the same time, abstain from all manner of positive actions whatsoever. Hence it comes to pass that prohibitions or negative precepts must by every one, in all times and places, be all actually observed: whereas those which enjoin the doing of an action allow room for human prudence and discretion in the execution of them ...

The universal observation of *pre*scriptions is precluded because it is not the case that one *always* can perform the act(s) required to fulfill *pre*scription(s). Empirical circumstances can stand in the way of the performance of an act required to obey a *pre*scription. Something could prevent me, for example, from keeping my promise to sing for Jones, e.g., my larynx has been removed. The other and more serious problem is that of not being able to fulfill several *pre*scriptive duties at one. This is a logical problem, for nothing empirical need be considered at all. Because of "their number" or "mutual inconsistency", I may not be able, logically, to perform the acts requisite to obey two or more *pre*scriptions.

Berkeley then must find a class of rules all of whose members can always be obeyed. We can never say of a member of this class of rule either that it could not be obeyed because of some physical circumstance, or that it could not, logically, be obeyed because of conflict with another rule of the same type. I have concocted a Berkeleian argument in order to show how Berkeley's conclusion that we ought always obey *proscriptive* laws of nature rests in part upon the premise that "'ought' implies 'can'".

(1) We ought to do that which promotes the public good (Greatest Goodness Principle).

(2) Only by obeying moral rules [rules which have a necessary connection with the public good] can we promote the public good (Principle of Rule-Utilitarianism).

(3) We ought *always* to do only that which we can *always* do to promote the public good [1, and universalized form of "'ought' implies 'can'"].

(4) We ought always to obey the moral rules which can always be obeyed [2, 3].

(5) The moral rules which always can be obeyed are those which can be obeyed simultaneously [definition of universality of rule-obedience in *PO* 26].

(6) The moral rules which can be obeyed simultaneously are those which designate acts which can be performed simultaneously [definition of simultaneity of rule-obedience in *PO* 26].

(7) We ought always to obey the moral rules designating acts which can be performed simultaneously [4, 5, 6].

(8) Omissions are the acts which can be performed simultaneously [*PO* 26].

(9) We ought always to obey the moral rules designating omissions, viz. *proscriptive* rules [7, 8].

Those cases wherein we always can behave in accordance with what we "will" reduce to those cases in which we will to not-do some sort of physical behavior. Berkeley maintains that everyone can always realize his intention to not-lie or not-steal simply because such inention is realized in "non-behavior". In the case of *prescriptions*, on the other hand, "accidental circumstances" must be taken into account. In such cases it is not always empirically possible for one to realize his intentions in behavior, let alone behave in two logically inconsistent ways. Thus might it be impossible for me to give to the needy and honour my debts within my limited means. In the case of obeying *proscriptions*, however, "act" is equivalent to the "mental act" of willing, intending to "not do". In observing *prescriptions*, on the other hand, "act" is equivalent to "mental *and* physical act" what Berkeley calls "positive action" (line 14,

PO 26). No physical circumstance can prevent or hinder one from performing a mental act and one can (logically and empirically) refrain from doing any number of things simultaneously.

At this point an obvious objection comes to mind : *pro*scriptions and *pre*scriptions are transformable into one another. It may be urged that Berkeley is focusing on an accidental feature of moral propositions and claiming that something significant (universal obligation and non-universal, limited obligation) follows from it. Thus, it might be argued, the prescription "you ought to foster life" is obvertible to the proscription "you ought not kill" ; the proscription "you ought not lie" is obvertible to the prescription "you ought to tell the truth". If this is the case, then Berkeley's logical distinction between proscriptions and prescriptions evaporates.

It seems to me, however, that at the very least not all *pro*scriptions are equivalent to their prescriptive transformations. "You ought not lie" for example, does not entail "you ought to tell the truth". One could obey the former (proscription) without obeying the latter, prescriptive transformation. On the other hand, the *pre*scription "you ought to tell the truth" *does entail* the *pro*scription "you ought not to lie". This seems to be the case in general. Rules as *pre*scriptions entail their proscriptive counterparts, but *pro*scriptions do not entail their prescriptive transformations ; therefore, the two are not logically equivalent or "obvertible". It is further questionable whether any *pro*scription is obvertible to a *pre*scription.

Consider another example, one which strikes a Berkeleian note : "do not commit suicide" is not obvertible to "continue living". We have a duty to obey the first because we have the *power* to refrain from taking our own lives. We do not have the power to *prevent* our own death, however, so are not morally obligated to "continue living".

In addition, not telling the Gestapo a lie concerning the whereabouts of someone is neither a necessary nor sufficient condition for that person's death. Surely the one who pulls the trigger is in some sense a necessary condition for the man's death *at that time*, as well as being a sufficient condition (given natural physical laws). We are obligated to do only that which we can do, that which is in our power. This is the "'ought' implies 'can'" dictum once again. Its significance features in both Kant's and Berkeley's ethics and underlies Berkeley's *pro*scription/ *pre*scription distinction.

Berkeley claimed to have written a treatise on ethics, the capstone of his philosophical system, while in Italy. Whether he did or not remains a question for historians and sleuths to determine. But, judging from what indeed he wrote about morality and human decision-making we have a rather substantial corpus of discourses and dialogue to go on. The thread which runs through all his discussion, the concept which underlies his most important principles and recommendations is that of universalization. We must employ a universalization procedure to vindicate rule-utilitarianism, to determine moral law, and to justify our universal obligation to obey a subclass of those moral laws. Although defective in several assumptions and hardly explicit enough to be wholly satisfying, when understood in this light, Berkeley's work in ethics is refreshingly inventive and characteristically of contemporary importance.

Iowa State University.

BERKELEY'S SOCIAL THEORY: CONTEXT AND DEVELOPMENT

By David E. Leary*

I. *Berkeley's Social Theory and its Intellectual Background*

George Berkeley's social thought has been overlooked. The reason seems obvious. Berkeley has been regarded principally as a link between John Locke and David Hume. Consequently, his works relating to the British empirical tradition and to his immaterialism have received primary attention while his works dealing with ethical and public issues have been regarded as secondary. This has led to a distortion of Berkeley's own scale of priorities. He repeatedly stressed that he was primarily concerned with the condition of the real and concrete world which surrounded him. That this real and concrete world is immaterial and is constituted in our ideas of it were indeed important propositions for Berkeley, but they were only steps toward a consistent philosophy that was intended to convince his readers of the essential relation of man to his world, society, religion, and God. Berkeley's goal was always to educate the public to "a Zeal for Religion and Love of their Country."[1] He was concerned primarily with how people lived their lives, how they related to one another and to their God; he was concerned with their metaphysical beliefs largely to the extent that they bore on these issues.

This paper is an investigation of Berkeley's social thought, particularly as it is grounded upon Berkeley's quite explicit, but neglected, social theory, which is revealed in an essay written by Berkeley in 1713 for Steele's short-lived *Guardian*. Originally untitled, this short essay has been labeled "The Bond of Society" in Luce and Jessop's critical edition of Berkeley's works. Its significance was noted by Harry Elmer Barnes in 1948, but Barnes's comment has not brought the essay the recognition it deserves. This is all the more unfortunate since, as Barnes says, Berkeley's essay is "one of the most suggestive essays in the whole history of social philosophy."[2]

---

* The author would like to thank Keith Michael Baker of the University of Chicago for his helpful comments on the first draft of this article.

[1] Berkeley, "A Proposal for the better supplying of Churches in our foreign Plantations" (1725), *Works*, VII, 348. All references to Berkeley's works are to the critical edition of his collected works: A. A. Luce and T. E. Jessop, eds., *The Works of George Berkeley, Bishop of Cloyne*, 9 Vols. (New York, 1948-57). In the notes this source will be referred to simply as *Works*.

[2] H. E. Barnes, ed., *An Introduction to the History of Sociology* (Chicago, 1966), 52.

"The Bond of Society" is a good title for this essay in which Berkeley's major concern is to comprehend the nature of social phenomena as an integral part of "the whole scope of creation."[3] The essence of Berkeley's argument is that there is "a certain correspondence" or "similitude of operation" between the natural world and the world of man. Just as natural philosophers now agree that natural bodies exert "a mutual attraction upon each other," so too, says Berkeley, can we observe "a like principle of attraction" in the moral world of man. In fact, the "social appetite in human souls is the greatest spring and source of moral actions"; it is the very bond of society.

In this very brief summary the intellectual context of Berkeley's social theory is clearly manifest. The natural philosopher to whom Berkeley alludes is, of course, Sir Isaac Newton, and it is against the background of Newtonian mechanics that Berkeley analyzes social dynamics. The key concept in Berkeley's analysis is the "principle of attraction" whereby men "are drawn together in communities, clubs, families, friendships, and all the various species of society." Based on this fundamental analogy of social attraction (or "appetite") with natural gravity,[4] Berkeley sketches a model of society which can account for both the common sociability of man and the unique individual differences in the attraction among men. For instance: "As in bodies, where the quantity is the same, the attraction is strongest between those which are placed nearest to each other, so it is likewise in the minds of men, *caeteris paribus*, between those which are most nearly related." Thus does Berkeley account for the fact that those who habitually live closer together are more tightly bound together in the various social relations which we observe in the human world.

Beyond this, Berkeley offers a further explanation of individual differences in the behavior of men. Individual idiosyncrasies (including anti-social and asocial behaviors) are explained by Berkeley as the results of the "private passions and motions of the soul" which "obstruct the operation of that benevolent uniting instinct implanted in human nature." These passions are analogous to the "rectilinear motions" in the natural world which in cooperation with "the general laws of gravitation" account for the orbits of the "several great bodies which compose the solar system." Just as the tendency to rectilinear (centrifugal)

---

[3] Berkeley. "The Bond of Society" (1713). *Works*, VII, 225-28. As is true of all of Berkeley's writings, this essay is a superb example of concise expression. Unquestionably it speaks for itself better than any exposition can, and so the reader is encouraged to consult it directly. Since the essay is very short, quotations in the following discussion will not be cited.

[4] Since Berkeley thinks of man's sociability as analogous to Newton's "mutual attraction" or gravity, it is interesting to note that Newton originally thought of gravity or attraction (especially in his alchemical experiments) as "sociability." Cf. Frank E. Manuel, *A Portrait of Isaac Newton* (Cambridge, 1968), 68.

motion counteracts the pull of gravity, which by itself would draw these great bodies "all into one mass," so too the passions of men serve to balance the influence of the "social appetite in human souls." Social dynamics, like natural mechanics, are the result of the interaction of individual and common tendencies.

This social theory is remarkable for several reasons. It is not only the first attempt to apply Newtonian mechanics to the analysis of social phenomena, but it is very possibly the first self-consciously "scientific" theory of social behavior. That is, it is based upon, and fulfills, the criteria of Berkeley's philosophy of science. It proposes "uniform laws of nature" which describe the "ordinary course of things"[5]; or, in Berkeley's favorite metaphor for science, it provides "a grammar for the understanding of nature."[6] The intellectual context of Berkeley's philosophy of science is again Newtonian science. It was through his critique of Newtonian science in the *Philosophical Commentaries* (1708-09) that Berkeley developed a consistent understanding of what science is and what it offers.[7] While it is not necessary to give the details of Berkeley's philosophy of science, two points from that analysis will be useful here.

First, according to Berkeley, science does not preclude freedom, i.e., the freedom of the Spirit. The Spirit of God is radically free; the Spirit of Man is relatively free. God can will a change in the uniformity of the natural world at any time; man cannot do so, but he is free to will a change in the human world.[8] This fact, the freedom of man's spirit, is another factor which influences the social behavior of man. Although Berkeley does not specify the influence in "The Bond of Society," it is clearly the cause of the ultimate dysanalogy between the natural and human worlds. Man can, as he says, become "a sort of [moral] monster or anomalous production" despite the "reciprocal attrac-

---

[5] Berkeley, *A Treatise concerning The Principles of Human Knowledge* (1710), *Works*, II, 54.

[6] Berkeley, *Siris* (1744), *Works*, V, 120.

[7] Berkeley's *Philosophical Commentaries* (1708-09), *Works*, I, 7-106, are the notebooks in which Berkeley laid the foundation for his later philosophical works. In his *Principles of Human Knowledge* (1710), *De Motu* (1721), his letters to Samuel Johnson (1729-30), and *Siris* (1744), he continued to develop the critique of Newtonian science which he set forth in these notebooks, but his basic philosophy of science was clearly delineated well before he wrote "The Bonds of Society" in 1713. Regarding Berkeley's philosophy of science, cf. Richard J. Brook, *Berkeley's Philosophy of Science* (The Hague, 1973) and Geoffrey James Warnock, "Science and Mathematics," in his *Berkeley* (Harmondsworth, 1953), 198-212.

[8] Cf. Berkeley, *Philosophical Commentaries, op. cit.*, 77 (#626), 101 (#850); *Principles of Human Knowledge* (1710), *Works*, II, 69-70; and Berkeley's letter to Johnson (1729), *Works*, II, 280. Berkeley planned to present a detailed discussion of man's freedom in Part II of *Principles of Human Knowledge*, but he apparently lost the manuscript of that part and never rewrote it.

tion in the minds of man" which is "originally engrafted in the very first foundation of the soul" as "the great spring and source of moral actions."

Secondly, according to Berkeley, science is not concerned merely with understanding reality. In fact, he did not think that science could give descriptions that are true in any absolute sense; rather, he felt that science gives descriptions which are useful, which give us "a sort of foresight, which enables us to regulate our actions for the benefit of life."[9] Thus Berkeley's philosophy of science was explicitly pragmatic and aimed at the *application* of science. This helps explain Berkeley's conclusions at the end of "The Bonds of Society." When he says that his thoughts about the nature of social dynamics "do naturally suggest" several particular conclusions, he is not merely tagging on some extraneous considerations. Rather the three social concerns he reveals in his conclusions reflect the pragmatic motives he had in developing his social theory. Upon these concerns he hoped to shed light and have a practical effect. His first conclusion is that, "as social inclinations are absolutely necessary to the well-being of the world, it is the duty and interest of each individual to cherish and improve them to the benefit of mankind." Secondly, he concludes that "it makes a signal proof of the divinity of the Christian religion, that the main duty which it inculcates above all other is charity," which is the virtue which contributes most to man's sociability, which in turn is the root of man's moral goodness. And therefore, his third conclusion is that "our modern Freethinkers" who "insinuate the Christian morals to be defective" are gravely in error. Just as the essay as a whole gives the basic premises of Berkeley's social theory, his three conclusions give a pithy indication of his three major social concerns—the disruption of society, the crisis of Christian faith and virtue, and the rise of modern free-thinking. We shall investigate the background of these concerns in the next section.

II. *Berkeley's Social Concerns*

Berkeley's threefold concern about society, religion, and modern free-thinking did not develop by chance. Berkeley lived in a world alive with changes which were rending the very fabric of the political, religious, and spiritual order, and these changes were more than evident within the "cloistered" confines of his own life.[10] The very halls of Trinity College, Dublin, which he entered in 1700 and at which he sub-

[9] Berkeley, *Principles of Human Knowledge*, op. cit., 54. Also cf. *Siris*, op. cit., 112.

[10] The biographical facts in this paper are generally available and commonly known and therefore will not be footnoted. My sources are A. A. Luce, *The Life of George Berkeley* (New York, 1968); T. E. Jessop, *George Berkeley* (London, 1959); John Wild, *George Berkeley: A Study of His Life and Philosophy* (Cambridge, 1936); Luce and Jessop's editorial comments throughout

sequently became a tutor and lecturer, still bore the marks left by the soldiers who had used them as a barracks. Despite the Act of Settlement in 1701, the political unrest in Ireland, England, and Scotland was still very real. The new Hanoverian line was not dearly beloved by the Tories, and Jacobite sympathies and hopes were still strong. At the same time the political turmoils of many years—and Marlborough's wars over a few years—had contributed to a very sizeable national debt and economic instability. And this political and economic disorder was accompanied by various signs of "moral decay." In short, social order was tentative at best.

Berkeley's concern about the state of society is reflected in a number of his writings before 1713. His notebooks (*Philosophical Commentaries*, 1708-09) show a preoccupation with the working out of a motivational-ethical theory upon which social order could be based.[11] In 1709, in a letter to Sir John Percival, he reveals his knowledge of, and his own ruminations about, political theory.[12] These same interests are further developed in his three sermons on "Passive Obedience," published in 1712 to quiet the suspicions that he had been preaching in favor of the Jacobite cause.[13] However, the publication of the actual, rather than rumored, words of his sermons did little to win him friends among the Whigs.[14] Rather than quieting public controversy over his political affiliations, his published sermons made him politically visible and earned him the pains of political discrimination. Specifically, his implicit critique of the new Lockean theory of limited obedience to government made him suspect to the Whigs who subsequently kept him for many years from receiving any clerical preferment. But he did not on that account moderate his views, and he bore his situation and consequent poverty as best he could. Berkeley's political involvement, therefore, was more than simply theoretical.

Meanwhile, the political tensions in early eighteenth-century British society were supplemented by religious tensions. Though not as violent

---

Works; and Colin Murray Turbayne, "Introduction," in George Berkeley's *Principles, Dialogues, and Philosophical Correspondence,* ed. by C. M. Turbayne (Indianapolis, 1965), vii-xxxiv.

[11] These notes in *Philosophical Commentaries* were to be the basis of the lost Part II of *Principles of Human Knowledge,* regarding Moral Philosophy. Berkeley's *Alciphron* (1732) can be viewed as a substitution for the lost manuscript.

[12] Berkeley, "Letters," *Works,* VIII, 21-23.

[13] Berkeley, "Passive Obedience," *Works,* VI, 15-46. This work is relevant to our interests, particularly regarding the development of Berkeley's ethical and motivational ideas.

[14] Ironically, since Berkeley preached obedience to civil authority, he was actually arguing *for* the Hanoverian-Whig cause, as opposed to the Jacobite-Tory cause. However, he argued on very non-Whiggish grounds, and that did not agree well with the Whigs. Such were the insecurities of the time.

and bitter as before, Catholic and Protestant rivalries still existed and were still a factor in the continuance of political unrest. But more important and dreadful to Berkeley than this inter-Christian conflict was the new phenomenon, as he perceived it, of the disaffection of a significant number of people from traditional Catholic and Protestant beliefs and practices and the development of new forms of religion. From Berkeley's viewpoint, this rise of atheism and deism added further strains to the traditional cultural order.

It was within this context that Berkeley was ordained an Anglican deacon in 1709 and a priest in 1710. Given his religious convictions, his attitude toward the rise of religious infidelity and atheism is not surprising. Yet it has not always been sufficiently recognized that Berkeley's concern about the rise of "irreligion" was a major motive behind the development of his philosophical system. This is clearly seen in the numerous notations in his *Philosophical Commentaries* which are concerned with the proof of an *immediately present and sustaining God*,[15] and it is made quite explicit in the subtitle of his major work, *A Treatise Concerning The Principles of Human Knowledge* (1710). The subtitle reads: "Wherein the chief causes of error and difficulty in the Sciences, with the grounds of Scepticism, Atheism, and Irreligion, are inquired into."[16] The final paragraphs of *The Principles of Human Knowledge* conclude that God's existence is capable of proof and that "after all, what deserves the first place in our studies, is the consideration of *God*, and our *duty;* which to promote . . . was the main drift and design of my labours. . . ." Therefore, "having shewn the falseness or vanity of those barren speculations, which make the chief employment of learned men," Berkeley hopes he has been able to "dispose them to reverence and embrace the salutary truths of the Gospel, which to know and to practice is the highest perfection of human nature."[17] This was not just the standard pious conclusion intended for the edification of the public. Berkeley had tried his best to develop a philosophy which would help restore and heal religious belief. He had done so on a level of philosophical discourse which omitted specific references to the doctrines and the proponents of doctrines which he was combatting, but it is nonetheless clear that, besides outright atheism, the "barren speculations" which he opposed were those of the deistic "free-thinkers." In particular, he must have had in mind Toland's *Christianity not Mysterious* (1696) which had brought great attention and controversy to the topic of rationalistic religion. Berkeley closed his *Three Dialogues between Hylas and Philonous* (1713) with similar antideistic and anti-

---

[15] Berkeley's stress on a God who continues to sustain and be involved with his creation is obviously presented in opposition to the deistic conception of a removed God who watches over a mechanically self-operating universe.

[16] Berkeley, *Principles of Human Knowledge, op. cit.*, 1.   [17] *Ibid.*, 113.

skeptical conclusions, and he directed a number of his essays in the *Guardian* against free-thinkers and skeptics.[18] Berkeley voiced his opposition to such "irreligion" in even more specific terms in his later "popular" works.

From this brief review it should be apparent that Berkeley's conclusions (about the disruption of society, the crisis of Christian faith and virtue, and the rise of modern free-thinking) at the end of "The Bonds of Society" were not simply a spelling-out of the logic of that essay. We shall now see how the changing social context of eighteenth-century life prompted Berkeley to further elaborate his social theory in a number of writings and projects which can be viewed as theoretical and practical extensions of "The Bond of Society."

III. *The Elaboration of Berkeley's Social Theory*

In October 1713, just two months after he published "The Bond of Society," Berkeley left London for a year's stay on the Continent as the chaplain of the Earl of Petersborough. When he returned in 1714, he hoped to receive a clerical appointment, but the memory of his "Passive Obedience" was still alive, and the Whigs, who had just come into power, blocked Berkeley's attempts to procure a living. Despite this discrimination, Berkeley wrote an anonymous article in 1715 which in effect supported the Whig ascendency, not in order to win the favor of the Whigs but in order to secure social order, which was extremely fragile. With Jacobite rebellion an immanent threat, this article, "Advice to the Tories who have taken the Oaths," appeals to the Tories to fulfill their moral duty to respect their oaths of allegiance and their responsibility to preserve public and religious order. It demonstrates Berkeley's continuing concern about the state of society and religion.[19]

It also develops some of the ideas set forth in "Passive Obedience" and "The Bond of Society." Specifically, it presents a further development of the argument for passive obedience to the sovereign, and it describes the role of "passion" and religion in, respectively, destroying and preserving the public order. Even more clearly than in Berkeley's 1713 essay, "passion" is associated with anti-social behavior; religion, with the fundamental social virtues. The symbiosis of social order and religion, a theme which is implicit in "Passive Obedience" and "The

---

[18] In fact, Berkeley's general purpose in the essays as a whole was to oppose the free-thinkers. Cf. esp. "Minute Philosophers," "Shortsightedness," "The Christian Idea of God," and "Immortality," all written in 1713, *Works*, VII, 206-09, 210-21, 222-24. Berkeley's *Three Dialogues between Hylas and Philonous* (1713), written in an attempt to introduce his philosophical doctrines to a wider audience, is found in *Works*, II, 163-263.

[19] "Advice to the Tories who have taken the Oaths" (1715), *Works*, VI, 53-58. A Jacobite rebellion did break out and was suppressed in Scotland, Sept. 1715.

Bond of Society," is more clearly elaborated here. In fact, the argument turns on itself when Berkeley pleads that social order must be preserved in order that Christianity be saved; and Christianity must be saved not just because of its "truth," but also because of its "usefulness" —its usefulness in preserving the social order! Despite this circularity in argument, Berkeley's theme is worth noting since it underlines a conviction which received fuller treatment in many of his later works: the state of society and the state of religion are intimately and directly related. Religion, in essence, fosters the "social appetite" and also aids the control of "private passions" which are inimical to social welfare. Social order, in turn, provides a setting in which the "private passions" are less likely to be aroused and "social appetite" is more likely to be fulfilled.

Before Berkeley could develop this theme, however, he needed to find a means to a living. After two years of fruitless search for an appointment, he left London again and began a second Continental tour, this time for four years as the tutor of the son of the Bishop of Clogher. When he returned to London in 1720, he found London once again in great social, political, and economic disorder. In fact, London seemed on the verge of collapse. The immediate cause was the bursting of the South Sea Bubble, the final event of a financial speculation scheme which led to the economic ruin of many. But Berkeley, in "An Essay towards preventing the Ruin of Great Britain" (1721), maintained that this particular event was only the result of a long decline in the country's morals and religion. Wanton licentiousness, rather than true liberty, had become the accustomed *modus operandi*; material gain had become the goal of all endeavor; and the simple, religious virtues upon which the English nation had risen were disappearing more and more each day. The problem was that "the passions of men" were being "violently" aroused by the hope of personal gain, leading to all sorts of private and public vices, while "public spirit, that glorious principle of all that is great and good," was being lost.[20]

This analysis is readily identifiable as an application of Berkeley's social theory. "Passion" is the father of individualism, and individualism, the father of public disorder. "Social appetite" or "public spirit" is the source of good. Therefore, since religion fosters the "public spirit," the reintroduction of "a true sense of religion" is the first step that should be taken to reestablish the public weal. Up to this point in his argument, Berkeley has extended his prior discussion but added nothing new. However, this essay of 1721 is significant because it goes further. Berkeley proceeds to list a number of concrete, practical suggestions regarding how the doom of England can be avoided. The significance of these measures is that they are designed to accomplish two simultaneous

---

[20] "An Essay towards preventing the Ruin of Great Britain" (1721). *Works*, VI, 71, 79.

goals—to foster "public spirit" (and allay "private passions") while at the same time restoring economic feasibility. The specific suggestions are beyond our scope here, but they are well worth perusal for the insight they give into Berkeley's economic and psychological acuity. Economic improvement, Berkeley implicitly realizes, depends to a great extent on psychological factors. For example, whereas cynicism and egoism, as well as the love of luxury and public vulgarities, reduce the sense of social cohesion and the desire to work for the common weal, "simplicity of manners" and attitudes contributes to the "public spirit" which motivates "every man's interest to support that of the public."[21] One must be conscious of such factors and foster them while developing economic strategies. Strategies alone are not enough. Berkeley returns to this implicit theme in later writings, making it much more explicit.

This general analysis of the public ills and his concrete suggestions were not merely theoretical for Berkeley. As he continued to seek some kind of ecclesiastical appointment, at first in London and then in Dublin, where he became involved in administration and teaching at Trinity College, Berkeley collected his ideas into a practical scheme which he felt would greatly benefit the public good. Based upon his conviction that Christianity fosters the natural social virtues which form the basis of "public spirit," and that "public spirit" is the basis of a healthy society, Berkeley turned his thoughts to religious education. If young children were properly introduced to the fullness of Christianity, Berkeley reasoned, society would soon be grounded again on solid virtues. Berkeley grew increasingly enthusiastic about the possible pragmatic results of religious education. However, he also became increasingly depressed about the "moral decay" of Great Britain. Consequently, under the influence of several missionary societies, he turned his sight to the New World as the place to realize his plan for religious education. In 1722 he began communicating his ideas to friends; in 1725 he published a fully developed "Proposal for the better supplying of Churches in our foreign Plantations, &c."[22]

His plan was to found an ideal Christian settlement in Bermuda which would include a College for the education of both natives and settlers from the American mainland. The proposal caught the public imagination, was popularly discussed, and, through much effort on Berkeley's part, received the approval of all the necessary authorities, including the King and Parliament, and a pledge of £20,000 from the national Treasury. After several years of preparation, enlisting people interested in his scheme, Berkeley set sail to America in September 1728.

[21] *Ibid.*, 82.   [22] "Proposal," *op. cit.*

His plan was never realized. After a two-and-a-half-year wait in Rhode Island, Berkeley learned in 1731 that the necessary grant of money was never to be paid. Returning disappointed to London, he passed two more years seeking ecclesiastical preferment. While doing so, in 1732, he published a work he had written in America. This work, written in dialogue form and entitled *Alciphron, or the Minute Philosopher*, was his longest work since *Three Dialogues between Hylas and Philonous* (1713).[23] It tied together the various strands of thought which he had developed since "The Bond of Society," and thus it represents the most important theoretical extension of his social philosophy since that essay. In it we can see the mature form of his critique of free-thinking and its relation to the ills of society; and his mature theory of social action can be culled from its pages.

Berkeley criticizes free-thinking in *Alciphron* through the dialogues of two fictional characters who represent the third Earl of Shaftesbury and Bernard Mandeville. Shaftesbury, in his *Characters* (1711), had proposed a "high" version of free-thinking ethical doctrine; Mandeville, in *The Fable of the Bees, or Private Vices Public Benefits* (1714), had proposed a "low" version. Berkeley wanted to contrast the deficiencies of both types of free-thinking approaches with the genuine "utility" of traditional Christianity. As in his "Advice to the Tories" (1715), Berkeley divides his defense of Christianity into considerations of its "truth" and considerations of its "usefulness," and he puts greater emphasis in his argument on the latter, again reflecting his primarily pragmatic concern.[24] In fact, the central issue of the book is whether Shaftes-

---

[23] *Alciphron, or the Minute Philosopher* (1732), *Works*, III, 21-330. The term "Minute Philosopher" was coined by Berkeley earlier. In 1713 he wrote an essay on "Minute Philosophers," *op. cit.*, in which he referred to the narrowness of mind of free-thinkers who busy themselves about the "minute particularities of religion" while missing the benefit of the whole of it. The context of Berkeley's concern about free-thinking, whether atheistic or deistic in form, was basically the same in 1732 as in 1713, except that in the meantime free-thinking had become even more popular. In fact, it was at the height of its influence after the publication of Tindal's *Christianity as Old as the Creation, or the Gospel a Republication of the Religion of Nature* (1730). Berkeley received Tindal's book too late to incorporate its doctrines into his text in any specific manner, but his critique was thorough enough to include Tindal's work within its scope. The timeliness of his critique in *Alciphron* is attested to by the fact that this was Berkeley's first work to provoke an immediate public reaction from its opponents.

[24] In fact, Berkeley points out that the objects of faith are mysterious *per se* (just as the objects of science!—"force" being no less mysterious than "grace"). But though the "truth" of a particular religious "idea" cannot be known or demonstrated, that "idea" can be shown to be "useful." E.g., take any given man and "do but produce in him a sincere belief of a Future State [i.e., heaven or hell], although it be a mystery, although it be what eye hath not seen, nor ear heard, nor hath it entered into the heart of man to conceive, he shall, nevertheless, by virtue of such belief, be withheld from executing his wicked project" (*Alci-*

bury's system, Mandeville's system, or traditional Christianity promotes best the public good.²⁵ Berkeley, of course, proceeds to demonstrate that Christianity does. First, he disposes of Mandeville's ethics with little difficulty by uncovering the absurdity in Mandeville's contention that public good results when everyone seeks his own private pleasure (in other words, that public good comes from private vice). Both facts and logic oppose such an idea. He also points out the lack of appreciation for reason and freedom in Mandeville's ethics. Contrary to Mandeville, he maintains that the use of reason is as natural and satisfying as the pleasure of sense.

Berkeley's critique of Shaftesbury is more significant because it provides an amplification of the social theory Berkeley presented in 1713. At that time Berkeley had asserted that men have an inborn "social appetite" which is "the great spring and source of moral actions." Confronted with Shaftesbury, Berkeley must clarify that statement in order to differentiate his approach from Shaftesbury's, which speaks of a natural "moral sense" in man which can lead him to a virtuous life. If virtue is "natural," what can religion add to man's moral life? Why is Shaftesbury's ethics insufficient? Because, Berkeley indicates, it is not in fact likely to motivate men to proper behavior. Men may have a natural "social appetite," but they also have "private passions," and these latter need to be kept under control while the former is somehow motivated. Mere altruism is not equal to the task; one needs the encouragement, beliefs, and training of religion. Thus, Christianity is more "useful" in promoting the good of mankind.

This argument from "utility" is only half of Berkeley's critique of the deists and only a part of *Alciphron*, but it is enough to indicate that the dialogues of *Alciphron* presuppose a more complex theory of social action than presented in 1713 and that this new motivational scheme is an elaboration, rather than a contradiction, of the earlier theory. "Social appetite" is still seen as natural, but the experiences in Berkeley's life have made him more realistic, or pessimistic. He now sees "social appetite" as fragile, needing the maintenance and strengthening of the religious outlook and motives. This development, however, fits within the structure of the 1713 social theory. It expands the details and not the terms of the discussion.²⁶

---

phron, op. cit., 303). This does not mean, of course, that he did not believe that Christianity was the "true" religion and could be proven so.

²⁵ For Berkeley, the "public good" constituted the goal of morals. This idea is developed extensively in other works too; cf. *ibid.*, 63-64.

²⁶ The discussion of the development of Berkeley's motivation scheme has been simplified here. The full story must look at the complexities already implicit in his 1713 essays "Pleasures" and "Happiness," *Works*, VII, 193-97, 214-17, where Berkeley distinguishes "natural" from "phantastical" pleasures and clari-

As for *Alciphron* as a whole, it indicates that by 1732 Berkeley had developed his critique of free-thinking to such a point that it helped him clarify an old theme, the role of religion in preserving social order. Religious training in social virtues and religious beliefs in God's Providence, in an afterlife, and in punishment—these were now clearly seen as the specific facets of religion which contribute to the effective maintenance of public order.[27]

The publication of *Alciphron* stimulated a good amount of public controversy. As this controversy diminished in 1734, Berkeley finally received the appointment he had sought for so long. At the age of forty-nine, he was made Bishop of Cloyne in Ireland. At this age and in this position we might expect him to retire to a comfortable country life, but in fact it was from this time on that the activities of Berkeley proved conclusively that social concerns were the central concerns in his life. In a position of some social power at last, Berkeley busied himself with his episcopal duties, began writing a series of tracts on public issues concerning the welfare of Ireland and the state of her economic development, made appearances before Parliament, and inaugurated a series of concrete reforms in the lands under his jurisdiction. These practical reforms included agricultural improvements, the founding of a spinning-school, and the creation of jobs for vagrants. The theoretical developments, which led him to plead with Parliament for certain national reforms, such as the creation of a National Bank, were contained in *The Querist* (1735-37) and "A Letter on the Project of a National Bank" (1737).[28]

The Querist in particular is a gem of economic insight. In it Berkeley uncovers the psychology of poverty even further than he had in "An Essay towards preventing the Ruin of Great Britain" (1721). Again, as in *Alciphron*, the issue is motivation. How can the poor be motivated to work? And again it is the inculcation of the simple virtues of "honesty and industry" that makes the difference. Healthy material advancement is seen as dependent upon moral growth. Through the proper moral incentive and a judicious division of labor, Berkeley hoped to fulfill the goals of total employment and equitable distribution of products. The experiments on his own lands justified his plans and hopes

---

fies the goal of man as the happiness of mankind rather than that of any individual.

[27] These are not new ideas for Berkeley, but they are newly integrated into the discussion of social action.

[28] *The Querist* (1735-37) and "A Letter on the Project of a National Bank" (1737), *Works*, VI, 105-53, 185-88. It is important to stress that Berkeley's social activism was not simply a function of his new role as Bishop. The social "experiments" he tried on his own lands, the jobs he provided, and his door-to-door solicitude for his people were far beyond the line of duty.

for reform, but he was unable to effect as great a change on the national scene as he wished.

Berkeley remained busy with these and other practical social concerns, and his pen continued to move, until his death in 1753.[29] In fact, as bishop and member of Parliament, Berkeley took particular care to comment and give advice regarding a variety of issues. "A Discourse addressed to Margistrates and Men in Authority" (1738) was directed to magistrates and members of Parliament; letters were sent to the Anglican and Roman Catholic clergy counselling civil obedience during the Jacobite rebellion in 1745; a further "Word to the Wise" was addressed to the Roman Catholic clergy in 1749; and "Maxims concerning Patriotism" appeared in 1750.[30] In addition to these writings, Berkeley's sermons contain significant material related to the explication of his social philosophy.[31] However, it is unnecessary for us to investigate in detail any of these writings now. We have reviewed them quite enough to document our contention that Berkeley's life and work were dominated by his social concerns and that his understanding of social reality, as originally set forth in "The Bond of Society," was theoretically elaborated and practically applied in subsequent years.

IV. *Conclusion*

In 1713, when Berkeley first presented his social theory in "The Bond of Society," he was concerned about the disruption of society, the crisis of Christian faith and virtue, and the rise of modern free-thinking. Berkeley presented these concerns as only loosely related. Christianity was to be commended—in fact, considered "divine"—for encouraging sociability, and free-thinkers were to be considered wrong for accusing Christianity of opposing friendship. Christianity was good; free-thinking, bad. This much was clear, but there was no systematic explication of the various relationships between society, religion, and free-thinking. In the years following 1713 Berkeley analyzed and described these relationships

---

[29] For example, in response to the epidemics of 1739 and 1740, Berkeley began several years of experimentation which resulted in his infamous, but very sincere, advocacy of tar-water as a medicinal cure-all that could be readily available to the public. Vol. 5 of *Works* contains Berkeley's numerous writings which attempted to popularize this remedy; cf. esp. *Siris* (1744), 27-164. Another practical project Berkeley undertook was to raise his own militia in 1745 to oppose renewed Jacobite rebellion. Cf. Luce, *The Life of George Berkeley, op. cit.,* 177.

[30] All of the writings referred to can be found in *Works,* VI. It was rare for an Anglican Bishop to address Roman Catholics, and even rarer to get a positive response as Berkeley did.

[31] Cf. esp. "On the Will of God" (1751), *Works,* VIII, 129-138.

much more completely, continuing to use the basic conceptual dichotomy between "social appetite" and "private passions" and developing a more refined understanding of the role of learning and motivation in social life. Through this analysis, Berkeley came to define in much greater detail the factors involved in the positive relation between Christianity and social order, and he expanded his critique of free-thinking to the point where he could explain to his own satisfaction the factors involved in the negative relation between free-thinking and social order. In both cases, the crucial factor was motivation; and in both cases, the common concern was social order.

This concern with social order was more than purely intellectual. Having used the conceptual tools of his social theory to analyze the different kinds of social dynamics motivated by Christianity and free-thinking, Berkeley tried to put his theoretical understanding to practical use. First he suggested a program of moral-economic reforms, and then he worked diligently to implement his scheme of religious education. But it was not until he had a position of social power that he could fully translate his theory into practice. And this he did, to the best of his ability.

The major purpose of this paper has been to show that Berkeley had a social theory, that this social theory arose within a definable social and intellectual context, and that it provided the basis for theoretical and practical elaboration in a number of later writings and projects in Berkeley's life. In particular, we have seen that the social context of Berkeley's own life provided the pragmatic motivation to develop, and to continue to develop, his model of society and social dynamics while his critique of Newtonian science provided the intellectual context in which that model was articulated.

However compelling the demonstration of these theses has or has not been to the individual reader, this paper should at least have made it possible to view Berkeley's works from a perspective different from the traditional one. Specifically, it has suggested that there is a unity among what are usually considered Berkeley's "minor" and "occasional" pieces, and it has implied that Berkeley was much more consistently concerned with social theory (and the *application* of social theory) than has generally been acknowledged. Berkeley was not an idle, solitary, dreaming philosopher, a stereotype which still seems extant though it has been attacked in the literature. Nor was he simply a link between Locke and Hume. He was an open-eyed observer of, and participant in, the world in which he lived, and his response to that world motivated his philosophical concerns. Even his *Essay towards a New Theory of Vision* (1709), which we did not discuss in the text and which may seem to be purely theoretical, served also to establish a foundation for his applied philosophy, i.e., his Christian apologetics and his social theory.[32] And his most famous work, *A Treatise concerning The Principles of Human Knowledge* (1710), served the same purpose. Indeed, after perusing his entire collected works, it is difficult to avoid the conclusion—which Berkeley himself voiced on several occasions—that his central concern was always to educate his fellow countrymen to be "good Christians and loyal subjects."[33] In this endeavor, his analysis of social dynamics played an essential role.

University of New Hampshire.

[32] *New Theory of Vision* (1709), *Works*, I, 161-236, established the basis of Berkeley's radically empirical philosophy upon which he based his philosophy of science, his proof of the existence of God, and his social theory. The purpose of Berkeley's theory of vision is made quite explicit in his later "popularization," *The Theory of Vision Vindicated,* the full title of which is *The Theory of Vision or Visual Language shewing the immediate Presence and Providence of a Deity Vindicated and Explained* (1733), *Works*, I, 249-76.

[33] "Passive Obedience," *op. cit.*, 15.

IV.—BERKELEY AS A MORAL PHILOSOPHER.

By Hugh W. Orange.

In his polemic against Abstract Ideas and Atheism, Bishop Berkeley presents the curious with a critical problem of a certain historical importance. He claims for the doctrines laid down in *The Principles of Human Knowledge,* that they will " abridge the labour of study, and make human sciences far more clear, compendious, and attainable than they were before " (§ 134). This claim he proceeds at some length to substantiate, in the provinces of Natural Philosophy and Mathematics, deferring the consideration of the benefits which would accrue to Moral Philosophy, by the banishment of Abstract Ideas, for a " more particular disquisition " (§ 144). The promise of a directly ethical disquisition he cannot be said to have redeemed; and the clause which admitted its necessity was, in his second edition of *The Principles,* omitted. It has therefore been left for his commentators to elucidate the " hint," which he declares will suffice (§ 100) to let any one see that " the doctrine of abstraction has not a little contributed towards spoiling the most useful parts of knowledge ".

Even without his promise, the method by which he proceeds to divide the sciences shows that Moral Philosophy must logically be included among those which are to be aided and abridged; not to mention an explicit declaration, in his *Common Place Book,* that Truth is of three kinds: Natural, Mathematical, and Moral. We know how, in the light of his discovery, he has handled the first two kinds; as regards the last, in the absence of a particular disquisition, this " hint " and his writings as a whole are all the materials we have for a solution of the question of the relation of Berkeley's ethical theories to his *Principles of Human Knowledge.*

This relation has been described by Prof. Fraser as a ' curious and close analogy,' which he thus interprets in a note to the third dialogue of *Alciphron* (vol. ii. p. 107), summing up the fundamental principles of Berkeley's ethical system as follows:—' That the general well-being of all men, " of all nations, of all ages of the world," is what the infinitely good God intends to be promoted " by the concurring actions of each individual "—that this end is to be accomplished by the observance of universal rules which have a corresponding tendency—and that faith in divine moral government and man's immortality is necessary to make the rules efficacious'.

An attentive criticism may show, more fully, the connexion of these principles with one another; and establish a still closer and more curious resemblance between Berkeley the moralist and Berkeley the metaphysician.

If we are to understand the historical significance of the scattered materials which his writings offer for the construction of a particular disquisition on ethics, it is very necessary to approach them with an idea of what may be appropriately expected from an ethical writer of his day. In every writer, the stress and the emphasis are only to be caught from the contemporary controversies; and in Berkeley, more than in any other, it is impossible, without a perception of the stress, to make anything but a confused and chaotic medley of discords never resolved and suspensions held continually in suspense. A controversial bishop may say much about the pleasantness of the paths of virtue, and yet not be a hedonist. An eager preacher of the eighteenth century may turn a vigorous appeal upon the rewards offered in a future life; and yet it need not follow that he is to be classed as a mercenarian of the nineteenth century. It is necessary to look to what a man is denying, if we would learn the scope and the accent of what he is asserting; and it is equivalent to a transgression of generic differences, or, as Aristotle would term it, ἀπαιδευσία, to deduce a nineteenth-century conclusion from a premiss casually given in English eighteenth-century ethics.

The danger of applying the catchwords of the present to the thought of the past, has never been better illustrated than by the inappropriateness of the title 'Theological Utilitarian' to Berkeley as a moralist. It is in this phrase that Prof. Fraser has summed up the 'fundamental principles' which were quoted above.

There is something, it is true, in Berkeley's works which sounds very like 'the greatest good of the greatest number': let us call it Utilitarian. The bishop has also written much about God; let us qualify him, therefore, as 'Theological'. To a writer so flexible, and so copious in the improvisations which controversy demands, it would be equally easy to justify the application, by this method, of almost any other modern philosophical nickname; and equally profitable. There is one sense, and one sense only, in which the phrase 'Theological Utilitarian' has an intelligible meaning; and in that sense it is not applicable to Bishop Berkeley. It is intelligible, if it is to imply a view of the nature of good as consisting in pleasure: of the test of good as that which brings most pleasure in the end; of the chief obligation of morality as the pleasure or pain to be meted out for an infinite number of years in a future life, or, as Bentham calls it, the religious sanction. In this sense, it is the 'otherworldliness' of which Coleridge and George Eliot speak; it is the venal morality which bargains for eternal life, at the cost of unreasoned virtue. The Hindoo who threw himself before the car of Juggernauth, that he might realise the *summum bonum* in a paradise of sensualism, was a Theological Utilitarian. Subtler forms of the creed are represented by Lord Tennyson, in his character of St. Simeon Stylites:—

> 'Who may be made a saint, if I fail here?
> Show me the man hath suffered more than I.
> For did not all the martyrs die one death?
> For either they were stoned, or crucified,
> Or burn'd in fire, or boiled in oil, or sawn
> In twain beneath the ribs; but I die here
> To-day, and whole years long, a life of death. . . .
> Surely the end! What's here? a shape, a shade,
> A flash of light. Is that the angel there
> That holds a crown? Come, blessed brother, come.
> I know thy glittering face. I waited long;
> My brows are ready. What! deny it now?
> Nay, draw, draw, draw nigh. So I clutch it. Christ!
> 'Tis gone: 'tis here again; the crown, the crown!'

It is in this sense, only, that the words have an intelligible meaning, and as a form of Egoistic Hedonism. It has been said that every man has his price: assuredly, the Theological Utilitarian's is Heaven. What is good? That which will enable me to avoid the pit, and clutch the crown. The sanction is personal pleasure or pain. Benevolence is, indeed, possible, as a useful bid for the prize, but below the skin it must be hedonistic too; for if I extend it to a willingness to forego the real pleasure which turns the balance, the crown, then the morality is brought to a self-contradiction. That which will take me to Heaven, must always be my definition of good.

This is the familiar and intelligible sense of the phrase which Prof. Fraser has applied to Berkeley; and it is the name for a creed which has certainly been preached, whether or not it has ever been held. If it is to be made to cover Berkeley, careful distinction must be made between him and all others to whom it has been applied. It must be held to indicate an anticipation by Berkeley of many of the criticisms brought to bear upon Bentham and his followers; an acceptance of a definition of good, as 'that which tends to the greatest amount of happiness, for the greatest number of men,' and the addition of a sanction, probably inconsistent, to overcome the difficulty of converting Hedonism into desire for others' good; this sanction being conveyed in a theological threat. Instead of being purely dogmatic, it submits the nature of good to arbitration ·and analysis, but reserves the sanction for revelation. In the one case, 'good' is the condition of entrance into heavenly bliss. In the second case, we are instructed to study the welfare of men in general, in order that we may know our duty: if we ask what claim this duty has on us, argument gives way to dogma; reason is ratified by the theology of threats.

It is, probably, in this latter sense, that the phrase Theological Utilitarian has been used by Prof. Fraser. Some support for such a reading of Berkeley's works may, no doubt, be discovered in the manifold varieties of his utterances; it may, or may not, be a complete account and synthesis of them. But, in that case, what becomes of the 'close and curious analogy' which is said to exist, between his ethical system and his system of human knowledge? How is there a parallel between the grounds of reality and of obligation? or a similarity in the relations of God and the world? What point, what aspect, is there in such a moral creed, which reminds us of anything peculiar to Berkeley in his conception of the material world? How is the God visually apparent in 'this mundane system,' analogous to the Judge who holds aloof from a natural morality, until the dread moment for enforcing it? According to Berkeley's metaphysical writings, God is so far the most clear and primary reality, that we only know ourselves by our knowledge of Him. In this reading of his ethical system, the reality of good depends upon the pleasure-sensations of men; and we can go all the way, without God, in the discovery of the nature of good, by the process which the word Utilitarian suggests. God is only necessary as the original willer that the formulæ of universalistic hedonism should be correct, and the ultimate avenger of their validity. If there be any analogy in these two conceptions of God and of the world, it is rather curious than close.

The clue to a different interpretation of this analogy is found in that part of *Alciphron* in which the moral doctrines of Shaftesbury are criticised. According to Green, in morals Berkeley 'ought to have regarded Shaftesbury as his yokefellow'; and indeed, if Berkeley's system were based on nothing but the fleeting ideas of the pleasure and pain of individuals, then his antagonism to Shaftesbury's recognition of principles of beauty and proportion among these ideas, would be hard to understand. And yet there is no part of *Alciphron*, in which the spirit of opposition runs higher, than in the criticisms, personal and literary, which are levelled against the " crazy nobleman," Cratylus, and his reduction of virtue to a relish, or a certain *je ne sais quoi* of appreciative contemplation. The antagonism is not more determined, even when the theory of abstraction, or of the existence of matter, is the subject of dispute.

If we carefully inspect the arguments which Berkeley brings to bear upon the doctrine that 'virtue is beauty,' we may discover the line which his particular disquisition would have taken, upon the leading moral controversies of the day.

One of the foremost issues was the debate, as to the faculty which apprehends moral truth. Even at the present day, we occasionally come across lingering traces of the belief, that to explain the origin of a sentiment is to deny its validity: and at the time when Locke's dictum was universally accepted, that truth consists in the perception of the agreement or disagreement between ideas, it was natural, that those to whom the universal certainty of moral truth seemed vitally important, should endeavour to argue down the dangerous supposition, that we apprehend moral truth by any other faculty than that by which we see that two and two make four. It seemed that, unless the claim of virtue could be put as high as the claim of the multiplication-table, universal obligation must give way to individual caprice; and in no other way could scepticism more grieve the enthusiasm of the orthodox, than by urging the claims of the faculty which feels to influence the man who is about to act. An eternal and immutable morality rests upon an intellectual system of the universe; and though, in later days, a skilful handling of the other subject of dispute, the relation of God to morality, could reconstruct a binding and yet intelligible ethics, upon a partly sentient faculty of conscience, yet in Berkeley's day the time had not come for these damaging admissions to 'the enemy'. Moral views prevailed, as to the moral faculty. So when Hume mischievously remarks, that 'belief is rather a state of the sentient, than of the cogitative part of man,' he is aiming the deadliest of all blows at the truth of the matter of such belief. And when he says, as he does distinctly say, that it is a moral sense, and not the faculty of reason, which distinguishes right and wrong, he is speaking in direct allusion to a critical ethical topic of his day.

Hume's denials are a guide to Berkeley's assertions. By

what faculty is moral truth apprehended? Very distinctly Euphranor implies, that the "notion" is "an object of the discursive faculty". And if moral truth is also moral beauty, the very fact of its being beautiful, proves, all the more, that, as beauty, it is an object of the understanding. That is the line of the argument which, at first sight, seems disposed to take the turn of denying Shaftesbury's position, that virtue is beauty. Berkeley does not deny it: he accepts, and asserts it. Virtue is beautiful, and is, therefore, not the object of a moral sense, but apprehended by the discursive faculty. Virtue is beauty, and must, therefore, rest, as beauty does, upon a mind. "We do not see beauty, strictly speaking," says Euphranor; "we infer it." "We see it by reason, through the means of sight; consequently, beauty, in this sense, is an object, not of the eye, but of the mind" (*Alciphron*, iii., § 8). The long digression upon architecture, which follows, is summed up to precisely the same effect. "I should now, methinks, be glad to see a little more distinctly the use and tendency of this digression upon architecture." "Was not beauty the very thing we inquired after?" "It was." The necessity of some real principle of beauty is then demonstrated; beauty implies an end; an end, "forasmuch as without thought there can be no end or design," implies a mind, which rules over the universe and the moral actions of men. Thus the outward show and appearance of virtue is made to yield by analysis a metaphysical proof of the "spirit which governs and actuates this mundane system"; and it is with the moral world, exactly as it is with the material, that its *esse* is *percipi*. The parallel is complete, as to the faculty called into play. We have here a "new theory" of ethical vision. The eye does not "see"; it furnishes to the mind, materials for seeing, "the canopy of heaven, and the choir and furniture of earth"; so, in the moral world, "the comparing parts one with another, the considering them as belonging to one whole, and referring this whole to its use, or end, should seem the work of reason: should it not?"

The analogy between Berkeley's ethical system, and his *Principles of Human Knowledge*, is this:—The material world consists only of ideas; the *esse* of matter is *percipi*; the only true substance, spirit. But, inasmuch as we find, that the ideas of different spirits vary, that ideas are void of force, and that each spirit has not control over its own ideas; since, in short, these ideas demand a metaphysical ground of unity, source of energy, and basis of reality—we infer God, as the universal spirit percipient of consistent truth, the permanent reality, and the source of energy. All that is not spirit, is idea; and the difference between true and false ideas, between life and illusion, is, that the true ideas are also God's ideas, and He is the one Spirit who sustains, consistently, and for ever, the many ideas which come and go in the minds of men. To know the truth, is to have the same ideas as God. "Laws of nature" are observations, for practical purposes correct, of the order in which he is pleased to manifest this succession of ideas.

So, in the moral world, we have "laws of nature," which are approximately demonstrated; we can learn them by certain signs, and recognise the voice of God in the orderly proportion of moral phenomena (*Passive Obedience*, § 8). To do the good, is to have the same ideas as God. This world only shows a multiplicity of moral perceptions, pleasures and pains, which cannot explain themselves; the human spirits who perceive them, perceive also the limits of their power over them, and require some independent ground of their validity; they perceive their own differences of moral ideas, and require some criterion of good and bad; they find it in the Spirit who holds all truth and reality together. Of moral, as of other ideas, some are permanent; some are individual fancies and aberrations. Good is true, and real, and life : evil is false, and illusory, and death.

"A spirit is one simple, active, undivided being : as it produces ideas it is called the will; as it thinks, or otherwise operates upon them, it is called the understanding." In each of these aspects, God is related to the human spirit. Good is predicated of will; truth is predicated of the understanding. Ideas are true, or good, when the human spirit is at one with the divine.

By such an analogy Berkeley might well have claimed for his "particular disquisition," that all the complications of human conduct are solved by the same metaphysical *Deus ex machina* who had solved all the problems of knowledge. First, the question, as to the faculty which apprehends right and wrong, is set at rest : moral laws are laws of nature; but there is no value or force in them as laws, save in so far as they are the orderly expression of God's ideas. Both in natural, and in moral philosophy, these generalisations are to be attained by means of the use of reason. In the *Discourse on Passive Obedience*, a single moral "law of Nature," "Thou shalt not resist the supreme power," is submitted, as an instance, to this process; and is identified by means of the marks which are proper to such a law—importance, universality, niceness, or difficulty. To reason and to argumentation are left—first, the very being of laws of nature; secondly, the criterion, whereby to know them; and, thirdly, the agreement of any particular precept with that criterion (§ 29). And so far are these laws from being the *a posteriori* conclusions of Utilitarian calculation, that " these propositions are called *laws of nature*, because they are universal, and do not derive their obligation from any civil sanction, but immediately from the Author of nature Himself. They are said to be *stamped on the mind*, to be *engraven on the tables of the heart*, because they are well known to mankind, and suggested and inculcated by conscience. Lastly, they are termed *eternal rules of reason*, because they necessarily result from the nature of things, and may be demonstrated by the infallible deductions of reason " (§ 12).

But there was another question at issue for a moral philosopher of Berkeley's day; and the manner in which he gathers up his solution of this ethical question, in his own peculiar metaphysical theory, would have been one of not the least attractive parts of the " particular disquisition ". Ever since the day of Descartes, and, possibly, long before, the relation of God to morality had been a difficulty for the dogmatic. Could God, if He had chosen, have appointed a different moral order? Is good in its nature independent, or is it merely good because God wills it? Descartes had said, that if He so chose, God could will that good should be evil, and evil good. The anxiety of the thinkers of those days, not to place anything on a footing of independence towards God, often becomes even grotesque; as in the case of the argument as to the nature of space—that it could not be infinite, or else there would be two infinite beings, and space would be a rival to God's omnipotence. But, still, the view, that morality was not absolute, but, so to speak, a divine derivative—the bare possibility that God might revoke the delegated validity of virtue—was to many moralists the more disagreeable alternative; and amongst those who endeavoured to explain, that without any limit to God's omnipotence, it was, at the same time, impossible for Him to put bitter for sweet and sweet for bitter, to call good evil and evil good— was Cudworth, author of the *Eternal and Immutable Morality*. In this book, posthumously published just when *Alciphron* was ready for the press, the nature of fate is discussed with great erudition, and the relation of God to morality settled by means of a subtle distinction between God's reason and God's wisdom.

Now it is obvious that the difficulty here again arises from a supposed dualism of good objective and good subjective; and it is easy to guess how Berkeley would have handled any such distinction. When he " hints," that the doctrine of abstraction has contributed not a little towards "spoiling the more useful parts of knowledge" (*Principles*, § 100), we are but dull learners, and suffer in vain from his reiteration, if we do not understand, that to Berkeley "abstract ideas" mean a reference to some objective reality "apart from the mind," and that with such dualisms he has a short way. He defines existence as perception, and the distinction of internal and external disappears. There can be no good independent of a mind, and, therefore, no rival to God's omnipotence. As for the supposition that God might have willed good to be something different from what it is, such an hypothesis merely amounts to the absurdity of imagining, or trying to imagine, a negation of the law of identity. Good is that which is present in the mind of God; it is impossible to imagine that evil, or that which is absent from His mind, should be present in it as well; and in *Siris* (§ 320), he thus plainly states this corollary, 'Evil, defect, negation, is not the object of God's creative power'.

We have seen that, in *The Principles*, Berkeley makes the distinct statement, that his metaphysical theories will have a direct bearing upon moral philosophy; that such a connexion is strictly in keeping with other passages in which he speaks of the nature of moral truth; that he foreshadows a particular disquisition upon the subject, but, meanwhile, leaves his readers with a " hint " which he hopes will suffice to let any one see, that the abolition of abstract ideas will mean a reform in ethics. We have seen that Prof. Fraser has drawn attention to a ' curious analogy,' existing between Berkeley's ethical and metaphysical theories, although, in the short summary in which he has intended to express the analogy, he has rather obscured it by the use of a phrase which either denies, or else inconsistently asserts, a connexion between ethics and metaphysics. We have recognised that in moral, as in natural philosophy, Berkeley must intend his abolition of abstract ideas as the prelude to an idealism in which God is both the ultimate and the immediate reality; a system of which it is the " main drift and design " " to inspire his readers with a pious sense of the presence of God " (*Princ.* § 156). We have seen, furthermore, that this hint of a connexion between ethics and metaphysics, as an alliance to the great advantage of the former, is not a mere idle boast on the part of Berkeley; but that, in the *Discourse on Passive Obedience*, he addresses himself to a demonstration, in a single instance, of the identity between a moral law and a law of nature. We have amplified this demonstration by once more stating the peculiar meaning attached, in his system, to the words " law of nature "; and we have been warranted in so doing by the result which is given by a close and exact attention to the criticism, in *Alciphron*, of the saying of Shaftesbury, that virtue is beauty.

Those parts of Berkeley's writings, from which the present argument is mainly supported, are justly said by Prof. Fraser to be the most important statements of Berkeley's moral philosophy. But of the many services which this commentator has rendered to the readers of his author, not the least valuable is his observation of the development and progress of Berkeley's idealist principles. And it is, similarly, not the least curious part of the close analogy that exists between Berkeley's ethical and his metaphysical principles, that precisely the same advance which is found in his conception of nature may be traced, also, in his conception of morality.

The 33rd section of the *Discourse on Passive Obedience*, which was only added in the third edition, might be quoted in illustration of this development in reference either to ethics or to mathematics :—

"In morality the eternal rules of action have the same immutable universal truth with propositions in geometry. Neither of them depends on circumstances or accidents, being at all times and in all places, without limitation or exception, true. 'Thou shalt not resist the supreme power' is no less constant or unalterable a rule, for modelling the behaviour of a subject towards the Government, than 'Multiply the height by half the base' is for measuring a triangle. And, as it would not be thought to detract from the universality of this mathematical rule, that it did not exactly measure a field which was not an exact triangle, so ought it not to be thought an argument against the universality of the rule prescribing passive obedience that it does not reach a man's practice in all cases where a Government is unhinged or the supreme power disputed."

The mystic pantheism of *Siris*, is the most remarkable instance of the development of Berkeley's principles, from a staring dualism of Spirit and Idea, into a conception of God which incorporates "ideas," in the Platonic sense, in a logical chain of graduated universality, with the *anima mundi*, the expression of them all; and ascends from tarwater, acid, salt, and sulphur, "by a regular connexion and climax, through all these mediums, to a glimpse of the first mover, invisible, incorporeal, unextended source of life and being". So of ethical study Berkeley dedicates, in the *Siris*, the later growth as well as the first fruits; and we advance, from the earlier conception of law, as a synthesis of the succession of ideas in a personal God, a spirit limited, because distinct from ourselves, into a mystical identification of God with law and order (§ 334) and the elevation of the principle of order, or λόγος, into membership of the Trinity (§ 361).

GEORGE BERKELEY'S THEORY OF ECONOMIC POLICY AND CLASSICAL ECONOMIC LIBERALISM

FRANK PETRELLA
College of the Holy Cross

INTRODUCTION

Although the contributions of George Berkeley, Bishop of Cloyne, to the science of political economy have been the subject of frequent studies, his commentators have ignored any comprehensive view of his theory of economic policy and its relation to the form and content of his harmony of interests doctrine.[1,2] The latter is important not only because it sheds light on Berkeley's brand of Mercantilism and its logic of government intervention in the economy, but also because it reveals Berkeley, the persistent interventionist, anticipating the classical *harmonielehre* implied in the system of natural liberty.[3]

BERKELEY AND ENGLISH MERCANTILISM

There is no question of Berkeley's Mercantilism. His works are marked with typical themes of the later mercantilist period. Singular among them is his concern with monetary questions rather than problems of value. Vickers, for example, has noted Berkeley's great attention to the prescriptions of monetary policy for solving the problems of poverty and unemployment.[4]

Another theme central to Mercantilism is found in Berkeley's view that labor was both the material and efficient cause of wealth. As he asks in the *Querist*,

> Whether the four elements, and man's labour therein, be not the true source of wealth?
> Whether it were not wrong to suppose the land itself to be wealth? And whether the industry of the people is not first to be considered, as that which constitutes wealth, which makes even land and silver to be wealth, neither of which would have any value but as means and motives to industry?[5]

Corollary to the importance of labor in accumulating wealth, is the necessity of maximizing its use. Again in the *Querist*,

> Whether, if human labour be the true source of wealth, it doth not follow that idleness should of all things be discouraged in a wise State?
> Whether the great and general aim of the public should not be to employ the people?[6]

The importance of labor in Berkeley's economic thought led to his expression of another mercantilist theme, the export-of-work doctrine and its stress on the exporting of labor-intensive goods and importing of land-intensive goods.

> Whether it be not even madness to encourage trade with a nation that takes nothing of our manufacture?
> Whether it would not be wise to order our

---

[1] T. W. Hutchison, for example, sees Berkeley's economics as a fine "summons to national action" to face the economic problems of his day. T. W. Hutchison, "Berkeley's Querist and Its Place in the Economic Thought of the Eighteenth Century," *The British Journal for the Philosophy of Science*, May 1953, p. 52.

[2] Ian D. S. Ward examines Berkeley in his relation to contemporary Keynesian thought while Joseph Johnston and Douglas Vicker stress Berkeley's place in the development of monetary and aggregate economics. Ian D. S. Ward, "George Berkeley: Precursor of Keynes or Moral Economist of Underdevelopment?," *Journal of Political Economy*, February 1959; Joseph Johnston, "Locke, Berkeley and Hume as Monetary Theorists," *Hermathena*, No. 40, 1940; and Douglas Vickers, *Studies in the Theory of Money, 1690-1776* (Philadelphia: 1959), Chapter 8.

[3] For a discussion on the way in which Mercantilism as a system anticipates Classical Liberalism, see W. D. Grampp, "The Liberal Element in English Mercantilism," *Quarterly Journal of Economics*, November 1952.

[4] Douglas Vickers, *op. cit.*, p. 141.

[5] A. A. Luce and T. E. Jessop, (eds.), *The Works of George Berkeley Bishop of Cloyne* (9 vols. London, 1953), VI, pp. 105, 108. Hereafter cited as *Works*, etc.

[6] *Works*, VI, pp. 108, 132.

trade as to export manufacturers rather than provisions, and of those such as employ most hands?"[7]

Ultimately, however, it is Berkeley's comprehensive view of state economic functions which classify him as a mercantilist. His 'state's agenda' was broadly based in its concern for the creation and circulation of the money supply, the maintenance of transport facilities, labor legislation which coupled with the appropriate monetary and fiscal policy would insure full employment, state promotion of important industries not developed by the private sector and general coordination of foreign and domestic trade.

THEORY OF ECONOMIC POLICY: THE FUNCTIONS OF THE LEGISLATOR

When speaking of the state proper, as if at some high level of abstraction, Berkeley's conception of government economic functions appears compatible with the nominal state role of early classical liberalism. The state, aside from fostering industry in its members, must encourage and protect property. Without the security of property, Berkeley doubts, "Whether in that case the wisest government, or the best of laws can avail us?"[8] However, the similarity between Berkeley's view of state economic activity and some early and naive laissez-faire quickly disappears as he focuses on the process of formulating a state economic agenda in the legislature, the art of legislating and the role and responsibilities of the legislator.

The authority of the legislature to intervene in economic and social affairs is related first to the principal goal of the economy. The "great and general aim of the public" is the employment of all the people. In turn, the general aim becomes the test of public institutions, "Whether in all public institutions there should not be an end proposed, which is to be the rule and limit of the means? Whether this end should not be the well-being of the whole? And whether, in order to this, the first step should not be to clothe and feed our people?"[9]

Second, the authority of the legislature is necessary given the inability of men to agree on the relative importance of human actions and its concomitant, the futility of individual action.

So insufficient is the wit or strength of any single man, either to avert the evils or procure the blessings of life, and so apt are the wills of different persons to contradict and thwart each other, that it is absolutely necessary several independent powers by combining together, under the direction... of one the same will: I mean the law of the society. Without this there is no politeness, no order, no peace..."[10]

The legislator's function, then, is to achieve some harmony of interests from the cacophony of individual interests. There was, however, nothing natural or automatic about this process. Berkeley's *harmonielehre* depends on a course of legislative action always strewn with obstacles and is, therefore, unlike other harmony doctrines which see unrestrained egoism automatically reconciling conflicts or sympathy moving individuals to agree on the general good.[11]

Instead, Berkeley sees both sympathy and egoism as inimical to the harmony of interests. "Self-love," the most universal of all principles, "and the most deeply engraven in our hearts," is, he feels, a disrupter of *harmonielehre*. "Whether this capricious tyrant, which usurps the place of reason, doth not... delude... the usurers, stockjobbers, and projectors, of content to themselves from heaping up riches... without (their) having a proper

---

[7] *Works*, VI, pp. 118, 119.
[8] *Works*, VI, pp. 105, 161.
[9] *Works*, VI, pp. 132, 116.
[10] *Works*, VI, p. 25.
[11] For different views on *harmonielehre*, see Elie Halevy, *The Growth of Philosophic Radicalism* (New York: 1928), pp. 13–18, and Lionel Robbins, *The Theory of Economic Policy in English Classical Political Economy* (London: 1953), pp. 23–26.

regard to the use, or end, or nature of things?" The principle of sympathy, although more laudable, can be more dangerous if it is made the sole rule of our actions since it is "... more plausible, and apt to dazzle and corrupt the mind with the appearance of goodness and generosity." [12]

Aware of the potential dangers of both egoism and altruism, Berkeley then considers the best means of achieving a harmony of interests.

> The well-being of mankind must necessarily be carried on one of these two ways. Either, first, without the injunction of any certain universal rules of morality, only by obliging every one upon each particular occasion to consult the public good, and always to do that which to him shall seem, in the present time and circumstances, most to conduce to it. Or, secondly, by enjoining the observation of some determinate, established laws, which, if universally practiced, have, from the nature of things, an essential fitness to procure the well-being of mankind.[13]

He rejects the first alternative for a number of reasons. First, the public good may be distorted or hidden by a malicious egoism or a misguided altruism. Secondly, even the best and wisest of men could not know every necessary circumstance of a situation before weighing their actions against the public good. Third, such a rule necessarily encourages subjective estimates of public welfare and produces no definite standard of conduct. Next, these subjective rules of behavior are difficult to detect, "Every man's particular rule is buried in his own breast, invisible to all but himself," and may vary from time to time. Finally, the first method leads to chaos, not *harmonielehre*, for without agreement even between the actions of good men, "... the best actions may be condemned, and the most villainous meet the applause. In a word, there ensues the most horrible confusion of vice and virtue, sin and duty...." [14]

Therefore, only by the universal "observation of some determinate, established laws," can the harmony of interests be established. However, this way of achieving the common good necessarily depends on the activities of the legislator. Although all men are obliged "... to trace out the divine will, or the general design of Providence with regard to mankind," it is the legislator who 'reads' the will of God as revealed in His creation and guides human behavior by rules and laws intended to accomplish the divine design.[15]

The high status and critical role of the legislator in Berkeley's theory of economic and social policy formation is apparent. The legislator's calling is analogous to the minister's. He becomes a steward of souls in the political order, a mediator of public happiness which originates in God, a cultivator of "divine impressions in the minds of all men" under his care. In another vein, Berkeley saw the legislator as a "benevolent physician" who contends with "... a State or body politic as with the human body, which lives and moves under various indispositions, perfect health being seldom or never to be found," and cures the consequences of man's passions in society.[16]

The calling of the legislator and its attendant responsibilities are not come by lightly, for example, by birth. Like the ministry and medicine it presumes preparation. Writing in the *Querist* on the marks of the legislator, Berkeley says,

> Whether our peers and gentlemen are born legislators? Or whether that faculty be acquired by study and reflection?
> Whether to comprehend the real interest of a people, and the means to procure it, doth not imply some fund of knowledge, historical, moral and political, with a faculty of reason improved by learning?
> Whether, therefore, a legislator should be content with a vulgar share of knowledge? Whether he should not be a person of reflexion and thought, who hath made it his study to understand the

---

[12] *Works*, VI, pp. 19, 130–131, 23.
[13] *Works*, VI, p. 21.
[14] *Works*, VI, pp. 21–22.

[15] *Works*, VI, pp. 20–21.
[16] *Works*, VI, pp. 212, 133, 202.

true nature and interest of mankind, how to guide men's humours and passions, how to incite their active powers, how to make their several talents co-operate to the mutual benefit of each other, and the general good of the whole?"[17]

Although the legislator's role in establishing *harmonielehre* is central, it is complemented by the duty of all citizens to submit to God's law as they are traced on earth by his lectors, the legislators. This obligation is the "bond and cement of society" and "that precept which enjoins obedience to civil laws...is a moral obligation on the conscience and derived from the universal voice of nature and reason."[18]

Up to this point, Berkeley is still the mercantilist, convinced of both the necessity and efficacy of government intervention into the economic and social life of the community. It is true that he is ill at ease with the Hobbesian view of nature especially as it is found in Mandeville; but, although he rejects Mandeville's pessimistic view that the vices of naturally and incorrigibly selfish men are the root of society's prosperity, Berkeley accepts his optimism concerning the manageability of selfish men:

> Man is an animal formidable both from his passions and his reason; his passions often urging him to great evils, and his reason furnishing means to achieve them. To tame this animal, and make him amenable to order, to inure him to a sense of justice and virtue...in short, to fashion and model him for society, hath been the aim of civil and religious institutions, and in all times the endeavour of good and wise men.[19]

In short, Berkeley assumes the principle of the artificial identification of interests, which says that egoism and *harmonielehre* are incompatible; therefore, the legislator must bring about an artificial harmony of interests. However, Berkeley's form of the principle is more Christian than Mandeville's, or, generally, that of other mercantilists of the period. Although both Mandeville and Berkely agree that man's selfish nature can be controlled and directed as billiard balls on a table, Berkeley, unlike Mandeville, feels that man can be acted upon by the legislator and institutions so that his social and economic behavior will embody the divine will of God.[20]

Berkeley's rejection of Shaftesbury's ethical theory and its appeal to sentiment seems to confirm his mercantilist views on the efficiency of government intervention and puts him at odds with emerging liberal thought: "... our present impending danger is from the setting up of private judgment, or an inward light, in opposition to human and divine laws."[21] Still, the thought of George Berkeley contains a formulation of *harmonielehre* which anticipates the system of natural liberty and the harmony of interest doctrine of classical economic liberalism.

HARMONIELEHRE AND THE SYSTEM
OF NATURAL LIBERTY

Classical Economics

The system of natural liberty found in the works of Adam Smith typifies the theory of economic policy in the classical school. Ultimately, Smith's theory of policy has its roots in his *The Theory of Moral Sentiments*, especially in the relation between the cardinal virtues, prudence and justice.[22] Prudence, Smith defines as "the

---

[17] *Works*, VI, pp. 120, 134.
[18] *Works*, VI, p. 31.
[19] *Works*, VI, p. 202.

[20] *Works*, VI, p. 216. Also, *Works*, III, *Alciphron*, Dialogue II, "On The Ethics of Mandeville", pp. 65-111.
[21] *Works*, VI, p. 217. Also *Works*, III, *Alciphron*, Dialogue III. "On The Ethics of Shaftesbury," pp. 112-140. Berkeley's rejection of Shaftesbury removed him from that stream of thought culminating in Adam Smith's *Theory of Moral Sentiments*, a work which in part forms the basis of early classical economic Liberalism as enunciated through the *Wealth of Nations*. See A. L. Macfie, "Adam Smith's Moral Sentiments as Foundation for His Wealth of Nations," *Oxford Economic Papers*, October 1959, and O. H. Taylor, *A History of Economic Thought* (New York: 1960), Chapters 2-4.
[22] Adam Smith, *The Theory of Moral Sentiments* (London and New York: 1892).

intelligent care of one's own health, wealth and happiness"; *justice* is "a scrupulous refusal ever to hurt or injure anyone else, in the pursuit of one's own interest or advantage."

The starting point of Smith's theory of government activity in the economic order involves the interdependence of prudence and justice in the proper moral and institutional environment. That is, the intelligent care of one's own health and wealth or rational self-interest tends to achieve the requirements of justice and the harmony of interests between individuals and groups in economic society *only* if the economic and social institutions are properly arranged.²³

For Adam Smith, the proper institutional order assumed a system of law detailing the requirements of justice, an operative and effective moral code, private property, a system of free contracts and the presence of an effective competition.²⁴ Within such a framework, men's social sympathies could be properly developed and attuned to one another so as to achieve the relation between prudence and justice. If the institutional order were perverted, for example, through the presence of monopoly, government intervention would be needed to restore one of the preconditions of a completely functioning system of natural liberty. Without intervention, monopoly goes unregulated, and the rational pursuit of our self-interest, unchecked by the competitive market structure, leads inevitably to injustice.

The importance of institutional precedents in a system of natural liberty are more evident in the economic thought of Edmund Burke, since in Burke, unlike Smith and other classical economists, there is a more dramatic and often loud contradiction between his pronouncements on the benefits of pure laissez-faire and his detailed practice in the art of public regulation. However, in each instance where Burke advocates government intervention, he assumes, if only implicitly, the absence or malfunction of legal, moral and market precedents necessary for the achievement of *harmonielehre*.²⁵

George Berkeley

For Berkeley, the harmonious resolution of individual and group conflicts in society by the legislator also depended upon a set of important conditions. Foremost was a *system of morality* which ensured obedience to civil laws as a matter of moral obligation. Without it, the legislation of *harmonielehre* is jeopardized, "Some perhaps may imagine," said Berkeley, "that the eye of the magistrate alone is sufficient to keep mankind in awe." Not so. If every man set out to do mischief, there could be no living in the world. Related to the moral precedent in Berkeley's system of natural liberty was the ubiquitous function of *religion*. Organized religion was "... the centre which unites, and the cement which connects, the several parts or members of the political body." There was no magistrate so ignorant, he felt, to ignore religion's role as the "great stay and support of a state." ²⁶

The economic well being of society also depended upon the existence and practice of religion. Religion along with industry

---

²³ O. H. Taylor, *op. cit.*, pp. 69-71, and A. L. Macfie, *op. cit.*, pp. 215-216. Both men point to a relation between prudence and justice in Smith and unlike Jacob Viner's, "Adam Smith and Laissez-Faire," *The Journal of Political Economy*, April 1927, they see a more formal relation between *The Wealth of Nations* and *The Theory of Moral Sentiments*.

²⁴ Lionel Robbins, *op. cit.*, pp. 23-26, and Warren J. Samuels, "The Classical Theory of Economic Policy: Non-Legal Social Control," Part I, *Southern Economic Journal*, July 1964. Unlike Robbins, Samuels stresses the non-legal forces of social control, for example, morality, religion, custom and education as vital ingredients in the institutional framework of the system of natural liberty.

²⁵ See my, "Edmund Burke: A Liberal Practitioner of Political Economy," *Modern Age*, Winter Issue, 1963-1964.

²⁶ *Works*, VI, pp. 31, 202, 210, 208.

and frugality, Berkeley thought, made a nation happy and flourishing. The process of economic reform too, must recognize God and religion. Without this explicit awareness, "...the finger of God will unravel all our vain projects...."[27] So too, economic reformers must do more than legislate acts embodying the divine will; they must live out God's will. Without good example, the harmony of interests is threatened.

> It is not so much the execution of the laws as the countenance of those in authority that is wanting to the maintenance of religion. If men of rank and power, who have a share in distributing justice, and a voice in the public councils, shall be observed to neglect divine worship themselves, it must needs be a great temptation for others to do the same. But if they and their families should set a good example, it may be presumed that men of less figure would be disposed to follow it.[28]

However, the central element in Berkeley's system of natural liberty was the psychology of the learning process and its role in shaping his version of the harmony of interests. In Berkeley's views on the educative process, we see the concept of the "instilled notion" become both the means of insuring obedience to law and harmony in society, and a way of resolving his apparently contradictory acceptance and rejection of the role of conscience in determining individual action.

Knowledge was important to Berkeley both for utilitarian and intellectual reasons, "Men's behaviour is the consequence of their principles...in order to make a State thrive and flourish, care must be taken that good principles be propagated in the minds of those who compose it." Also, for Berkeley, it was a noble pursuit, "I will freely own," he says, "a judicial and impartial search after truth is the most valuable employment of the mind." Although economically useful and meritorious for its own sake, education is, ultimately, the keystone to order and harmony in society. Without it, man's appetites and passions reign. It is even vain to depend on the constitution and structure of a state if there is "...a prevailing disorder in the principles and opinions of its members." With a proper educative process, judgment, order and harmony rule.[29]

For Berkeley, the educative process was the 'instilling of notions', that is, the implanting of ideas and attitudes, hopefully at an early age where they can take the deepest root and exert the greatest influence. These notions may be acquired in an active or passive manner, "...either by private reason and reflection, or taught and instilled by the general reason of the public, that is, by the law of the land."[30]

When an individual does not assume the responsibility of educating himself by acquiring 'notions' through the use of private reason, or when the individual is not qualified by age or has neither "...disposition nor leisure for faculties to dig in the mine of truth themselves...," then it is the duty of the legislator, by definition one who is responsible and able to inform himself, to implant the proper notions, that is, those ideas and institutions which are most conducive to the public good. It is true, Berkeley acknowledges, that ideas or notions once implanted by law rather than acquired through reason become prejudices, that is "notions or opinions...assented to without examination"; however, this does not make prejudices false and notions true, rather, "...the former are taken upon trust, and the latter acquired by reasoning."[31]

It is also true, he continues, that the necessity of implanting opinions seems more evident historically than the experience of men acquiring notions: "...if you look through the world, you shall find but few of

---
[27] *Works*, VI, p. 71.
[28] *Works*, VI, p. 221.
[29] *Works*, VI, pp. 201, 218, 201–02, 203.
[30] *Works*, VI, pp. 204, 203.
[31] *Works*, VI, pp. 218, 203, 205–206.

these narrow inspectors and inquirers, very few who make it their business to analyse opinions and pursue them to their rational source...." Berkeley is not suggesting here that only the wealthy and leisure class, or only the extremely intelligent are capable of using reason. However, given the unequal distribution of income, leisure and talent, frequently it is only the talented and wealthy who have the opportunity to acquire the necessary knowledge for properly directing their actions in society. This opportunity, given to some by chance of birth, is not, however, automatically fulfilled. For every man, despite the most difficult of circumstances, Berkeley seems to hold out the possibility of self-education: "... where there is a sincere love of truth and virtue, the grace of God can easily supply the defect of human means." For, "Providence hath made provision for our wellbeing... The good and gracious God hath furnished us with faculties to perform our duty: he hath given us the light of nature and reason to discern it." [32]

Berkeley's theory of notions also sheds some light on his apparent rejection of the role of conscience. Speaking of the tension between law and conscience, he comments,

... and out present impending danger is from the setting up of private judgment, or an inward light, in opposition to human and divine laws. Such an inward conceited principle always at work and proceeding gradually and steadily, may be sufficient to dissolve any human fabric of polity or civil government.[33]

However, Berkeley cannot be completely opposed to "inner principles" or he should logically reject those notions based upon private judgment and acquired, even by the legislators themselves, through private reason. Possibly, he is opposing here only those notions which contradict existing human and divine laws.[34]

Actually, Berkeley accepts both the autonomy of conscience and the necessity of law in achieving the harmony of interests in society. Generally, the process of discovering the divine plan for man on earth cannot be left to one individual, or the "inner lights" of separate individuals.[35] It is the legislature, or legislators acting in concert, which is best equipped to maintain the harmony of interests by creating civil laws, or implanting notions and institutions, which embody God's will.

However, the laws of God's nature are not entirely external to any given individual,

These propositions are called laws of nature because they are universal, and do not derive their obligations from any civil sanction, but immediately from the Author of nature himself. They are said to be stamped on the mind, to be engraven on the tables of the heart, because they are well known to mankind, and suggested and inculcated by *conscience*. Lastly, they are termed eternal rules of reason, because they necessarily result from the nature of things, and may be demonstrated by the infallible deductions of reason.[36]

For Berkeley, then, it seems that where there exists a functioning moral order, organized religion and a belief in God and God's nature and providence, and a "sincere love of truth and virtue," then *conscience and private reason conjoin to distill from our nature the 'notions' necessary for establishing and maintaining harmonielehre.*

Berkeley and Classical Harmonielehre

The view that Berkeley's system of natural liberty anticipates the classical system must be carefully defined. The proposition does not mean that Berkeley was, potentially, a classical economist. It is clear from his concern with monetary affairs and advocacy of numerous specific public policies that he must be classified as a later mercantilist. Instead, the proposi-

---

[32] *Works*, VI, pp. 205, 218; VII, 91–92.
[33] *Works*, VI, p. 217.
[34] Naturally, Berkeley is assuming that some individuals at least can discern good notions, whether privately acquired or implanted, from bad notions.
[35] See above, p. 5.
[36] *Works*, VI, p. 23. (My Italics)

tion means that Berkeley, despite his interventionism, was predisposed to assign the individual a widening role in determining the means of social and economic policies, provided the presence of a proper institutional order.

However, the position that Berkeley had a concept of *harmonielehre* which, in some way, anticipates the system of natural liberty in Classical Liberalism, is not shared by others. For example, I. D. S. Ward views Berkeley as a consistent interventionist who rejects the harmony of interest doctrine and consequently, laissez-faire. T. W. Hutchison sees Berkeley as the thorough Mercantilist. At the same time, however, Hutchison notes a contradiction between Berkeley's religious and intellectual liberalism and his illiberal economic views but makes no attempt to resolve it. On the other hand, it is W. D. Grampp who first notes how Mercantilism anticipated many important elements of classical economics including the place of the state in the economic organization of society. However, Grampp does not examine the process of "state's agenda" in Berkeley or how Berkeley's theory of policy represents a transitional element between later Mercantilism and early Classical Liberalism.[37]

There are a number of elements in Berkeley's system which are consistent with Classical Economic Liberalism. For example, although he stresses the need for law in society, Berkeley admits some areas do not come under the discretion of law. He felt that a number of rules regulating human affairs could "... be either totally abrogated or dispensed with; because the private ends they were intended to promote respect only some particular persons ... who ... in different postures of things, may prosecute their own designs by different measures, as in human prudence shall seem convenient." Only "negative precepts," he thought, "must by everyone, in all times and places, be actually observed." In contrast, Berkeley, facing squarely the complexity of most human situations, realized that general laws which "enjoin the doing of an action," must "allow room for human prudence and discretion in the execution of them, it for the most part depending on various accidental circumstances...."[38]

So convinced was Berkeley of the limitations of law, that he hoped for other means of redressing public injustice: "But would it not be better to heal the source, and, by an inward principle, extirpate wickedness from the heart, rather than depend altogether on human laws for preventing or redressing the bad effects thereof?"[39]

Another characteristic of Berkeley's system of natural liberty which is compatible with Liberalism is his emphasis on the importance of the individual in determining the common good of society. *Harmonielehre*, he asserted, is an end "... which God requires should be promoted by the free actions of men..."; and, this freedom "... is the greatest human blessing that a virtuous man can possess...."[40]

An understanding of the content of *harmonielehre* also, for Berkeley, depends uniquely on the individual.

There is some analogy between the methods of grace and the ordinary course of nature. Providence hath made provision for our welbeing both in this life and in that which is to come: ... The good and precious God hath furnished us with faculties to perform our duty: he hath given us the light of nature and reason to discern it; ... he strengthens and assists our weak endeavors with his grace; *and hath planted a conscience in the breast of every man which never fails to check and admonish him*.[41]

Corresponding to this privilege of knowing the common good is the individual's obligation to pursue it: "... as social inclinations are absolutely necessary to the well-

---

[37] Ian D. S. Ward, *op. cit.*, p. 32; T. W. Hutchison, *op. cit.*, p. 76; W. D. Grampp, *op. cit.*, p. 62.
[38] *Works*, VI, pp. 26, 31.
[39] *Works*, VI, p. 209.
[40] *Works*, VI, pp. 33, 70.
[41] *Works*, VII, pp. 91–92. Italics added.

being of the world, it is the duty and interest of each individual to cherish and improve them to the benefit of mankind...."[42]

The means to the harmony of interests, for Berkeley, center about three categories: cooperation, innate social sympathies, and the relation between private reason and conscience. In an analogy to geographic specialization, he says, "As different countries are by their respective products fitted to supply each other's wants: so the all-wise providence of God hath ordered that different men are endowed with various talents whereby they are mutually enabled to assist and to promote the happiness of one another." Reinforcing this principle of cooperation are the "seeds of mutual benevolence" implanted in our souls and the natural tendency in man toward community and *harmonielehre*. Drawing upon Newton's principle of universal attraction, Berkeley notes the "benevolent uniting instinct implanted in human nature," which draws men into "communities, clubs, families, friendships, and all the various species of society."[43]

But, it is the interaction of knowledge and conscience which is the principal agent of *harmonielehre*. It is knowledge which leads us to the realization of *harmonielehre*: "Knowledge does naturally produce in us a zeal towards that which is excellent, and a detestation and abhorrence of whatsoever is known to be evil.... Knowledge is the lamp of the soul that guides its faculties to proper objects and regulates their respective operations"; it is conscience which "never fails to check and admonish" man in his use of reason. Without conscience, there can be no order: "...what hold can the prince or magistrate have on the conscience of those who have no conscience?" Indeed, "...who thinks his own authority sufficient to make him respected and obeyed... Obedience to all civil power is rooted in the religious fear of God: it is propagated, preserved, and nourished by religion. This makes men obey... in sincerity of heart."[44]

Berkeley's views on the primacy of conscience casts an interesting light on the role of law and the legislator in achieving the harmony of interests. His position states that law in itself cannot command harmony; and suggests, instead, that the law is a sign, a symbol, almost an *a posteriori*, which only reflects the more vital relation between conscience and reason and the establishment of *harmonielehre*.

As we have seen earlier, Berkeley's harmony of interests, like that of Classical Liberalism, presupposes a correct moral, religious and institutional order. So too, the proper functioning of reason and conscience also presume a right order in society, especially in the religious institutions: "Religion hath in former day been cherished and reverenced by wise patriots and lawgivers, as knowing it to be impossible that a nation should thrive and flourish without virtue, or that virtue should subsist without conscience, or conscience without religion...." Here, Berkeley suggests a strong functional dependence between *harmonielehre* conscience and religion. Therefore, whenever private reason or conscience are insufficient, or when the necessary relation between them is obstructed or perverted, these deficiencies or obstructions to *harmonielehre*, as in the Classical system, can be corrected by the efforts of the legislator.[45]

Berkeley's view of the harmony of interests sheds some light on contradictory and ambiguous elements in his thought. For example, his view of *harmonielehre* explains how Berkeley can accept the primacy of conscience in the right institutional environment; yet, reject the "inner

---

[42] *Works*, VII, p. 227.
[43] *Works*, VII, pp. 35, 227, 226.
[44] *Works*, VII, pp. 21, 92; VI, pp. 209, 208.
[45] *Works*, VI, p. 69.

lights" of Shaftesbury's doctrine when it is taken over by the "free-thinkers" of Berkeley's time and placed in a context which denies God and organized religion.[46]

Again, Berkeley's process of *harmonielehre* shows how in the essay on *Passive Obedience* he is able to deny the consultation of conscience and affirm in its place, the obedience to law. Knowing Berkeley's view that the common good, as embodied in God's will and revealed in the laws of nature, is stamped on the mind of all men and "inculcated by conscience," it is difficult to explain his dismissal of conscience unless we assume the absence, implicit in Berkeley's reasoning, of institutional precedents which insure the effective operation of private reason and conscience. As before, the presence of obstructions demands the function of the legislator until the imperfections are removed.[47]

Finally, Berkeley's conception of *harmonielehre* might also explain why a great deal of his economic writings appear illiberal. His two major economic works, *The Querist* and *An Essay Towards Preventing The Ruin of Great Britain*, addressed in the first instance to the economic and social plight of an impoverished and uneducated Ireland, and in the second, against the spirit of avarice and excess in Great Britain *circa* the South Sea Bubble escapade, are situations characterized by the absence of a proper institutional order needed to insure the establishment and maintenance of Berkeley's system of natural liberty. It is natural, then, that he should call for the wise, benevolent and "overseeing" legislator to restore *harmonielehre*.[48]

Berkeley's desire to assign the individual more responsibility for his own destiny and the future of society is very evident and theoretically systematized in his works.

However, we should not conclude that he was on the verge of dispensing with the services of the legislator. In his own time, he was still frightened and appalled by the many real obstacles to his system of natural liberty, obstacles which demanded considerable government intervention and reform before individual men could be left to their own devices in achieving *harmonielehre*.

If we consider the blindness and infirmity, the folly and passions of mankind, how little most men understand their true interests, and how backward they are to pursue and to practise, even what they know to be so, it will be very evident, that we are too imperfect creatures to be governed by our own wills.... Hence it is, that all political societies have found it necessary, to oblige each individual member, to conform his civil life and actions, to the will or decrees of the community, rather than leave him to be governed at his own pleasure.[49]

Berkeley's theoretical vision of a more liberal society is to be viewed more as a hope than a fact. A few stanzas of a poem written by Berkeley on the occasion of the founding of a college in the new world strongly suggest his anticipation of this new and more liberal society.[50]

The Muse, Disgusted at an Age and Clime,
  Barren of every glorious Theme,
In distant Lands now wait a better Time,
  Producing Subjects worthy Fame: ...

In happy Climes the Seat of Innocence,
  Where Nature guides and Virtue rules,
Where Men shall not impose for Truth and Sense,
  The Pedantry of Courts and Schools:

There shall be sung another golden Age,
  The rise of Empire and of Arts,
The good and Great inspiring epic Rage,
  The wisest Heads and noblest Hearts.

Not such as Europe breeds in her decay;
  Such as she bred when fresh and young,
When heav'nly Flame did animate her Clay,
  By future Poets shall be sung.

---

[46] *Works*, VII, pp. 198–202.
[47] *Works*, VI, pp. 15–46.
[48] *Works*, VI, "An Essay Towards Preventing the Ruin of Great Britain," pp. 67–85; "The Querist," pp. 87–181.

[49] *Works*, VII, p. 131.
[50] *Works*, VII, p. 373. After great efforts on his part, St. Paul's College in Bermuda was founded in 1725 with Berkeley as the first President.

Chapter 8

George Berkeley

George Berkeley, Bishop of Cloyne, missionary, social philosopher, and reformer, commands a higher place in the history of economic analysis than either of the other authors we are considering in this section under the title of *The Inflationists*. The kinship of Berkeley's work is closest with that of Law. There is a generic similarity between them in that they addressed comparable prescriptions of monetary policy to the solution of depression, poverty, and unemployment. They each retreated from the inhibiting metallist assumptions of the earlier classical mercantilism.

The significance of Berkeley's *Querist*[1] for the development of monetary analysis has been only scantily recognized in the historical literature.[2] A more adequate recognition has had to await the shift of emphasis of macro-economic analysis to the neo-mercantilist positions of the last two decades of the present century. This has made possible the estimate by Johnston, for example, who concludes that "in his analysis of the nature of money itself, and of the function of gold in relation to it, Berkeley . . . takes high rank as one of the most modern and 'advanced' of monetary thinkers."[3]

---

1. Published in three parts in 1735, 1736, and 1737. Reference, unless otherwise stated, will be to the Johns Hopkins University reprint, ed. J. H. Hollander. Berkeley's only other work bearing on the matters discussed here is his *Essay towards preventing the ruine of Great Britain* (London, 1721).

2. Cf. T. W. Hutchison in *The British Journal for the Philosophy of Science* (May 1953), p. 68 ff., for a discussion of the manner in which the characteristic theoretical predilections of the nineteenth-century economists avoided an adequate recognition of the message of the *Querist*.

3. J. Johnston in *Economic History* (1938) on "The Monetary Theories of Berkeley," pp. 21–24. Cf. ibid., p. 24: "In his emphasis on the importance of consumption as a factor in the production of wealth, in

141

ANALYSIS

It has been suggested that Berkeley, in the development of economic thought as in the history of philosophy, may be described as "the successor of Locke and the predecessor of Hume."[4] Such a conclusion might follow from his development of two of the concepts which had been raised in the last decade of the previous century. These were, firstly, the concept of the circulation of money *per se* as having autonomous and even causal significance for monetary analysis, and secondly, the associated concept of money as a determinant variable in the explanation of the level of economic activity. In these matters, as in the question of the definition of money and the description of monetary institutions, Berkeley pushed the logic of his predecessors to an advanced and coherent level. In conjunction with his work in the *Querist*, the theoretical developments of the later eighteenth century present a cogent case for relative theoretical completeness.

The 1690's and the 1730's were two of the most fluid and formative decades in the history of the theory of money. The work of John Law in the first and third decades of the eighteenth century had made an important contribution, and Berkeley's work in the following decade depended heavily on deeper validities of Law's essays, even though the practical excesses of the latter's monetary management were attacked and condemned. Berkeley joined with Law in deducing the theoretical and policy implications of the newly developed emphasis on the medium-of-exchange function of money. The functions of money being more adequately understood, the examination of monetary circulation became more important than a sterile preoccupation, in the earlier regulatory mercantilist fashion, with the acquisition and protection of a supply of gold and silver. As Berkeley says:

---

his realisation of the vital part played by the quantity of money in the promotion of commerce and enterprise, Berkeley must be regarded as a precursor of Keynes."

4. Hollander's reprint, p. 3, quoting Balfour's "Biographical Introduction" to *The Works of George Berkeley* (London, ed. George Sampson, 1897-1898). The statement in the text is correct in many ways, but we disagree with Hollander's further observation that "the continuity is less apparent with respect to specific doctrines than in the matter of that common sense rationalism which distinguishes the best economic thought of the eighteenth century." Berkeley's work does, in fact, exhibit an important doctrinal continuity. With the "common sense rationalism," of course, there can be no disagreement. This has been noted in other places; e.g., Hutchison, *op. cit.*, p. 53 (cf. his citation of Fraser); and Schumpeter, *op. cit.*, p. 294.

Whether the prejudices about gold and silver are not strong but whether they are not still prejudices? (3/86)[5]

The redefinition of money as a "ticket" or a "counter,"[6] involving the logical priority of the medium-of-exchange function of money, led naturally to the consideration of money as an equilibrating variable in the total economic system. The circulation of money, however defined, had become more important than the mere consideration of the supply and value of metallic money itself.[7]

In taking this position, Berkeley stands not simply as "the successor of Locke and the predecessor of Hume," but as the logical successor of the definitional monetary economics of the 1690's and the precursor of the more satisfying dynamic monetary analysis of the third quarter of the eighteenth century. Berkeley is in an intermediate position in the sense that after him two things remained to be done. Firstly, it was necessary to build a sharper analysis of the *structure* of monetary flows;[8] and secondly, this newer analysis needed to be integrated with the theory of the value of money to form a general theory of money and the monetary process. The

---

5. The reference here is to the *Querist*, Part 3, Query 86. Similar references throughout will be given in this form.

6. E.g., 3/89, 3/181, 1/23. This is also in the tradition of Barbon's cartalist argument. Cf. *supra*.

7. The development of the theory of money which did in this way take place in the eighteenth century was not the only possible logical development from the earlier medium-of-exchange analysis. The economists of the following century chose to argue the alternative possibility, namely, the relevance of money to the theory of value but its irrelevance to the determination of the effective level of economic activity, and this constituted a principal reason why the theory of money was at that time shunted onto a wrong and unfruitful track. The resultant division of economic theory into logically independent compartments of real and monetary economics did much to inhibit not only the theoretical maturity of economic thought, but also its social and practical applicability. In addition to the references cited in Part One and T. W. Hutchison *supra*, cf. J. B. Say, *A Treatise on Political Economy* (ed. 1812), Sec. 3, p. 167, and *ibid.*, Chap. XV. Cf. also Becker and Baumol in *Economica* (Nov. 1952), and references there cited.

8. This was achieved to a comparatively high degree in Cantillon's *Essai sur la nature du commerce en général* and to a lesser extent in David Hume's essays. Cantillon in particular was concerned with examining, for example, not only the static relationship between the supply of money and the level of prices in the pure Lockeian tradition, but also the nature of the *causal* relationship and the way in which a change in the rate of flow of money brought about a new stable level of prices. The later writers, in other words, were concerned in varying degrees with the *movement between* one equilibrium situation and another. The nature of the time path between the two positions, moreover, depended on the nature and origin of the stimulus to change itself.

derivation of the theory of monetary flows proceeded logically from Locke's earlier two-sector analysis. This latter had turned on the twofold proposition that the effective amount of money in circulation determined in one context, in the commodity sector of the economy, the operative level of commodity prices and the effective level of trade activity; and it determined at the same time in the financial sector the equilibrium loan price at which the money supply was activated in trade. The argument was that money was borrowed in order that trade might take place. In the eighteenth-century synthesis the theory of money is generalized in the sense that the conditions obtaining in what we have called the commodity sector are relevant in a direct and *causal* manner to the operative conditions in the financial sector. This generalization was dependent, moreover, on a parallel development in the theory of the rate of interest. Cantillon, Hume, and in a similar degree Steuart, showed that the theory of interest involved more than the static supply and demand for money equations of many of the earlier authors. It was not sufficient to argue, they claimed, that an increase in the supply of money would necessarily lead to a reduction in the rate of interest. The outcome depended on the way in which the increased supply of money influenced the level of trading activity and thus the level of the demand for loan money for trading purposes.[9] The conditions of demand for loan money were not independent of the conditions of its supply.

Furthermore, at the same time as a more general theory of money was established at this point, the analysis of the commodity sector was also broadened to conclude that the effective price level of commodities depended not simply on an equational relationship between the supply of money and the supply of goods in the Lockeian sense, but on the conditions of supply as influenced by trading profitabilities on the one hand, and on the level of effective monetary demand on the other.

This brief discussion of the development of the theory of money

---

9. This extension in the financial sector analysis, or in the theory of interest, followed naturally from a theoretical concern for the level of the demand for money. The concept of the demand for money is here similar to that expressed in the theory of banking which grew in the earlier decades of the century (as in Berkeley) from a needs-of-trade doctrine of money requirements. That is, in the same way as the needs-of-trade conception of the demand for money was earlier relevant for the theory of the *availability* of money, it became relevant later in the pre-classical literature for the theory of the *price* of money.

in the eighteenth century indicates the intermediate position which Berkeley's *Querist* occupied. Two preliminary questions might be asked relative to Berkeley's own contributions to the theory. Firstly, in what sense can the *Querist* be said to be "consciously theoretical," as that term describes much of the literature prior to the 1730's? The answer is not unambiguous. Berkeley was concerned closely with an urgent, pressing problem of unemployment and poverty. His work moves on the level of policy and prescription rather than on that of positive analysis. Yet his proposals, self-consistent and integrated as they are, possess a compelling logic which derives from the analytical insight which informed them. On a superficial view the *Querist* is a loosely strung series of nine hundred questions relating to the causes and cures of the country's depressed conditions. Their arrangement is haphazard and disorderly. Yet there emerges from them a comprehensive program of economic reform which was based on a genuine perception of the issues of monetary analysis. The *Querist* is a work in applied economics. But it is applied economics in the tradition of the best literature of the eighteenth century. Its applications were based on closely reasoned theorems and analogies.

The second preliminary question relates to the way in which, as was suggested above, Berkeley's work is to be accorded a higher place in the history of analysis than that of Law, the other important monetary inflationist of the early eighteenth century. The answer exhibits the similarities and differences between them. Both wanted to solve comparable problems of depression by raising the level of monetary circulation. Both saw that the best means of doing this was by issuing bank money. They both reacted against the earlier mercantilist prejudices in favor of a metallic money supply. Having perceived the functional efficacy of paper money-substitutes, they each saw that the old laborious method of foreign trade surpluses was neither the only nor the best way of increasing the money supply. But at this point their respective positions diverge. Law proceeded to argue from this important point that his monetary inflation at home would not have any unfavorable effects on the balance of payments because the increased monetary circulation would call forth an increased production of commodities at a constant or diminishing price level, and this would lead to an increase in exports, a more favorable balance of payments, and thereby a further increase in the supply of money. Thus the circle of expansion would commence again. Two of Law's important arguments, it was noted earlier, were those we transcribed as the internal elasticity of supply of goods and the external elasticity of demand for them. International economic relations remained important for Law, as they had been for the century of mercantilist literature before him.

For Berkeley, on the other hand, this was not so. For him, the analysis of the circulation of money was incorporated into the economics not of an open, but of a closed, economy. Berkeley is the father of the monetary economics of a closed economy. He was concerned with "domestic commerce,"[10] "inward trade,"[11] and the possible conditions of prosperity "even though we had no foreign trade."[12] It may appear today that the closed economy argument is to be regarded as the first approximation and that of the open economy as the subsequent approximation to the analysis of full or general economic equilibrium. The paradoxical statement is true, however, that Berkeley's arguments should be seen as the more considerable achievement at the stage in the development of thought at which he wrote. This was so because the analysis represented at that time, and against its own intellectual background, a further extension of the revolt against the earlier prejudices and policies of regulatory, bullion-collecting mercantilism. It was so also because by this method, and on its own level of assumptions, the closed economy argument was best able to demonstrate the nature and expansive potential of a growing monetary circulation. And in this way a foundation was laid for the further advances accomplished in the decades that followed.

II

The employment objective

The conditions of unemployment and depression against the background of which the *Querist* was written have been described in numerous places.[13] We are interested at present in Berkeley's own conception of the relevance to these situations of the theory of the money-flow process and his descriptions of monetary institutions. As to the objective of the analysis, he asks

10. *Querist*, 3/266.
11. *Ibid.*, 3/265.
12. *Ibid.*, 1/112.

13. E.g., cf. J. Johnston, *op. cit.*, and T. W. Hutchison, *op. cit.* Cf. also Chapter 2 above.

Whether the great and general aim of the publique should not be to employ the people? (2/162)

and as to the function of monetary regulations and monetary institutions:

Whether all regulations of coin should not be made, with a view to encourage industry and a circulation of commerce, throughout the kingdom? (3/140)

Whether there be any vertue in gold or silver, other than as they set people at work, or create industry? (1/32)

Such an attitude proceeds from the perception of the logical priority in analysis of the functions of money. The purely analytical question at this point was "whether the *effect* is not to be considered, more than the *kind* or quantity of money?"[14] In the same sense as the primary consideration was that of functional efficacy, the criterion of efficacy was the employment-creating effects of the circulation itself.[15]

Berkeley shared the view common to his time that the source of wealth and power lay in a large and actively employed population. But in the same way as John Bellers had done, he saw that it was not people, but "regularly labouring people,"[16] who were the source of national wealth and strength.

Whether the main point be not to multiply *and employ* our people? (2/178)[17]

---

14. *Op. cit.*, 3/292. The important distinction here is between the *effect* and the *kind*, and the further idea of quantity is relevant to Berkeley's separate discussion of the importance of the velocity of circulation of money. Cf. *op. cit.*, 1/22: "Whether therefore less money swiftly circulating be not, in effect, equivalent to more money slowly circulating?"

15. Cf. *infra* for Berkeley's transition from this point to the discussion of paper money and his insistence on the significance of the "local value" which such money-substitutes could acquire and retain. E.g., 3/87: "Whether paper doth not by its stamp and signature acquire a local value and become as precious and scarce as gold?"

16. John Bellers, *op. cit.*, p. 124.

17. Our italics. In the same year (1735) as Berkeley published the first edition of Part I of the *Querist*, William Hay made the very same point in his first edition of *Remarks on the laws relating to the poor; with proposals for their better relief and employment* (London, 2nd ed., 1751): "The wealth of any nation must originally flow . . . from the number of inhabitants . . . the more populous a country is, the richer it is, or at least may be," p. 19. Our italics. Hay continues also: "If it must be allowed, that increasing our people would be an addition to our wealth, then it will follow, that employing our poor will be so too," *ibid.*, p. 24.

Whether there can be a greater reproach, on the leading men and the patriots of a country, than that the people should want employment? (2/194)

The lamentable fact which faced the social reformer so clearly was the all-too-frequent paradox of poverty "in the midst of plenty":

Whether we are not in fact the only people, who may be said to starve in the midst of plenty? (3/101)

and

Whether there ever was in any part of the world, a country in such wretched circumstances, and which, at the same time, could be so easily remedied, and nevertheless the remedy not applied? (3/79)

But it is recognized that the solution is largely a monetary one, and it is asked

Whether, without the proper means of circulation, it be not in vain, to hope for thriving manufactures and a busy people? (3/187)

At the same time, however, the problem as Berkeley saw it was not exclusively a monetary problem, and he recognized clearly the obstacles to progress raised in many instances by the sheer disinclination of the people to work. Much has been made in the historical literature of this so-called "perverse supply curve of labour"[18] as it characterized the underlying economic conditions of the early eighteenth century.[19] Berkeley also noticed the same conditions:

Whether the bulk of our Irish natives are not kept from thriving, by that cynical content in dirt and beggary, which they possess to a degree beyond any other people in Christendom? (1/19)[20]

---

18. Cf. T. W. Hutchison, *op. cit.*, pp. 55–58, and references there cited. *Vide* also D. C. Coleman in *The Economic History Review* (April 1956) on "Labour in the English Economy of the Seventeenth Century."

19. Joshua Gee, for example, puts the case in his *The Trade and Navigation of Great Britain Considered* (London, 1729). "It has been remarked by our clothiers and other manufacturers, that when corn has been cheap they have had great difficulty to get their spinning and other work done; for the poor could buy provisions enough with two or three days' wages to serve them a week, and would spend the rest in idleness, drinking etc. But when corn has been dear, they have been forced to stick all week at it . . . ," *op. cit.* (2nd ed., 1730), p. 38.

20. One can almost hear the philanthropist turned cynic in "Whether a tax on dirt would not be one way of encouraging industry" (2/196).

Whether great profits may not be made by fisheries; but whether our Irish who live by that business, do not contrive to be drunk and unemployed, one half of the year? (3/258)

"Great profits" in and of themselves were not necessarily adequate incentives to effort. Other incentives were required. These, Berkeley saw, lay in the stimulation of new economic wants and in the development of new consumer fashions.[21] In general terms,

Whether the way to make men industrious, be not to let them taste the fruits of their industry? (2/181)

What is important at present, however, is that given these considerations, and given the need of "artificial helps . . . to redress our evils . . . in a land where industry is most against the natural grain of the people,"[22] Berkeley finds that the most important and the most efficient "helps" are monetary ones.

Whether of all the helps to industry that ever were invented, there be any more secure, more easy, and more effectual than a National Bank? (3/106)

From the recognition that the real economic problem was that of unemployment, the *Querist* proceeds to consider the explanation of the monetary means to the achievement of a satisfactory employment situation.

III

The circulation of money

Berkeley's primary view of money has been referred to as a functional view.[23] More particularly, the *Querist* asks

Whether money be not only so far useful as it stirreth up industry, enabling men mutually to participate the fruits of each others labour? (1/5)

And furthermore,

---

21. Cf. 1/9 ff. In conjunction with the observations in the following text, these conclusions point to the proposition, which is implicit in Berkeley and explicit in later writers, that the important thing for the theory of monetary equilibrium at a high level of activity is not simply the presence of a large supply of money, but the presence of a high level of monetary demand.
22. 3/105.
23. *Vide op. cit.*, 3/292.

150   ANALYSIS

Whether gold and silver be not a drug where they do not promote industry? Whether they be not even the bane and undoing of an idle people? (3/283)

The important thing, in other words, was that money should circulate. In terms similar to those of John Locke, Berkeley recognized the dragging, debilitating effects of a stagnation in the circulation of money:

Whether money lying dead . . . would not be as useless as in the mine? (1/269)
Whether it be not evidently the interest of every state, that its money should rather circulate than stagnate? (3/177)
Whether the public is not more benefited by a shilling that circulates, than a pound that lies dead? (3/183)
Whether the sure way to supply people with tools and materials, and to set them at work, be not a free circulation of money, whether silver or paper? (1/265)

and finally:

Whether money circulating be not the life of industry; and whether the want thereof doth not render a state gouty and inactive? (3/8)

References such as these could be multiplied at length. Berkeley is in this way drawing attention to the cornerstones of the theory of money in the eighteenth century. There is the Lockeian conception and fear of money that "lies dead"; there is the subsequent conception of circulation as having autonomous significance; and, to complete the trilogy of ideas at this preparatory stage of analysis, there is also the Lockeian idea of the "quickness of circulation."

Whether therefore less money swiftly circulating be not, in effect, equivalent to more money slowly circulating? or whether if the circulation be reciprocally as the quantity of coin the nation can be a loser? (1/22)

The discussion of the velocity concept in Locke's *Consequences* . . . left some doubt as to whether he conceived of velocity as itself an autonomous and causal variable. It was not clear whether a change in velocity was assumed to have direct and observable effects on dependent variables in the system, such as the price level and the level of activity. Here in Berkeley, however, there is no ambiguity. A change in the rate of circulation "reciprocally as the quantity of

GEORGE BERKELEY 151

the coin" can itself exert direct effects on the monetary system. More explicitly, it is asked

> Whether an inward trade would not cause industry to flourish, and multiply the circulation of our coin, and whether this may not do as well as multiplying the coin itself? (3/265)

And associated with these ideas also was the further Lockeian idea of the significance for policy of the structure of payments habits:

> Whether silver and small money be not that which circulates the quickest . . . ? (3/172)
>
> Whether all things considered, it would not be better for a kingdom that its cash consisted of half a million in small silver, than of two millions in gold? (3/173)
>
> Whether business at fairs and markets is not often at a stand, and often hindered, even though the seller hath his commodities at hand, and the purchaser his gold, yet for want of change? (3/179; cf. 1/227.)

It is from this nexus of ideas that there emerges the central proposition: "Money circulating" is "the life of industry" (3/8). And by money was meant either "silver or paper" (1/265). Berkeley was not in any sense shackled by "prejudices about gold and silver" (3/86). If, indeed, the metallist denotation of money be insisted upon, Berkeley, at the very beginning of the *Querist*, shifts the analytical emphasis from the notion of money to that of its circulation. He asks "Whether any other means, equally conducing to excite and circulate the industry of mankind, may not be as useful as money" (1/6).

What, then, does Berkeley understand as money?

> Whether money is to be considered as having an intrinsic value, or as being a commodity, a standard, a measure, or a pledge, as is variously suggested by writers? And whether the true idea of money, as such, be not altogether that of a ticket or counter? (1/23; cf. 3/89.)

This clearly isolates the medium-of-exchange function of money. Granted also the function of money as a measure of values in exchange, that is as a measure of a "compounded proportion, directly as the demand, and reciprocally as the plenty" (1/24), Berkeley continues:

> Whether the terms Crown, Livre, Pound sterling etc. are not to be considered as exponents or denominations of such proportion? and whether

■ 161 ■

gold, silver, and paper are not tickets or counters for reckoning, recording, and transferring thereof? (1/25)

Whether the denominations being retained, although the bullion were gone, things might not nevertheless be rated, bought and sold, industry promoted, and a circulation of commerce maintained? (1/26)

To look at these basic monetary conceptions in another way, Berkeley's understanding of the *function* of money itself involves a twofold idea. By this means "industry [is] promoted" and the "circulation of commerce maintained." Here in explicit terms is the twofold objective of the nascent economic science of the late seventeenth and the eighteenth centuries. The objective was firstly to reach a high level of activity and employment and secondly to maintain that high level under stable conditions. In the same section of his work Berkeley puts the proposition in a form which associates with it the previously mentioned attitude to the question of the most efficient *forms* of money.

Whether to promote, transfer, and secure this commerce . . . be not the sole means of enriching a people, and how far this may be done independently of gold and silver? (1/39)

Logically, the conception is thus three-sided. The function of monetary circulation, and thus the objectives of a theoretical explanation, lay in its ability to "promote," "transfer," and "secure" a satisfactory level of "commerce of industry" (cf. 1/38–39). This statement can be taken as a convenient summary by the *Querist* of its own analytical preoccupations. The meaning of the word "transfer" subsists in Berkeley's conception of the priority of the medium-of-exchange function of money as we have looked at that already. In what follows we shall look more closely at the question of the "promoting" and the "securing" of commerce.

IV

The induced and magnified effects of monetary expenditure

Having thrown off the shackles of earlier metallist prejudices, Berkeley, as did also John Law in the theoretical parts of his work, saw the need to maintain a careful balance between the supply of and the demand for money. This in no sense precluded the monetary authorities from operating upon the demand conditions in such a way as would enlarge the scope for the use of money in trade and thus the demand for it. Indeed, it was at this very point that the inflationists made their important contribution to the economics of monetary equilibrium at a high level of activity. But given the demand for money—that is, the autonomous and the induced trading demand—it was important that the conditions of supply should be adjusted, by appropriate policy action where necessary, to the demand situation. And conversely, given the elasticity of supply of nonmetallic money, it was important that the demand for it should be maintained at a level appropriate to the real economic needs of the community. The notion of the resultant monetary balance is put, for example, as follows:

Whether counters be not referred to other things, which so long as they keep pace and proportion with the counters, it must be owned the counters are useful, but whether beyond that to value or covet counters, be not direct folly? (2/119)

The issues here raised, the "folly" of a maladjusted demand for money, refer to both of the two sources of monetary disease: the underutilization of currency on the one hand and its overissue on the other. The question of underutilisation Berkeley has already referred to in the discussion of the circulation of money. The other question of the overissue of money was also examined.

The point at which this was relevant was, as might be expected, Berkeley's criticism of the excesses of policy of the arch-inflationist of the preceding decade, John Law, to whose work, on a theoretical level, the *Querist* is clearly indebted. The expression of monetary demand, Berkeley recognized, depended partly on the public's possession of money wealth. There existed, and had to be taken into account, something of a money illusion. After examining the excesses of John Law's schemes of money creation, and after pointing out that "by a glut of paper, the prices of things must rise," Berkeley continues:

Whence also the fortunes of men must encrease in denomination, though not in value; whence pride, idleness and beggary. (1/215)

The money-wealth illusion was a disincentive to productive effort, and it led ultimately to the general lowering of the prosperity of the economy. This situation, moreover, induced directly a wasteful import demand for luxury commodities and led to the kind of strain on the country's balance of payments which, in other contexts, the *Querist* was at pains to condemn and correct.

Against this background of a balanced level of monetary circulation the *Querist* indicates two further lines of investigation. The first relates to the way in which an impulse or impetus to monetary circulation has, to a greater or lesser degree, a sustaining effect on economic activity. The second relates to the ways in which, by way of monetary and fiscal policy, the authorities might operate on the determinants of the economic system to produce a balance or equilibrium at a high level of activity.

Berkeley begins his discussion of these points with an example of what has been referred to in subsequent times as "Crusoe economics."[24] The concept of interdependent monetary relations then rested firmly on the economic concepts of the division of labor and the specialization of production. These latter were logically antecedent to the emergence of an exchange economy. And the emergence of monetary relationships themselves developed a more complicated economic nexus of the "creating of wants" (1/20), the associated stimulus to industry, and the widening of the area of exchange. Against this background the conclusion follows:

Whether other things being given . . . the wealth be not proportioned to the industry, and this to the circulation of credit, be the credit circulated or transferred by what marks or tokens so ever? (1/21)

Within this context the circular nature of the flow of money becomes clear:

Whether the same shilling circulating in a village may not supply one man with bread, another with stockings, a third with a knife, a fourth with paper, a fifth with nails, and so answer many wants which must otherwise have remained unsatisfied? (3/185)

Or again,

Whether the small town of Birmingham alone doth not, upon an average, circulate every week one way or other, to the value of fifty thousand pounds? But whether the same crown may not be often paid? (3/203)

More particularly,

---

24. *Vide* 1/48, 1/49, 3/100. The form of argument was not uncommon at this time and was employed on the grand scale again by Sir James Steuart in his socio-historical analysis. Cf. *infra*.

Whether money, though lent only to the rich, would not soon circulate among the poor? (3/94)[25]

And,

Whether facilitating and quickening the circulation of power to supply wants be not the promoting of wealth and industry among the lower people? And whether upon this the wealth of the great doth not depend? (3/186; cf. 2/244.)

The idea of the circular flow of money is in this way broadened to include the propagation of monetary demand, with its expansive effects on employment and activity.

Whether the industry of the lower part of our people doth not much depend on the expense of the upper? (2/229)
What would be the consequence, of our gentry affected to distinguish themselves by fine houses rather than fine cloaths? (2/230)[26]

Whether building would not peculiarly encourage all other arts in this kingdom? (2/232)
Whether smiths, masons, bricklayers, plaisterers, carpenters, joyners, tylers, plummers, glaziers would not all find employment if the humour of building prevailed? (2/233)
Whether, the ornaments and furniture of a good house do not employ a number of all sorts of artificers, in iron, wood, marble, brass, pewter, copper, wool, flax and divers other materials? (2/234)
Whether in buildings and gardens, a great number of day labourers do not find employment? (2/235)

25. This concept of the circular flow has been noted already in several of the earlier authors we have considered. Petty again has an interesting example of the point made here. Against current complaints that the king was bestowing on his own favorites the monies raised by taxation, Petty replies that "what is given to favourites may at the next step or transmigration, come into our own hands or theirs unto whom we wish well, and think do deserve it," *A Treatise of Taxes and Contributions*, p. 33. This is relevant again to the following discussion in the text above of the proposition that the employment of the poor depends on the expenditure or, as Barbon said, the "prodigality" of the rich. As to the question of the circular flow of money and monetary demand and its induced effects, the point is put again by John Cary in 1696. By the circulation of credit, he argues, employment would be provided "for industrious men ... which wheels being set again at work, will by their circular motion carry round many others," *An essay on the coyn and credit of England*, pp. 27-28

26. This is an oblique reference again to the substitution of expenditure on home-produced goods for expenditure on imports. Cf. *infra*.

156   ANALYSIS

Whether he who employs men in buildings *and manufactures* doth not put life in the country, and whether the neighbourhood round him be not observed to thrive? (2/243; our italics.)

Such arguments as these could be multiplied at length in illustration of Berkeley's proposition that the circulation of money, the stimulation of monetary demand, "promoted" industry and exerted magnified effects on the level of economic activity at large. The notion of the importance of the expenditure of the rich for the employment of the poor, was not at this time new in the economic literature. In particular, and in addition to the authors already considered in this connection, the importance of Mandeville's *Fable* . . . has become well known.[27] The issue will be considered again in connection with the positions in the theory of money of David Hume and Cantillon.[28]

Berkeley's argument at this point complained also against the wasteful expenditure of the rich on luxury imports. He saw clearly that a diversion of expenditure from imports to home-produced goods would have the beneficial effects not only of arresting and correcting the persistent tendency to deficit on the balance of payments, but of stimulating, in the manner already referred to, the level of employment and expenditure in the domestic economy.

---

27. Bernard de Mandeville, *The fable of the bees, or private vices, publick benefits* (Oxford, 1714); *vide* F. B. Kaye ed. 1924. A discussion of the work is given in J. M. Keynes, *General Theory* . . . , pp. 359–362. The important concept here at issue, however, was not without its critics in the eighteenth century. Mandeville's *Fable* . . . was attacked by George Blewitt in *An inquiry whether a general practice of virtue tends to the wealth or poverty, benefit or advantage of a people* (London, 1725). Blewitt points out that "the grand maxim on which this treatise (Mandeville's) of luxury is founded is, that consumption breeds riches . . . ," *op. cit.*, p. 50. A fair statement, but he unfortunately refers also to "the absurdity of supposing that frugality should enrich every single family, and empoverish a number of those families joined together in society," *ibid.*, contents page. The fallacy of composition seems always to have been a trap for economic analysts.

28. It is interesting that *Palgrave's Dictionary of Political Economy* (ed. H. Higgs, 1925), pp. 134–135, recognizes with reference to the passages from the *Querist* here under discussion, that "Like Cantillon, Berkeley ascribes paramount importance to the direction which unproductive consumption takes." It goes on to refer to this, however, as a doctrine "which may appear to our generation less certain, or less important, than Berkeley held." As to the fundamental attitude from which so much of Berkeley's monetary analysis proceeded the *Dictionary* says that "it savours now of heterodoxy to ask 'whether the true idea of money as such be not altogether that of a ticket or counter?'"

Whether by these means much of that sustenance and wealth of this nation which now goes to foreigners would not be kept at home and nourish and circulate among our own people? (2/236)

The issue is raised in numerous passages in the *Querist*.

Whether we are not undone by fashions made for other people? And whether it be not madness in a poor nation to imitate a rich one? (1/146; cf. 1/61, 1/120, 1/150, 2/159.)

Whether it be possible for this country to grow rich so long as what is made by domestic industry, is spent in foreign luxury? (3/225)[29]

At the same time as Berkeley recognized the potentially stimulating effects of diverting expenditure from imports to home-produced goods, he sought to achieve this end by the imposition of sumptuary laws on the one hand and a system of import duties on the other. Barbon earlier had considered the question of sumptuary laws and had concluded against their use.[30] His argument was that the use of such devices would, by reducing the country's expenditure abroad, reduce foreign demand for its exports and thus the level of activity in export industries. In Berkeley's case the argument for sumptuary laws (cf. 1/109, 1/152, 3/6) rested on the primary consideration of the diversion of the flow of monetary demand.

A similar comparison of views might be made in the matter of import taxes. Berkeley argued for their use for the same reason as in the foregoing case. Barbon had also argued in favor of import taxation, though for a very different reason.[31] He claimed it to be the case that import prohibitions would not necessarily act as a stimulus to production. Demand for comparable home-produced

---

29. The same attitude to the dissipation of wealth on luxury imports was prominent in the work of other authors of the period under review. Vide Roger Coke, *A Discourse of Trade* (1670), p. 40; Rice Vaughan's *A Discourse of Coin and Coinage* (in J. R. McCulloch's *A Select Collection of Scarce and Valuable Tracts on Money*), p. 36, links the point with the idea of a redundancy of money supply in the same way as Berkeley: ". . . if money were invented for the exchange of things useful to man's life, there is a certain proportion for that use, and there is as well a too much as a too little: Because that the want of money makes the life of the citizens penurious and barbarious, so the overgreat abundance of money makes their lives luxurious and wanton, by reason of the great commutability of all things for money . . ." Cf. also John Pollexfen, *A Discourse of Trade and Coyn*, p. 158, and John Bellers, *Works* (ed. Ruth Fry), p. 131.

30. Vide Barbon, *Discourse of Trade*, p. 36.

31. Vide Barbon, *op. cit.*, p. 37.

goods may be relatively inelastic and satiable. If, on the other hand, import taxes rather than prohibitions were imposed, this may encourage the well-to-do to spend on the importation of commodities the funds which would otherwise have remained idle. The receipt by foreigners of the funds thus expended would in turn facilitate their demand for the country's exports and thus assist again to maintain the level of its industrial activity.

Berkeley's attitude, on the other hand, rested more directly on his concern for a consistently high level of internal activity. His answer to the distressed condition of the woolen trades, which had followed from the English commercial policy of discrimination against Irish woolen exports, was that, along with the maintenance of internal demand in the ways already indicated, the structure of industrial activity should be altered to meet new economic demands. Petty almost a hundred years previously had advanced precisely the same argument with relation to the situation in England. He advocated the "introduction of new trades into England to supply that of cloth which we have almost lost."[32]

V

The determinants of expenditure

It was not only the case that Berkeley envisaged in this manner the cumulative effects of domestic monetary expenditure. He argued, on the policy level, that the authorities could influence the determinants of expenditure in such a way that the aggregate level could be sustained and increased if this should be necessary. The *Querist* submits a general statement of such policy objectives on at least four distinct levels: those of consumers' demand, private investment, public works, and state-controlled industries.

The more important argument in relation to consumers' demand, apart from the question of consumer education and the conditioning of wants, related to the redistribution of wealth and income as a means of maintaining a high level of consumption expenditures.

When the root yieldeth insufficient nourishment; whether men to not top the tree to make the lower branches thrive? (1/164)

Suppose the bulk of our inhabitants had shoes to their feet, cloaths to their backs, and beef in their bellies? Might not such a state be eligible

---

32. Petty, *A Treatise of Taxes and Contributions* (ed. Hull), p. 30.

for the public, even though the squires were condemned to drink ale and cyder? (1/118)

Whether to provide plentifully for the poor, be not feeding the root, the substance whereof will shoot upwards into the branches, and cause the top to flourish? (1/64)

Whether as seed equally scattered produces a goodly harvest, even so an equal distribution of wealth doth not cause a nation to flourish? (2nd ed., Query 214)

The second question of the level of investment activity was relevant again to the reconstruction of industry in such a way as to take account of new demand situations:

Whether it would not be more prudent, to strike out and exert ourselves in permitted branches of trade, than to fold our hands and repine, that we are not allowed the woollen? (1/79)

These suggestions were based firstly on proposals for governmental subsidies for the encouragement of new activities:

Whether there be any thing more profitable than hemp? And whether there should not be great premiums for encouraging our hempen trade? (1/82)

and secondly on the expectation of an adequate market for output and on the profitability of production:

Whether Ireland alone might not raise hemp sufficient for the British Navy . . . ? (1/83)

Whether if all the idle hands in the kingdom were employed on hemp and linen, we might not find sufficient vent for these manufactures? (1/85; cf. 1/92 ff.)

It was proposed in this connection that centers of technical education should be established and maintained at the public expense (1/70–72).

The third element of expenditure over which the authorities had control was the government's own expenditure on public works:

Whether private endeavours without assistance from the public are likely to advance our manufactures and commerce to any great degree? But whether, as bills uttered from a National Bank upon private mortgages, would facilitate the purchases and projects of private men, even so the same bills uttered on the public security alone, may not answer public ends, in promoting new works and manufactures throughout the kingdom? (3/316)

The kind of public works which might be financed was also indicated (2/248). Proposals were advanced for the employment of criminals and beggars on public works programs (1/57, 2/214) and the proposition was advanced that "the public hath . . . a right to employ those who cannot, or who will not, find employment for themselves" (2/216). Similarly:

> Whether temporary servitude would not be the best cure for idleness and beggary? (2/215)

This, of course, is not a proposal for the illiberal economic regimentation which, at first sight, it may appear to intend. Berkeley, the social reformer, here has his eyes on the well-being of the depressed masses of the Irish people, to the alleviation of whose misery the *Querist* was addressed. He argues, therefore,

> Whether it would be a hardship on people destitute of all things, if the public furnished them with necessaries which they should be obliged to earn by their labour? (2/213)
> Whether he who is chained in a jail or dungeon hath not, for the time, lost his liberty? And if so, whether temporary slavery be not already admitted among us? (2/218)

The final way in which the authorities might influence the determinants of expenditure was by a closer financial association between manufacturing activities and the proposed government bank. The suggestion was made of an indirect official participation in industry, though the implications were not worked out any further than is indicated in the following:

> Whether part of the profits of the Bank should not be employed, in erecting manufactures of several kinds, which are not likely to be set on foot and carried on to perfection, without great stock, public encouragement, general regulations, and the concurrence of many hands? (3/226)

The suggestions, furthermore, of latent economies of scale can be seen in this passage.[33] (Cf. 3/238.)

---

33. In connection with Berkeley's general attitude as discussed in the foregoing paragraphs, Joseph Johnston in his brief but excellent review (cf. *op. cit.*) concludes: "Berkeley saw that if the nation was to be set on its feet, the state must play a positive part in the direction of investment, that an adequate supply of money must be provided under public responsibility, and that there must be an increased internal consumption of those things which could be most readily produced, but for which there appeared to be no adequate economic demand," p. 21.

At the same time as Berkeley envisaged in this way the benefits and the methods of maintaining a high level of monetary circulation, he envisaged also a high degree of government management and direction of economic affairs. At this point his "economics of control" closely approaches the work of Sir James Steuart some thirty years later. There was no guarantee, in Berkeley's view, that a necessary and inherent harmony of interests would emerge from the conjunction of individual wants, objectives, and proposals. Berkeley and Steuart had no faith in the "hidden hand" of the later English classicists. It is true that Berkeley recognized the rights of individuals and of individual property (cf. 2/168), but it was at the same time the responsibility of the legislature, he argued, "to guide men's humours and passions" and

to incite their active powers . . . to make their several talents co-operate to the mutual benefit of each other, and the general good of the whole. (2/170)

The highest good for the community as a whole required, in the nature of the case, a co-operation in the design and implementation of economic policy. The *Querist* asks

Whether the particular motions of the members of a state, in opposite directions, will not destroy each other, and lessen the momentum of the whole, but whether they must not conspire to produce a great effect? (3/314)

More specifically, to accomplish the "general aim . . . to employ the people" (2/162), the proposed government control was to be based on a carefully planned system of recording and collecting statistics and economic information:

Whether if a man builds a house, he doth not in the first place provide a plan which governs his work? And shall the public act without an end, a view, a plan? (1/53; cf. 1/137, 1/214.)

Whether commissioners of trade or other proper persons should not be appointed, to draw up plans of our commerce both foreign and domestic, and lay them at the beginning of every session before the parliament? (3/269)

Whether registers of industry should not be kept and the public from time to time acquainted, what new manufactures are introduced, what increases or decreases of old ones? (3/270; cf. 3/271.)

Whether we are appraised, of all the uses that may be made of political arithmetic? (2/199)

The kinship of Berkeley's work at this point with that of Petty in the preceding century is clear.

VI

The closed economy

At several points of the foregoing arguments, the *Querist* has taken account of international trade and payments. It could be argued, indeed, that it erects a clear conception of a liberal system of international economic relations.

> Whether it be not the true interest of both nations, to become one people? (1/96)

But on a careful reading of the *Querist* it is clear that this is not the case. Berkeley reacted, as did John Law, from the metallist assumptions of the earlier mercantilism and argued for other means of increasing the effective supply of money than by straining for a foreign trade surplus. But his reaction took a different form from that of his liberal predecessors. Whereas the earlier writers incorporated their conceptions of international trade as a necessary part of their view of the economic system, with Berkeley this was not the case. His reaction from the earlier "prejudices" led him to apply comparable conceptions of the division of labor and specialization of production to the optimum structure of the internal economy itself.

> Whether anything can be more ridiculous than for the north of Ireland to be jealous of a linen manufacture in the south? (1/101; cf. 3/237–239.)

The source of this notion of an internal rather than an international freedom of trade was twofold. Firstly, it emerged from the sheer exigencies of economic depression which had called forth the *Querist*. And secondly, and analytically more important, Berkeley saw that the problem confronting the depressed and underemployed and therefore expansible economy was primarily a monetary one; and seeing this, he built an analysis of the nature and effects of monetary circulation upon the conception of the purely "local value" which certain kinds of money might acquire, quite apart from the use of traditional metallic monies. While such money as Berkeley proposed would not have a world-wide currency it was not in logic necessary that it should. The effect, analytically, of this theoretical conception, was that it made possible in a clearer form than had yet been achieved an emphasis on the structure of the circular monetary system. It emphasized the purely endogenous nature of the stimuli to economic expansion which were inherent in the structure of the system, given an initial stimulus to economic revival. It was not simply the case in the earlier mercantilist sense that, as Sir Dudley North had said, "Wealth . . . cannot be maintained without foreign trade." Wealth, economic prosperity, was realizable by an appropriately administered monetary reflation and expansion in the domestic economy. Subject to the administration and the direction of economic policy which Berkeley proposed, the process of expansion in the domestic economy was cumulative and self-reinforcing in character. He had asked

> Whether paper doth not by its stamp and signature acquire a local value and become as precious and scarce as gold? (3/87)

And furthermore,

> Whether a nation *within itself* might not have real wealth, sufficient to give its inhabitants power and distinction, without the help of gold and silver? (1/120; our italics.)

The precise manner in which Berkeley understood a change in the level and rate of monetary circulation to exert its beneficial effects has already been examined. The context of his argument gives a logical priority to the theory of internal economic activity. The objective is clear:

> Whether one may not be allowed to conceive and suppose a society, or nation of human creatures, clad in woollen cloaths and stuffs, eating good bread, beef, and mutton, poultry and fish in great plenty . . . inhabiting decent houses, depending on no foreign imports either for food or raiment . . . (1/129)

In conjunction with this objective and by way of reaction against the errors of the metallist assumptions, he asks further

> Whether the benefits of a domestic commerce are sufficiently understood, and attended to, and whether the cause hereof be not the prejudiced and narrow way of thinking about gold and silver? (3/266)

It was the case, of course, that Berkeley rested his analysis at this point on what he understood as the virtual self-sufficiency of the country in industrial resources and equipment (cf. 3/268, 1/114). It followed that the economic administration should "enquire how

164   ANALYSIS

far we may do without foreign trade, and what would follow on such a supposition" (1/135). And, as is said in the same context:

Whether, if there was a wall of brass a thousand cubits high around this kingdom, our natives might not nevertheless live cleanly and comfortably, till the land, and reap the fruits of it? (1/140)

Or to put the same conception on a higher theoretical plane:

Whether the exigencies of nature are not to be answered by industry on our own soil. And how far the conveniences and comforts of life may be procured, by a domestic commerce between the several parts of this kingdom? (1/116)

Foreign trade was placed in its correct logical order in the following way:

Whether the dirt, and famine, and nakedness of the bulk of our people, might not be remedied *even although we had no foreign trade?* And whether this should not be our *first* care, and whether, if this were once provided for, the conveniences of the rich would not soon follow? (1/112; our italics.)

The *Querist* thereby develops theoretically the manner in which a satisfactory level of activity and employment might be realized "even though we had no foreign trade" and examines secondly the "conveniences" which foreign trade might produce.

It was not the case, of course, that Berkeley overlooked entirely the benefits which adhered in international trade and exchanges (cf. 1/254, 1/124). But the important thing is that he did not incorporate his propositions in respect of foreign trade into his general activity analysis in any logically indispensable sense in the same way as earlier authors had done. His activity analysis was the analysis of an autonomous and self-determining economic system.

VII

Monetary institutions

The contributions which the *Querist* made in relation to the description and the functioning of monetary institutions are found in its detailed comments on the need for a National Bank and on the methods of its operation. We need not stay with the detail of Berkeley's proposals, as their theoretical significance has already been adequately emphasized. His interest in banking followed logically from all that has been said regarding his understanding of money and the significance of its circulation. The banking proposals themselves rested on the similar suggestions of John Law, though care was to be taken in the case of Berkeley's bank to avoid the errors into which Law's practice, as opposed to his theory, had fallen.

The proposed bank was to be a National Bank, not controlled by private shareholders, and was to be subject to minute regulations regarding cash holdings, management, audit of accounts, and note-issuing prerogatives. Berkeley significantly asks

> Whether the abuse of banks and paper money is a just objection against the use thereof? And whether such abuse might not easily be prevented? (1/199; cf. 1/225.)

On the contrary, there were positive advantages to be realized from the properly supervised conduct of banking operations. The actual proposals were very similar to those of Law in that the issue of notes was to be made on the security of mortgages of land.

> Whether the notes ought not to be issued in lots, to be lent at interest on mortgaged lands, the whole number of lots to be divided among the four provinces, rateable to the number of hearths in each? (1/233)

But safeguards against overissue were also proposed:

> Whether the same rule should not always be observed, of lending out money or notes, only to half the value of the mortgaged land? And whether this value should not always be rated at the same number of years purchase as at first? (1/239)
>
> Whether care should not be taken to prevent an undue rise of the value of land? (1/240)
>
> Whether the increase of industry and people will not of course raise the value of land? And whether this rise may not be sufficient? (1/241)
>
> Whether this may not be prevented by the gradual and slow issuing of notes, and by frequent sales of lands? (1/243)

It was noted in our earlier discussion of John Law's similar proposals that he had failed to see that the valuation of the security against which bank notes were to be issued would not remain independent of the issue of the notes themselves. This very point is here recognized in Berkeley, and a criterion by which to judge the adequacy of the note issue is proposed. It involves essentially a constancy of the valuation of land securities, apart from any appreciation in their relative economic values which might follow from the induced expansion of trade and economic activity. Admittedly, Berkeley leaves his criterion open to problems of definition and differentiation of these causes of change in value, but at the same time an important theoretical point had been recognized. Berkeley's scheme thus contained two criteria against which to judge the adequacy of the volume of money circulating in the economy. The first, which will be noted again in the following section, was a constant level of commodity prices, and the second is now advanced as a constancy in the valuation of asset securities.

Yet Berkeley went even farther in these proposals and suggested that bank notes might be issued on other adequate security in addition to that of land:

> Whether paper money or notes may not be issued from the National Bank, on the security of hemp, of linen, or other manufactures whereby the poor might be supported in their industry? (1/267; cf. Steuart in Chapter 12 *infra*.)

Berkeley did not, however, discuss as Law had done the question of the reflux of bank money and the cancellation of bank loans, though he did remark that one of the reasons for the failure of the comparable schemes in New England was "their not insisting upon repayment of loans at the time pre-fixed" (1/212). Berkeley did not need, however, to discuss in detail such a micro-economic proposition, for he had already established his twofold macro-economic criteria of the constancy of commodity prices on the one hand and of asset values on the other. So long as these criteria were satisfied, bank money could be issued on any genuine trade security, given only the adequacy of its security value.

VIII

The value of money

Berkeley's propositions relative to commodity prices and the theory of the value of money move on two distinct levels. In the first place, he describes the nature of the static money-price equation in much the same form as earlier writers had presented it. In the second place, the *Querist* contains the beginnings of an income theory of prices in the sense in which that shows the size of the money element in the quantity equation to depend on the monetary requirements of the total demand in the economy. In Berkeley, in other words, there emerges a dependence of the effective money supply on the level of aggregate demand, rather than, as hitherto, simply a dependence of aggregate demand on the total available supply of money. This depends on Berkeley's refined conception of the nature and function of money, and on his understanding of the role and potentialities of banking and the issue of paper money. The conception is not unrelated to his logical preoccupation with the "closed economy" argument which we have noted already.

One of the clearest statements of the static money-price equation is as follows:

> Whether, *ceteris paribus*, it be not true that the price of things increase, as the quantity of money increaseth, and are diminished as that is diminished? And whether, by the quantity of money, is not to be understood the amount of the denominations, all contracts being nominal for pounds, shillings and pence, and not for weights of gold and silver? (3/157)

This is in the Lockeian static tradition and makes explicit the same *ceteris paribus* assumption. The theory of market prices had also been presented at the beginning of the *Querist:*

> Whether the value or price of things, be not a compounded proportion, directly as the demand, and reciprocally as the plenty? (1/24)

The context in which this passage occurs makes it quite clear that demand is understood to be demand expressed in money terms.

The second proposition, that of the dependence of the supply of money on the total money requirements of industry and trade, had been suggested very early in the *Querist:* ". . . while industry begot credit, and credit moved to industry" (1/48). Then subsequently, in the context of a discussion of the issue of bank money:

> Whether by degrees, as business and people multiplied, more bills may not be issued, without augmenting the captital stock (of the bank) provided still, that they are issued on good security; which further issuing of new bills, not to be without consent of Parliament? (1/255)

In addition to this safeguard of parliamentary supervision, Berkeley laid down clearly defined theoretical maxims which were intended to serve as guides in actual practice:

> Whether there should not be a constant care to keep the bills at par? (2/123)

168 ANALYSIS

Whether therefore bank bills should at any time be multiplied, but as trade and business were also multiplied? (1/124; cf. 1/245.)

The level of trade activity and the resulting monetary requirements here constitute the independent variable and the volume of money supply the dependent variable in the argument.

Whether commodities of all kinds do not naturally flow where there is the greatest demand? Whether the greatest demand for a thing be not where it is of most use? Whether money, like other things hath not its proper use? Whether this use be not to circulate? Whether therefore there must not of course be money where there is a circulation of industry; and where there is no industry, whether there will be a demand for money? (3/288)

Recognizing the fact of this dependence, and having made his theoretical assumption of a constant price level, Berkeley was able to concentrate logically on the operative significance of increasing the money supply in this way. So much so that he drew an explicit distinction between the effects of an increase in money for genuine trade purposes, and an increase in the sense of an overissue in relation to trade requirements in the manner of John Law's grandiose schemes. It was not the circulation of a large supply of money as such which was troublesome, but the overissue as compared with the real requirements of trade and industry.

Whether, therefore, the circulating paper, in the late ruinous scheme of France and England, was the true evil, and not rather the circulating thereof without industry. And whether the Bank of Amsterdam, where industry had been for so many years subsisted, and circulated by transfers on paper doth not clearly decide this point? (1/283; cf. 1/262, 1/274.)

IX

The rate of interest

In the earlier mercantilist system of thought the preoccupation with a favorable balance of trade and payments found something of an indirect justification in the theory of interest with which it was associated. For it was by amassing a large supply of the monetary metals by means of a favorable balance of payments that low effective rates of interest would be produced, with consequent advantages for trade activity. Berkeley did not develop a theory of interest in any systematic way, but he did turn this mercantilist

GEORGE BERKELEY

argument against those who were objecting to his scheme for the establishment of a National Bank:

> If it be objected that a National Bank must lower interest, and therefore hurt the monied man, whether the same objection would not hold as strong against multiplying our gold and silver? (3/82)

Having escaped from the existing "prejudices" regarding gold and silver, Berkeley could afford in this way to undermine the exclusiveness at this point of earlier mercantilist thought. He himself had introduced a broader conception of a satisfactorily functioning monetary system.

In so far as Berkeley did conceive of the operative significance of a market rate of interest, however, his conception appears to have been similar to that of Locke. The latter had advanced a two-sector analysis in which the money supply was activated simultaneously in both of what we referred to as the loan and the goods markets. The primary reason for borrowing, Locke had pointed out, was the need to finance trade activity. The demand side of the loan market was made up almost exclusively of the needs of trade for working capital. Now in his very brief mention of interest Berkeley takes a similar position:

> Whether money though lent out only to the rich, would not circulate among the poor? And whether any man borrows but with an intent to circulate? (3/94)

But there is no fuller development in the *Querist* of the significance of interest. Perhaps the explanation of this omission lay partly in the fact of Berkeley's proposals for government monetary control and direction, implying, in the circumstances in which the *Querist* was produced, a greatly increased money supply and a lowered rate of interest. But there are obviously problems here which are not worked out. A more adequate development of the theory of interest is to be found in the authors whose work is considered in Section C of this Part, below.

GEORGE BERKELEY: PRECURSOR OF KEYNES OR MORAL ECONOMIST ON UNDERDEVELOPMENT?[1]

IAN D. S. WARD
University of California, Berkeley

Whether there be any Country in Christendom more capable of Improvement than Ireland?—*The Querist.*

As with Richard Cantillon prior to his rediscovery by Stanley Jevons in 1880, George Berkeley (1685–1750), bishop of Cloyne, has, with the passage of time, become a relatively forgotten personality in the annals of the history of economic thought. Although primarily a philosopher, "the successor of Locke and the predecessor of Hume," he was a man of wide intellectual and practical interests, one of which was political economy.[2] However, his interest in this field was not an isolated one in the sense of being unrelated to his fundamental teachings; in fact, his three major works of political economy[3] can only be fully appreciated if perceived as a synthesis of moral, philosophical, and economic doctrines in the form of practical policies directed toward the alleviation of the depressed conditions of contemporary Ireland and, to a lesser degree, England.

Berkeley's moral philosophy[4] is essentially theological utilitarianism. Arising out of a discussion of the nature of matter, he considered that the material universe consists of nothing but a series of free actions produced by the best and wisest Agent. Moral rules for society are deduced from the intention of the Creator and are directed toward promoting the welfare of all men at all times. "Nothing is a law merely because it conduceth to the public good, but because it is desired by the will of God."[5]

Although there is no necessary relationship between a man's philosophical and economic ideas,[6] there is no inconsistency between Berkeley's moral philosophy and his *ad hoc* economic views. In fact, the latter may be considered as an appendage of the former.

I shall note below that the moral

---

[1] I should like to express my appreciation to Professor J. M. Letiche for his suggestions and encouragement.

[2] J. O. Wisdom, "An Outline of Berkeley's Life," *British Journal for the Philosophy of Science*, IV, No. 13 (1953), 82, gives a good account of the span of his intellectual perception which he sums up thus: "So died scholar, psychologist, philosopher, man of letters, courtier, traveller, educational missionary, Christian apologist, bishop, mathematician, economist and amateur doctor."

[3] George Berkeley, "*The Querist*" (*1735–37*) ("A Reprint of Economic Tracts," ed. J. H. Hollander [Baltimore: Johns Hopkins Press, 1910]); George Berkeley, *An Essay towards Preventing the Ruin of Great Britain*, in *The Works of George Berkeley, Bishop of Cloyne*, ed. A. A. Luce and T. E. Jessop (9 vols.; London: Thomas Nelson & Sons, 1949–57), VI, 61–85; George Berkeley, *A Word to the Wise—an Exhortation to the Roman Catholic Clergy of Ireland*, ibid., pp. 233–49.

[4] *The Essay towards a New Theory of Vision* (1709), ibid., I, 171–239; *A Treatise concerning the Principles of Human Knowledge* (1710), ibid., II, 25–113; *The Three Dialogues* (1713), ibid., pp. 171–263; *The Theory of Vision or Visual Language, Vindicated and Explained* (1733), ibid., I, 251–79.

[5] George Berkeley, *Passive Obedience*, ibid., VI, 34.

[6] For an interesting, though perhaps extreme, treatment of this issue see J. A. Schumpeter, *History of Economic Analysis* (New York: Oxford University Press, 1955), pp. 28–32.

31

philosophical foundations of Berkeley's views may have led to his rejection of laissez faire, on the one hand, and his failure to develop a reasonably integrated body of economic analysis, on the other.

II

Following the publication of Keynes's *General Theory* in 1936, with its eulogy of the basic tenets of mercantilism, a reaction has set in against the former perfunctory treatment accorded to Berkeley. Johnston,[7] Wisdom,[8] Pauling,[9] and, more recently, Hutchison[10] have all seen in his works many anticipations of modern Keynesian economic doctrine, particularly in relation to the necessity of having a high level of government and private expenditure in order to reduce the deflationary gap existing in early eighteenth-century Ireland.

Hutchison's analysis of Berkeley is not an isolated work; it is part of a more general thesis, developed in his *Review of Economic Doctrines*, in which he stresses the importance of pre-classical political economists,[11] who, prior to their being "driven completely underground by Adam Smith's unconditional eulogy of the beneficence of savings ... and by James Mill's dogmatic rigmarole about the impossibility of general overproduction,"[12] had posed many of the problems and remedies of present Keynesian economics. Berkeley is a very prominent representative of this group in that his "main assumptions, analysis and programme ... are very closely similar in essential outline to those which Keynes argued for in the inter-war years; that is much more centralised monetary management, public works, and tariffs if necessary to protect the balance of payments, all with the objective of raising the level of employment and productivity above its depressed level."[13] To what degree is this a precise and accurate summing-up of Berkeley's main contributions to the development of economic thought?

III

Perhaps we can best seek a solution to this problem by considering whether or not Berkeley was aware of an unemployment problem per se or, more explicitly, whether he considered that the distressed nature of Ireland, at this time, could be attributed to a deficiency in the level of effective demand.

Evidence to support a positive reply to these questions is advanced by Hutchison in terms of Berkeley's acknowledgment, on pure economic grounds, of Mandeville's assertion of the unconditional beneficence of luxury. Drawing a distinction between Berkeley and Frances Hutcheson, who, he considered, was opposed to luxury on both economic and moral grounds, Hutchison develops the

---

[7] Joseph Johnston, "Locke, Berkeley and Hume as Monetary Theorists," *Hermathena*, No. LVI (1940), pp. 77–83. He speaks of Berkeley thus: "His Keynesian approach is striking."

[8] J. O. Wisdom, *The Unconscious Origin of Berkeley's Philosophy* (London: Hogarth Press, 1953): "His proposals are notable for their Keynesian approach."

[9] N. J. Pauling, "The Employment Problem in Preclassical English Economic Thought," *Economic Record*, XXVII, No. 52 (1951), 52–65.

[10] T. W. Hutchison, "Berkeley's Querist and Its Place in the Economic Thought of the 18th Century," *British Journal for the Philosophy of Science*, IV, No. 13 (1953), 52–77. Emphasis will be concentrated on this treatment, as it is the only scholarly and comprehensive analysis of Berkeley's economic analysis and policies.

[11] The main representatives of this notable band of "underconsumptionists" are Petty, Barbon, Berkeley, North, Mandeville, Steuart, Lauderdale, Boisguillebert, Quesnay, and Melon.

[12] T. W. Hutchison, *A Review of Economic Doctrines, 1870–1929* (Oxford: Clarendon Press, 1953), p. 348.

[13] Hutchison, "Berkeley's Querist and Its Place in the Economic Thought of the 18th Century," *op. cit.*, p. 74.

general thesis that "at a vital juncture in the second quarter of the eighteenth, Hutcheson pointed to the highroad of nineteenth century orthodoxy, while Berkeley, like most of his contemporaries and predecessors, kept along the low road, which, for almost a century and a half from Adam Smith to Keynes, was in Britain followed only by a minority of unorthodox 'cranks.' "[14] Thus to Hutchison, the Hutcheson-Smithian analysis of saving and investment, that saving is investment,[15] later to be extended and developed by James Mill and J. B. Say into "a law of markets," was markedly in contrast to the Berkeleyan attitude that "the level of aggregate effective demand could (not) be left to settle itself" and, therefore, "that money not spent in one way would (not) inevitably get spent in another." As a corollary "he would have rejected the economic analysis of saving and investment (or that saving is investment) on which Smith based his eulogy of parsimony."[16] This is essentially the crux of his argument.

The crucial point, and weakness, of this analysis concerns Berkeley's attitude toward luxury spending. Hutchison's contention that it is one of economic, as opposed to moral, support appears unfounded.[17] In both the *Essay*

and *The Querist* Berkeley never tires from pointing out that "a corrupt luxurious people must of themselves fall into slavery."[18] In his condemnation of the South Sea Bubble in England, Berkeley argued that

Men are apt to measure national profits by riches. It would be righter to measure it by the use that is made of them. Where they promote an honest commerce among men, and are motives to industry and virtue, they are, without doubt, of great advantage: but where they are made (as too often happens) an instrument to luxury, they enervate and dispirit the bravest people.... Frugality is the nourishment and strength of bodies politic. It is that by which they grow and subsist, until they are corrupted by luxury, the natural cause of their decay and ruin.[19]

It would, therefore, be extremely difficult to attribute to Berkeley the view that Ireland's economic difficulties were the consequence of a deficiency of expenditure by the luxurious class or that an increase in such expenditure would bring forth an increased rate of development. On the contrary, what was needed was an encouragement of industry and thrift.

Hutchison, hoping to expose the existence of a complete break between Berkeley and the classical economists, has failed to perceive the harmony in the approach adopted by Berkeley, Smith, and Hutcheson which sought not to consider the problem of whether or not saving is, or is not, investment, and thereby whether or not a deficiency of demand could arise, but more to analyze the relationship between productive and unproductive consumption (labor)—that

---

[14] *Ibid.*, p. 71.

[15] Hutchison contends that Frances Hutcheson's proposition that luxury expenditure is wasteful, that is, "that income not spent in one way will be spent in another," automatically led to the conclusion that there can be no deficiency of demand, and therefore that saving is investment (*ibid.*).

[16] *Ibid.*, p. 70.

[17] More recently, Bonamy Dobreté in an introductory note to Bernard Mandeville's *A Letter to Dion* (Liverpool: University Press of Liverpool, 1954) interprets Berkeley as essentially agreeing with Mandeville's view that "if men didn't spend their money on pleasure, there would be little wealth in the nation." This interpretation is essentially in agreement with that of Hutchison.

[18] *An Essay towards Preventing the Ruin of Great Britain*, in *Works*, I, 77.

[19] *Ibid.*, pp. 74–75. *The Querist* (II, 204) asks further: "What Folly it is to build fine Houses, or establish lucerative Posts and large Incomes, under the notion of providing for the Poor?" See also *Queries*, Vol. I, Nos. 63–64; Vol. II, No. 205; and Vol. III, No. 186.

is, not the relationship between savings and investment but of consumption and investment[20]. Luxury expenditure was to be deprecated as it, like all unproductive consumption (labor), failed to add to the annual wealth of a country and, as such, was decidedly inferior to industry and thrift which took the form of productive consumption (labor).[21]

We now appear to be in a dilemma. If Berkeley was not concerned with the problem of bridging the gap in the level of effective demand, then how can his countless references to the "problem of unemployment" be explained? The answer lies simply in the fact that it was not so much a problem of involuntary unemployment as voluntary unemployment that he was so concerned to alleviate. Although no clear direction is given in *The Querist* as to which of the two problems he was concerned with, except insofar as he stresses the existence of idleness,[22] any doubt is quickly swept aside in a later work, *A Word to the Wise*. Addressing the Roman Catholic clergy, upon whose shoulders, he maintains, the solution to the depressed state of Ireland largely rests, he despairs at the sight of "poverty in the midst of plenty," particularly when the blame rests upon the idleness of the people themselves. "Alas!, how many incentives to industry offer themselves in this island crying aloud to the inhabitants for work. ... Was there but the will to work, there are not wanting in this island either opportunities or encouragements."[23] It appears, therefore, that Berkeley's thoughts were directed against voluntary unemployment which he attributed to the low moral standards of the Irish people, inadequate remuneration for industry, and the widespread prevalence of luxury. This does not mean that he was unaware of the existence of any involuntary unem-

---

[20] It is this interest in productive as against unproductive consumption (labor) which explains the Query cited by Hutchison to defend his theory—that of "Whether the Industry of the lower part of our People doth not depend on the Expense of the Upper?" Berkeley is concerned here not with what should be but more with what he actually sees about him in contemporary Ireland. His thoughts on the matter can be best gauged from the quotation from *The Essay* cited above (No. 15).

This question of which economists perceived "the balance between saving and investment" has been a hotly debated one since Keynes, in his *Essays in Biography*, attributed recognition to Robert Malthus for having posed "the whole problem of the balance between saving and investment." G. S. L. Tucker (*Economic Record*, XXVII, No. 51 [1950], 331–32) and, later, Ronald Meek (*Review of Economic Studies*, XVII [1950–51], 156) have advanced a more accurate interpretation of the facts available in considering that "although Malthus (and other earlier under-consumptionists) stressed the importance of effective demand, he never seems to have appreciated the significance of the distinction between decisions to save and decisions to invest" (Tucker, *op. cit.*, p. 332). This is, as we have already seen, even more true of Berkeley.

[21] "Whether that small Town of Bearn, with its scanty, barren Territory, in a mountainous Corner, without Sea-ports, without Manufactures, without Mines, be not rich by mere Dint of Frugality?" (*The Querist*, Vol. III, No. 5.) Classical political economy was to have to wait another thirty years, after Smith's *Wealth of Nations*, before the complete economic justification for productive, as against unproductive consumption (labor), was to be developed by J. B. Say, in 1803, and later by James Mill (1808), referred to by Ricardo as "Mr. Mills Idea."

[22] *The Querist*, Vol. I, No. 44.

[23] *A Word to the Wise*, in *Works*, VI, 235–44. Stressing his despair of a people who would allow their country to be so distressed and still prefer idleness and beggary, Berkeley points to the existence of "lusty vagabonds strolling about the country, and begging without pretence to buy. Ask them why they do not labour to earn their livelihood and they will tell you, they want employment; offer to employ them, and they shall refuse your offer; or, if you get them to work one day, you may be sure not to see them the next" (*ibid.*, p. 244). Or in the form of a story-tale point out to the "Wise" the laziness of the Irish as follows: "Hark an Irishman in the field; if a coach or Horsemen go by, he is sure to suspend his labour and stand staring until they are out of sight. A neighbour of mine made it his remark in a journey from London to Bristol, that all the labourers of whom he inquired the road constantly answered without looking up, or interrupting their work, except one who stood staring and leaning on his spade, and him he found to be an Irishman."

ployment, although the tendency would be to consider that he was not so concerned.[24]

Thus, despite the persuasiveness of Hutchison's arguments, the view that Berkeley was, in some sense, a precursor of Keynes appears unfounded; it would indeed be strange if we expected him to be so, since the problems confronting them were of an entirely different nature. Bishop Berkeley directed his efforts to eighteenth-century Ireland, an underdeveloped area, in which the overriding problem was the "vicious circle of poverty."[25] Keynes, on the other hand, developed a theory directed to a short-run dislocation in the functioning of an industrialized and complex society. It would appear, therefore, that Hutchison, who wanted to gain recognition for Berkeley's insight into the practical problems of his day, has been guilty of "bending the rod too far the other way" in seeking to find in this Irish philosopher's thoughts the seeds of current economic doctrine.

IV

In interpreting Berkeley's proposals, I have attempted to give them some degree of continuity. Berkeley's writings were scattered in time and unsystematic in presentation, and this has perhaps contributed to a failure by some historians of economic thought correctly to understand his contributions.[26] However there is a sense of unity which provides the key to an understanding of his thoughts, that is, the application of philosophical, moral, and economic principles to the problems of an underdeveloped economy.

The level of economic development and the living conditions of the people were both depressed in eighteenth-century Ireland. "The house of an Irish peasant is the core of poverty; within, you see a pot and a little straw; without, a heap of children tumbling on the dunghill."[27] The basic problem was to raise the Irish economy out of "the circle of poverty," in which poverty bred idleness and idleness poverty. However, to Berkeley, it was a case of starving "in the midst of plenty,"[28] as Ireland was not lacking natural resources[29] which, if developed by an industrious people, would be sufficient to maintain a high living standard.

Defining wealth in terms of the "skill and industry of human labour ... which makes even Land and Silver to be Wealth,"[30] Berkeley emphasized that, in

---

[24] If he were aware of involuntary unemployment at all, it would almost certainly have been only sectional, since the domestic system was still predominant at this time. Even so, the absence of what we call a work force would make it extremely difficult to assess whether the unemployment was widespread or not.

[25] The key problems of such areas cannot be solved by monetary measures alone, such as increasing effective demand; primarily they are "real" problems, related to education, improvement in productivity and technique, increased investment and the quantity of capital, enlarged markets, and generally more advanced economic organization.

[26] The basic feature of Berkeley's philosophy is the fundamental role played by the Deity. It was not so much the inherent nature of man but the relationship of men to the Supreme Being which was important in determining the welfare of society. Hence Berkeley has no set of premises based upon individual choice on which to develop a system of economic analysis. His *ad hoc* economic views appear, therefore, only as they fit into his general philosophical framework. See also n. 51.

[27] *A Word to the Wise*, in *Works*, VI, 236.

[28] *The Querist*, Vol. III, No. 101.

[29] "Whether we are not as far before other Nations with respect to natural Advantages, as we are behind them with respect to Arts and Industry" (*ibid.*, Vol. II, No. 2).

[30] *Ibid.*, Vol. I, No. 40; see also *ibid.*, Vol. III, No. 273. As a criticism of earlier, and to a lesser extent contemporary, doctrine, Berkeley asks "Whether there can be a Greater Mistake in Politics than to measure the wealth of a nation by its Gold and Silver?" (*ibid.*, No. 282).

order to improve the conditions of the Irish economy, particular attention must be given to both the quantity and the quality of the labor force.[31] To increase the quantity of labor, he advocated such measures as the encouragement of immigration and the discouragement of emigration;[32] the setting of criminals, as well as women and children, to work; and, in an attempt to raise the birth rate, the granting of "some reward or privilege to those who have a certain number of children."[33] To improve labor productivity, Berkeley advocated not only a transference of labor from unproductive to productive employment but also increased remuneration and improved conditions of work designed to raise both the initiative and the physical productivity of labor.[34]

Given an abundance of natural resources, together with a large supply of productive labor, the wealth of an economy could be greatly increased through the application of the principles of specialization and exchange. Anticipating Adam Smith, Berkeley demonstrated a clear understanding of the significance of the division of labor. In *The Querist* he asks "Whether if each of these towns were addicted to some peculiar Manufacture, we should not find that the employing many Hands together on the Same Work was the Way to perfect our workmen?"[35] Further, one is able to find among his scattered thoughts an understanding of the advantages of territorial specialization. This in turn leads him to examine the importance of domestic trade and, as a corollary, the need for maintaining a network of good roads and navigable rivers.

Although Berkeley analyzes the problems of an underdeveloped area essentially within the framework of the domestic economy, he did not ignore completely issues relating to the external sector. However, in reading Berkeley, one has the feeling that the particular problems confronting Ireland during this period could be overcome without undue reliance upon international trade. In part, this attitude stems from Ireland's lack of self-determination in this sector; in part, it is a reaction to mercantilist writings.[36]

Whatever the reason, international trade policies play only a relatively minor role in Berkeley's development program. Perhaps, in view of this, it is not surprising that his analysis and understanding of this area of political economy is somewhat undeveloped and, at times, even contradictory. In places he appears to grasp the concept of international

---

[31] *Ibid.*, Vol. II, No. 178.

[32] "Whether the Industry of our People employed in foreign Land, while our own are left uncultivated, be not a great Loss to the Country?" "Whether it would not be much better for us, if, instead of sending our Men Abroad, we could draw Men from the Neighbouring Counties to cultivate our own?" (*ibid.*, Vol. III, Nos. 246, 247).

[33] *An Essay...*, in *Works*, VI, 72.

[34] "Whether hearty Food and warm Clothing would not enable and encourage the lower sort to Labour?" (*The Querist*, Vol. II, No. 179). See also *ibid.*, Vol. I, No. 20. In this way Berkeley hoped to reduce the prevalence of idleness or voluntary unemployment, which he considered to be one of the underlying problems at that time: he asks "Whether if human labour be the true source of Wealth, it doth not follow that Idleness should be discourag'd in a wise State" (*ibid.*, No. 44).

[35] *Ibid.*, Vol. II, No. 249.

[36] "Whether the Dirt, the Famine, and Nakedness of the bulk of the People, might not be remedied even though we had no Foreign Trade?" (*ibid.*, Vol. I, No. 112). See also *ibid.*, Vol. II, No. 257. Berkeley shows that he is keenly aware of the relative importance attributed to foreign rather than domestic trade when he asks "Whether the Benefits of Domestic Commerce are sufficiently understood, and attended to, and whether the Cause hereof be not the prejudiced and narrow Way of thinking about Gold and Silver?" (*ibid.*, Vol. III, No. 266).

specialization and absolute advantage;[37] nevertheless, he gives little evidence of subscribing to a free-trade doctrine (as, for example, was advocated earlier by North[38] and by Gervaise[39]). On the one hand, he considers, in certain queries, the gain to Ireland from taking advantage of its cheap labor by competing with the American colonies for the English market, while at other times he advocates a policy prohibiting the export of raw materials and food which he considers should be utilized domestically, thereby increasing employment. On this basis only finished products were to be exported. However, no clear-cut statement emerges, partly because his efforts were primarily directed toward the immediate ways in which the Irish economy had been adversely affected by foreign trade: first, the existence of excessive imports of luxury goods[40] and, second, restrictions upon Irish trade imposed by the English parliament, particularly with respect to the wool trade. However, one does find a complete rejection of policies directed toward increasing the supply of gold and silver through a favorable trade balance and of the use of foreign trade as a weapon of power politics. Unfortunately, in rejecting mercantilist ends, Berkeley seems, at the same time, to have reacted against the significant role attributed to foreign trade by earlier writers. And, in view of this, he appears to have underestimated the contribution which international trade, based upon the doctrine of absolute advantage, could make to the economic development of Ireland.

There seems little doubt that, during the period in which Berkeley resided at his bishopric of Cloyne, the Irish economy was subject to deflationary pressure which reflected a severe shortage in the quantity of money. Such a situation provided a check to the extension of specialization and exchange, for it was money which "stirreth up industry, enabling Men mutually to participate the fruits of each other's labour."[41] Demonstrating a sound understanding of the quantity theory, Berkeley advocated an increase in the quantity of money in an attempt not only to check the deflationary trend in the economy, and thereby stimulate industry, but also to lower the rate of interest. Lower interest, by increasing the value of land, would check the general decline in the pastoral and agricultural industries. Finally, in an attempt to increase the velocity of circulation, he favored the creating of units of currency of lower denominations.[42]

[37] "And whether there should not be great Premiums for encouraging our Hempen Trade; what Advantages may not Great Britain make of a Country where Land and Labour are so cheap?" "Whether Ireland alone might not raise Hemp sufficient for the British Navy? and whether it would not be vain to expect this from the British Colonies in America, where hands are so scarce and Labour so Excessively Dear?" (*ibid.*, Vol. I, Nos. 82, 83).

[38] Sir Dudley North, *Discourses upon Trade* (1691), ed. J. H. Hollander (Baltimore, 1934).

[39] Isaac Gervaise, *The System or Theorpy of the Trade of the World* ("A Reprint of Economic Tracts," ed. G. Heberton Evans [Baltimore: Johns Hopkins Press, 1954]).

[40] The Querist asks "Whether it be possible for this Country to grow rich, so long as what is made by Domestic Industry, is spent in foreign luxury?" (*The Querist*, Vol. III, No. 225). It is interesting to note "a letter from a Gentleman in Ireland" quoted in *The Gentlemens Magazine*, VII (1737), 48: ". . . that near £600,000 expended yearly for these unnecessary imports, does not shew a right management in the inhabitants of Ireland, who affect to style themselves poor, yet spend £30,700 a year for foreign silks. . . ."

[41] *The Querist*, Vol. I, No. 5.

[42] "Whether therefore less Money swiftly circulating be not, in effect, equivalent to more Money slowly circulating?" (*ibid.*, No. 22). Drawing an analogy with the circulation of blood, discovered by William Harvey in 1624, Berkeley asks "Whether the Natural Body can be in a State of Health and Vigour, without a due circulation in Extremeties,

The shortage of money was not to be met by an increase in the quantity of gold and silver but through the circulation of paper money, which "doth ... by its Stamp and Signature acquire a local Value, and become as Precious and Scarce as Gold?"[43] The view that money had no intrinsically determined value but was more of a ticket or counter serving the necessary function of an intermediary was an important antidote to much current mercantilist thought. Commenting upon the role of money in the process of exchange, Berkeley asks "Whether Power to command the Industry of others be not real Wealth? And whether Money be not in Truth, Ticket or Tokens for conveying and recording such Power, and whether it be of great Consequence what Materials the Tickets are made of?"[44] In order to facilitate an expansion in the quantity of money and provide an adequately controlled monetary system, he advocated the establishment of a publicly owned national bank which would "at once secure our Properties, put an End to Usury, facilitate Commerce, supply the want of Coin, and produce ready Payments in all Parts of the Kingdom?"[45] It was to be, to a large extent, through this institution that public policy was to be implemented.

When interpreting Berkeley's contributions within the context of a program directed toward the problems of an underdeveloped economy, one must not lose sight of his underlying message, which was essentially of a philosophical and moral nature, although with economic implications. The basic problem which faced both the Irish and the English people lay in their attitudes toward the moral values which lay at the foundation of society.[46] For example, it was the immoral speculation indulged in by the "idolatrous" English, in 1721, that culminated in the South Sea Bubble. Similarly, it was a lack of sound moral values that was responsible in large measure for the idleness and lack of initiative of the Irish people. From this foundation he argues that a people must sacrifice in order to attain a higher standard of living.[47] Idleness and luxury must be replaced by industry and thrift. Through the teaching of the clergy, increased education, and, finally, beautification of the environment,[48] supported by a policy of state public works,[49] Berkeley hoped

---

even in the Fingers and Toes? and whether the Political Body, any more than the Natural, can thrive without a proportionable Circulation through the minutest and most inconsiderable Parts thereof?" (*ibid.*, Vol. III, No. 190).

[42] "Whether the Prejudices about Gold and Silver are not strong, but whether they are not still Prejudices?" (*ibid.*, No. 86).

[43] *Ibid.*, Vol. I, No. 37.

[44] *Ibid.*, Vol. II, No. 12. See also *ibid.*, No. 129.

[45] "Whether the bulk of our Irish Natives are not kept from thriving, by that cynical Content in Dirt and Beggary, which they possess to a degree beyond any other People in Christendom?" (*ibid.*, Vol. I, No. 19).

[47] *A Word to the Wise*, in *Works*, VI, p. 233.

[48] "Whether a Tax upon Dirt would not be one way of encouraging Industry?" (*The Querist*, Vol. II, No. 196).

[49] The expression "public works" seems to have excited a number of economists, including Hutchison, into imagining a large-scale program of government expenditure directed toward the reduction of a deflationary gap. However, this interpretation appears to be unfounded. In the context of Berkeley's writing their significance is more of a psychological than of an economic nature. Hutchison cites the following query as supporting his interpretation: "Whether it would not be of use and ornament, if the Towns throughout this Kingdom were provided with decent Churches, Town-Houses, Market Places and paved Streets, with some Order taken for Cleanliness?" (*ibid.*, No. 248). The real meaning behind this query is found in the following passages of *An Essay . . .* , in *Works*, VI, 206–7: "Triumphal arches, columns, statues, inscriptions, and the like monuments of public services, have in former

not only to reduce idleness and luxuriousness but, equally important, to develop a craving for new wants, that is, for a higher standard of living. In the absence of a favorable sociological environment little could be achieved toward raising the level of economic development.

In contrast to the trend toward a laissez faire doctrine during the eighteenth century, Berkeley relied heavily upon the state for the implementation of his program. It was to be the function of the legislature to be responsible for such policies as the creation and circulation of money, the maintenance of transport facilities, the transference of labor from unproductive to productive employment, the direct promotion of important industries not developed by private interests, the establishment of academies to encourage manufacturing and commerce, and the general co-ordination of foreign and domestic trade. Paying homage neither to the doctrine of natural harmony nor to the more extreme Mandevillean interpretation that private vices are public benefits,[50] Berkeley is led inevitably to a philosophy of state intervention.[51] It was only in this way that the planned program required to meet the problems of an underdeveloped economy could be effectively implemented. Arguing for the establishment of a publicly owned national bank, he asks "Whether it can be expected, that private Persons should have more Regard to the Public, than the Public itself?"[52] and, further, "If a Country where the Legislative Body is not fit to be trusted, what Security can there be for trusting anyone else?"[53]

To what end were the wide range of policies advocated by Berkeley directed? He leaves little doubt that it is per capita rather than aggregate or national welfare that is important.[54] The well-being of a country was measured

---

[49] times, been found great incentives to virtue and magnanimity, and would have the same effects on Englishmen which they had on Greeks and Romans. These noble arts of architecture, sculpture, and painting do not only adorn the public but have also an influence on the minds and manners of men, filling them with great ideas, and spiriting them up to an emulation of worthy actions?" See also *The Querist*, Vol. II, No. 242.

[50] Bernard Mandeville, *The Fable of the Bees: or, Private Vices, Public Benefits*, ed. F. B. Kaye (2 vols.; Oxford, 1924).

[51] John Stuart Mill, reviewing A. C. Fraser's 1871 edition of *The Works of George Berkeley*, noted that one of the chief merits of Berkeley's *Querist* was "the distinctiveness with which he perceived, being much in advance of his age, that money is not in itself wealth, but a set of counters for computing and exchanging wealth." Mill commented further that "had he followed up this idea, he might have anticipated the work of Adam Smith" (see J. S. Mill, "Berkeley's Life and Writings," *Fortnightly Review*, No. LIX [N.S., November 1, 1871], p. 523). There appears to be little evidence to substantiate this view. Although it is true that much of Berkeley's economic analysis found expression in *The Wealth of Nations*, Mill failed to perceive the basic inconsistency involved in the philosophical framework of the two writers. Smith "believed men had God-created psychologies which made them operate in a beneficent manner. There was a Director of the Universe who created earth and heaven and then left it to run, having built into it psychological forces which would make it run on an even keel.... Government interference may be part of such a system, with justice being necessary only as an arbitrator and the role of the state not being potentially great" (see the forthcoming book by J. M. Letiche, *Balance of Payments and Economic Growth* [Harper & Bros., 1959], chap. i). To Berkeley, however, it is not the self-interest of human individuals but the pursuance of policies, embodying divine will, which are consistent with the happiness of all mankind within the framework of natural religion. In his *Passive Obedience* Berkeley stresses the vital role of government in the implementation of the moral rules which a flourishing society must follow. In Berkeley we have a doctrine of theological utilitarianism, whereas Smith may be regarded as a forerunner of secular utilitarianism.

[52] *The Querist*, Vol. III, No. 16.

[53] *Ibid.*, No. 49.

[54] "Whether the Number and Welfare of the Subjects be not the true Strength of the Crown?" (*ibid.*, Vol. I, No. 136).

in terms of the standard of living of its people.[55] In essence, therefore, we have, in the works of Berkeley, a concept of society which involves the blending of direct state intervention with the protection of the interests of the individual directed toward an increasing per capita welfare.

V

In a final evaluation of Berkeley's scattered works in political economy one must be careful not to exaggerate his contributions to economic analysis. Although he showed insight into a number of important concepts, for example, the division of labor, territorial specialization, the nature and function of money, and the distinction between productive and unproductive employment, his analysis lacks the over-all sophistication of his contemporary, Richard Cantillon. In contrast to Cantillon, Berkeley found economic analysis useful only to the extent that it contributed to his understanding of particular problems. Nowhere is there an attempt to explain the functioning of the economic system, and it is in this respect that Cantillon's *Essay* was a greater contribution to the history of economic analysis than Berkeley's *Querist*. On the other hand, there is no doubt that in his writings is found one of the earliest systematic attempts to apply economic analysis, within the framework of his moral and philosophical principles, to the problems of an underdeveloped economy. It is in this context that we must examine Berkeley's contributions and not, as recent economists have attempted to do, to seek anticipations of Keynesian doctrine.

[55] "Whether Plenty of all the Necessaries and Comforts of Life be not real Wealth?" (*ibid.*, Vol. II, No. 282).

TITLES IN THIS SERIES

1. David Berman, ed., *George Berkeley: Eighteenth-Century Responses*, New York: Garland Publishing, Inc., 1988, in two volumes.

2. Stephen R. L. Clark, ed., *Money, Obedience, and Affection: Essays on Berkeley's Moral and Political Thought*, New York: Garland Publishing, Inc., 1988.

3. Willis Doney, ed., *Berkeley on Abstraction and Abstract Ideas*, New York: Garland Publishing, Inc., 1988.

4. R.C.S. Walker, ed. *The Real in the Ideal: Berkeley's Relation to Kant*, New York: Garland Publishing, Inc., 1988.

5. Thomas K. Abbott, *Sight and Touch: An Attempt to Disprove the Received (or Berkeleian) Theory of Vision*, London: Longman, Green, Longman, Roberts, and Green, 1864.

6. D. M. Armstrong, *Berkeley's Theory of Vision: A Critical Examination of Bishop Berkeley's "Essay Towards a New Theory of Vision,"* Melbourne University Press, 1960.

7. Samuel Bailey, *A Review of Berkeley's Theory of Vision, Designed to Show the Unsoundness of That Celebrated Speculation*, London: James Ridgway, Piccadilly, 1842.

James F. Ferrier, "Berkeley and Idealism," London: *Blackwood's Magazine* (June 1842).

John Stuart Mill, "Bailey on Berkeley's Theory of Vision," London: *Westminster Review*, 38 (1842).

Samuel Bailey, *A Letter to a Philosopher in Reply to Some Recent Attempts to Vindicate Berkeley's Theory of Vision, and in Further Elucidation of its Unsoundness*, London: James Ridgway, Piccadilly, 1843.

James F. Ferrier, "Mr. Bailey's Reply to an Article in Blackwood's Magazine," Edinburgh and London: *Blackwood's Magazine* (June 1843).

John Stuart Mill, "Rejoinder to Mr. Bailey's Reply," London: *Westminster Review*, 39 (1843).

8. George Berkeley, *Philosophical Commentaries, Transcribed from the Manuscript and Edited, with an Introduction and Index by George H. Thomas: Explanatory Notes by A. A. Luce*, printed by Mount Union College, 1976.

9. A. C. Crombie, *George Berkeley's Bicentenary, The British Journal for the Philosophy of Science*, 4 (May 1953). Edinburgh and London: Thomas Nelson and Sons Ltd.

10. Alexander Campbell Fraser, *Life and Letters of George Berkeley, Formerly Bishop of Cloyne, and an Account of His Philosophy. With Many Writings of Bishop Berkeley Hitherto Unpublished*, Oxford, At the Clarendon Press, 1871.

11. G. Dawes Hicks, *Berkeley*, New York: Russell & Russell, 1932.

12. G. A. Johnston, *The Development of Berkeley's Philosophy*, London: Macmillan and Co., 1923.

13. A. A. Luce, *Berkeley and Malebranche: A Study in the Origins of Berkeley's Thought*, Oxford, At the Clarendon Press, 1934.

14. C. B. Martin and D. M. Armstrong, eds., *Berkeley: A Collection of Critical Essays. The Articles from "Locke and Berkeley: A Collection of Critical Essays"*, Garden City, New York: Anchor Books, Doubleday & Company, Inc., 1968

15. I. C. Tipton, *Berkeley: The Philosophy of Immaterialism*, London: Methuen & Co. Ltd., 1974.

DATE DUE

HIGHSMITH   #LO-45220